**ADV**

STUDENT EDITION

BREAKING THE FRENCH BARRIER

ADVANCED

Catherine Coursaget

Micheline Myers

Series Editor, John Conner

Student Edition

BREAKING THE BARRIER, INC.

THE LANGUAGE SERIES WITH ALL THE RULES YOU NEED TO KNOW

THE FASTEST PATH TO TRUE LANGUAGE FLUENCY

ACKNOWLEDGMENTS

A special thanks to Ken Bower, whose suggestions were extremely helpful as this book came to life. Barbara Peterson offered wise editorial suggestions. Anne Squire offered wonderful suggestions for this edition. Guillermo Barnetche provided stunning artwork. We also appreciate the efforts of Ann Talbot, who laid out the text stylishly.

AN INVITATION

*We invite you to join many of our readers who, over the years, have shared their suggestions for improvements as well as their personal knowledge of the Francophone world. In doing so, they have become our partners. We are grateful for their invaluable contributions as the evolution of **Breaking the Barrier** belongs, in part, to them.*

BREAKING THE BARRIER, INC.
63 Shirley Road
Groton, MA 01450
Toll Free: 866-TO BREAK (866-862-7325)
Fax: 978-448-1237
E-mail: info@tobreak.com
www.tobreak.com

Copyright © John Conner (2011 printing)

ISBN: 0-9712817-4-2

PREFACE

BREAKING THE FRENCH BARRIER is a core text, workbook and handy reference all-in-one. It can stand alone, or complement the multitude of French language resources currently available.

We believe the fastest path to fluency is built upon a rock-solid understanding of grammar. **BREAKING THE FRENCH BARRIER** provides the essential roadmap for this journey.

In the following twelve lessons, you will find country maps, vocabulary, a review of key grammatical concepts, explanations of new material, many practice exercises, as well as a review test. Sentences throughout the book highlight current people, places and events from the French-speaking world. You will find the tone of these pages informal and conversational — a one-on-one session between teacher and student.

WE LOOK FORWARD TO ACCOMPANYING YOU AS YOU BREAK THE FRENCH BARRIER.

BONNE CHANCE!

JOHN CONNER
Series Editor

CINDY BEAMS
Publisher

TABLE OF CONTENTS

LA FRANCE & LA CORSE

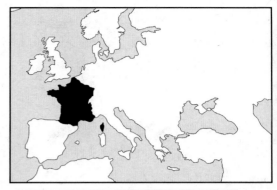

LA FRANCE

Capitale:	Paris
Population:	64.800.000
Gouvernement:	République
Chef d'état:	Président Nicolas Sarkozy
Monnaie:	Euro
Langue:	Français
Ressources:	Automobiles, cinéma, fromages, gastronomie, haute couture, télécommunications, textiles, tourisme, vins
Musique:	Hector Berlioz, Claude Debussy, Gabriel Fauré, Edith Piaf, Maurice Ravel
Principales richesses touristiques:	Les Alpes, l'Arc de Triomphe, la Cathédrale de Notre Dame, les châteaux de la Loire, la Côte d'Azur, le Mont Saint Michel, le Musée du Louvre, le Musée d'Orsay, la Provence, la Tour Eiffel, Versailles
Cuisine:	Bouillabaisse, cassoulet, confit de canard, coquilles St. Jacques, crème brûlée, escargots à la Bourguignonne, foie gras, "haute cuisine," poulet rôti, quiche lorraine, salade niçoise, soufflé au chocolat, soupe à l'oignon, tarte tatin, vin

FRANÇAIS CÉLÈBRES

Jeanne d'Arc
(SAINTE)

Napoléon Bonaparte
(CHEF MILITAIRE)

Colette (ÉCRIVAIN)

Marie Curie
(SCIENTIFIQUE)

Louis XIV (ROI)

Edouard Manet
(PEINTRE)

Claude Monet
(PEINTRE)

Auguste Rodin
(SCULPTEUR)

Jean-Jacques Rousseau
(PHILOSOPHE)

Voltaire
(ÉCRIVAIN, PHILOSOPHE)

Zinédine Zidane
(JOUEUR DE FOOTBALL)

VOCABULAIRE LEÇON UN

ADJECTIFS

aigu/aiguë	sharp
amer/amère	bitter
amoureux/ amoureuse	in love
beau/belle	beautiful ✓
bête	foolish, silly, stupid
blond/blonde	blonde ✓
bon/bonne	good ✓
bon marché	cheap
célèbre	famous
confortable	comfortable (for things)
coupable	guilty
différent/différente	different
difficile	difficult
doué/douée	gifted
ennuyeux/ennuyeuse	boring
faible	weak
fermé/fermée	closed
furieux/furieuse	furious, angry
impoli/impolie	rude, impolite
irlandais/irlandaise	Irish ✓
italien/italienne	Italian ✓
joli/jolie	pretty ✓
lent/lente	slow

meilleur/meilleure	better, best ✓
mignon/mignonne	precious, cute ✓
modeste	modest ✓
mouillé/mouillée	wet
né/née	born ✓
nouveau/nouvelle	new ✓
ordinaire	common, ordinary
paresseux/ paresseuse	lazy
pénible	annoying, a pain
petit/petite	little, small, tiny ✓
poli/polie	courteous, polite
préféré/préférée	preferred, favorite
propre	own, clean
rare	unusual, rare
salé/salée	salted
sérieux/sérieuse	serious ✓
seul/seule	alone, only ✓
supérieur/ supérieure	superior, better
vieux/vieille	old

 This symbol lets you know where you can practice along using the Audio CD set.

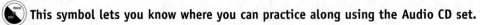

LEÇON UN

KEY GRAMMAR CONCEPTS

A) **Le présent de l'indicatif** → *The present tense*

B) **Les interrogatifs** → *Interrogatives*

C) **Les conjonctions** → *Conjunctions*

D) **Les pronoms sujets** → *Subject pronouns*

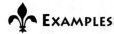 **A) Le présent de l'indicatif**

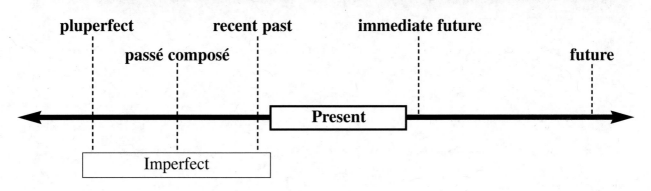

The **present tense** is used to describe actions that are currently happening, to note general conditions or traits, to describe habits, and, at times, to tell what will happen in the not-too-distant future.

Examples: *Émilie **passe** l'examen maintenant.*
Émilie is taking the exam now.

*Il **pleut** tout le temps en Bretagne.*
It rains all the time in Brittany.

*À l'école nous **faisons** du sport chaque après-midi.*
At school we play sports every afternoon.

*Demain je **vais** à Toulouse.*
Tomorrow I am going to Toulouse.

1) LES VERBES RÉGULIERS

PARLER	FINIR	ENTENDRE
je parle	je finis	j'entends
tu parles	tu finis	tu entends
on/il/elle parle	on/il/elle finit	on/il/elle entend
nous parlons	nous finissons	nous entendons
vous parlez	vous finissez	vous entendez
ils parlent	elles finissent	ils entendent

2) VERBES "BOTTE" ET CHANGEMENT ORTHOGRAPHIQUE

Some verbs undergo spelling changes in order to preserve the sound of a particular letter found in the infinitive.

For example, the *"nous"* form of *"manger"* is *"nous mangeons,"* not nous *mangons as you might expect.

With *"commencer,"* the present tense is *"nous commençons."* It is not nous *commencons! This change occurs because the letter *"c"* before an *"a," "o,"* or *"u"* sounds like the "k" in "kite," whereas in front of "i" and "e," it sounds like the "s" in "sun."

In order to maintain the correct sound of the verb, some verbs require a spelling change.

Let's look at the following diagram with examples of these "spelling changes":

Infinitive Ending	Sample Verbs	These letters change . . .	to these letters!
-cer	*commencer*	c	ç before *a, o,* or *u*
-ger	*manger*	g	*ge* before *a, o,* or *u*
-e/é + consonant + *er*	*acheter/célébrer*	e/é	è before mute *e*
-ter	*jeter*	t	*tt* before mute *e*
-ler	*appeler*	l	*ll* before mute *e*
-yer	*envoyer*	y	*i* before mute *e*

Notice the difference in the *"nous"* form for these verbs:

COMMENCER (to begin)		MANGER (to eat)	
je commence	nous commen**ç**ons	je mange	nous mang**e**ons
tu commences	vous commencez	tu manges	vous mangez
elle commence	elles commencent	il mange	ils mangent

In the following verbs, the forms with spelling changes seem to form a "boot."

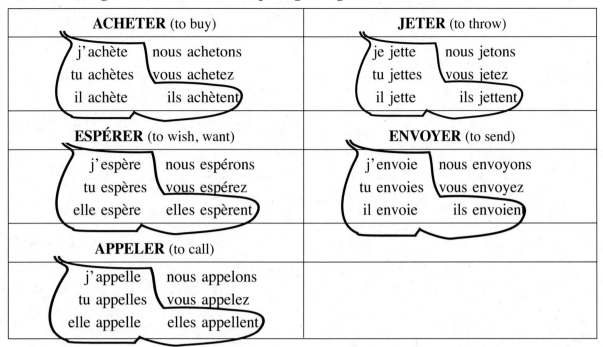

ACHETER (to buy)		JETER (to throw)	
j'achète	nous achetons	je jette	nous jetons
tu achètes	vous achetez	tu jettes	vous jetez
il achète	ils achètent	il jette	ils jettent
ESPÉRER (to wish, want)		ENVOYER (to send)	
j'espère	nous espérons	j'envoie	nous envoyons
tu espères	vous espérez	tu envoies	vous envoyez
elle espère	elles espèrent	il envoie	ils envoient
APPELER (to call)			
j'appelle	nous appelons		
tu appelles	vous appelez		
elle appelle	elles appellent		

3) LES VERBES RÉFLÉCHIS

In a reflexive construction, the subject and the pronoun refer to the same person or object.

The following pronouns are used for reflexive verbs:

Reflexive Object Pronouns	
me	nous
te	vous
se	se

EXAMPLES: *Je **me brosse** les dents chaque matin avant d'aller à l'école.*
I brush my teeth every morning before going to school.

*Ma grand-mère **se repose** après le travail.*
My grandmother rests after work.

*Mon père **se rase** avant d'aller au bureau.*
My father shaves before going to the office.

Here is the conjugation of a model reflexive verb:

se reposer (to rest)	
je **me** repose	nous **nous** reposons
tu **te** reposes	vous **vous** reposez
il **se** repose	ils **se** reposent
elle **se** repose	elles **se** reposent

4) LES VERBES IRRÉGULIERS

In addition to "boot" verbs and verbs with spelling changes, some verbs are completely irregular.

These are common verbs you must memorize:

ALLER (to go)		AVOIR (to have)	
je vais	nous allons	j'ai	nous avons
tu vas	vous allez	tu as	vous avez
il va	ils vont	il a	ils ont

BOIRE (to drink)		CONNAÎTRE (to be familiar with)	
je bois	nous buvons	je connais	nous connaissons
tu bois	vous buvez	tu connais	vous connaissez
elle boit	ils boivent	il connaît	elles connaissent

COURIR (to run)		CROIRE (to believe)	
je cours	nous courons	je crois	nous croyons
tu cours	vous courez	tu crois	vous croyez
elle court	ils courent	il croit	ils croient

DEVOIR (to owe, to have to)		DIRE (to say)	
je dois	nous devons	je dis	nous disons
tu dois	vous devez	tu dis	vous dites
il doit	ils doivent	il dit	ils disent

ÉCRIRE (to write)		ÊTRE (to be)	
j'écris	nous écrivons	je suis	nous sommes
tu écris	vous écrivez	tu es	vous êtes
il écrit	ils écrivent	elle est	elles sont

FAIRE (to do)		LIRE (to read)	
je fais	nous faisons	je lis	nous lisons
tu fais	vous faites	tu lis	vous lisez
il fait	ils font	elle lit	elles lisent

METTRE (to put, place) also: **promettre** (to promise)		OUVRIR (to open)	
je mets	nous mettons	j'ouvre	nous ouvrons
tu mets	vous mettez	tu ouvres	vous ouvrez
il met	elles mettent	elle ouvre	ils ouvrent

PARTIR (to go away) also: **dormir** (to sleep), **sortir** (to go out) and **servir** (to serve)		PEINDRE (to paint) also: **craindre** (to fear), and **éteindre** (to turn off a light or put out a fire)	
je pars	nous partons	je peins	nous peignons
tu pars	vous partez	tu peins	vous peignez
il part	ils partent	elle peint	ils peignent

POUVOIR (to be able to)		PRENDRE (to take) also: **apprendre** (to learn), **comprendre** (to understand)	
je peux	nous pouvons	je prends	nous prenons
tu peux	vous pouvez	tu prends	vous prenez
elle peut	ils peuvent	elle prend	ils prennent
RECEVOIR (to receive)		**SAVOIR** (to know)	
je reçois	nous recevons	je sais	nous savons
tu reçois	vous recevez	tu sais	vous savez
elle reçoit	ils reçoivent	elle sait	ils savent
VENIR (to come) also: **devenir** (to become), **tenir** (to hold)		**VOIR** (to see)	
je viens	nous venons	je vois	nous voyons
tu viens	vous venez	tu vois	vous voyez
elle vient	ils viennent	il voit	ils voient
VOULOIR (to wish, to want)			
je veux	nous voulons		
tu veux	vous voulez		
elle veut	ils veulent		

5) LES VERBES IMPERSONNELS

Certain verbs are used only in the 3rd person singular:

falloir: Il faut . . .	*neiger: Il neige.*	*pleuvoir: Il pleut.*
It is necessary . . .	It is snowing.	It is raining.

EXERCICES

1. Write the correct present indicative form of the infinitive in parentheses:

a. Nous ___parlons___ français pendant la classe. (parler)

b. Tu ___fais___ toujours un repas provençal le dimanche. (faire)

c. Marie et moi, nous ___essayons___ de construire un château de sable sur une plage de la Côte d'Azur. (essayer)

d. Tu _se rases_ trois fois par semaine. (se raser)

e. Je ne _sais_ rien. Je ne suis pas un élève doué. (savoir)

f. Le Prince Albert de Monaco _conduit_ sa propre voiture. (conduire)

g. Elles _sont_ irlandaises parce qu'elles sont nées à Dublin. (être)

h. Jean-Claude, un élève sérieux, _va_ souvent à la bibliothèque pour travailler. (aller)

i. Quand je vais au supermarché, je _choisis_ des produits biologiques. (choisir)

j. Est-ce que tu _pars_ seul ou est-ce que nous _voyageons_ ensemble? (partir/voyager)

k. Je _mets_ mes chaussettes mouillées dans le séchoir. (mettre)

2. **Translate these three verbs and then conjugate them in the present indicative:**

envoyer	entendre	se coucher
(to _____)	(to _____)	(to _____)
_____	_____	_____
_____	_____	_____
_____	_____	_____
_____	_____	_____
_____	_____	_____

3. There are six errors in the following paragraph. Underline and correct them:

Quand je travaille à la bibliothèque, je met mes livres sur la table. Mes amis qui sont paresseux ne voulent pas travailler avec moi parce que je n'aimes pas bavarder. Je leur dis: "Dites donc, vous êtes pénibles! On n'apprends rien quand on bavarde. Je connais le bibliothécaire et je vais lui parler si vous refusez de vous taire." Bien sûr, mes amis se mettent en colère contre moi, mais ça m'est égal. Je suis un bon élève et je recevois facilement de bonnes notes. Mes professeurs me respectent, mes parents m'aimes, mais je n'ai plus d'amis!

 B) LES QUESTIONS

HOW DO YOU ASK A QUESTION IN FRENCH?

1) WITH AN INVERSION

If the subject of a sentence is a pronoun *(je, tu, il, elle, on, nous, vous, elles, ils)*, you can swap around the subject and the verb to form a question.

EXAMPLES: *Que **faites-vous**?*
What are you doing?

***Chantez-vous** bien?*
Do you sing well?

*Qui **regardes-tu**?*
Whom are you looking at?

> **As-tu mangé** *du chocolat?*
> Did you eat any chocolate?

> **Les enfants sont-ils** *dans le jardin?*
> Are the children in the garden?

When the verb ends in a vowel and the subject pronoun begins with a vowel, you will insert a *"-t"* for phonetic purposes – to avoid two consecutive vowel sounds.

⚜ **EXAMPLES:** *Qu'apporte-**t-il** à la fête?*
> What is he bringing to the party?

> *Qui regard**e-t-elle**?*
> Whom is she looking at?

When the verb is in the *passé composé,* the subject pronoun is placed between the auxiliary verb (*"avoir"* or *"être"*) and the past participle.

⚜ **EXAMPLES:** *Avec qui es-**tu** sorti?*
> With whom did you go out?

> *Qu'a-t-**elle** acheté?*
> What did she buy?

> *Pourquoi ont-**ils** choisi ces chaussettes roses?*
> Why did they choose those pink socks?

When the subject is a noun, place that noun <u>before</u> the verb and then place the corresponding subject pronoun <u>after</u> the verb. This practice would be redundant in English, but is necessary in French.

⚜ **EXAMPLES:** **Caroline** *a-t-elle fini ses devoirs?*
> Has Caroline finished her homework?

> *Comment **Gustave** a-t-il eu cet accident?*
> How did Gustave have that accident?

> **Le Président** *parlera-t-il ce soir?*
> Will the President speak this evening?

❓◆❓ Do you remember why each of the above examples has a *"-t-"*?

---

2) WITH "EST-CE QUE"

Questions formed with *"est-ce que"* maintain the word order of an affirmative statement. It is an easy, very common way to ask a question.

EXAMPLES: *Est-ce que tu as mangé du chocolat?*
Did you eat some chocolate?

Est-ce que les enfants sont dans le jardin?
Are the children in the garden?

WHAT ARE INTERROGATIVES?

These words ask questions. Let's look at three types of interrogatives: interrogative pronouns, interrogative adjectives and interrogative adverbs.

1 **Interrogative pronouns**

Interrogative pronouns help us at the beginning of a question. Depending on the type of question, we will use a different word in French.

a) **Questions about <u>people</u>** → *Qui . . .* or *Qui est-ce qui?/Qui est-ce que?*

<u>Subject of a verb</u>

Qui?	or *Qui est-ce qui?*	Who?
Qui parle?	or *Qui est-ce qui parle?*	Who is speaking?

<u>Direct object of a verb</u>

Qui?	or *Qui est-ce que?*	Whom?
Qui avez-vous invité? or *Qui est-ce que vous avez invité?*		Whom did you invite?

<u>After a preposition</u>

(Preposition) **qui?**	or *(Preposition)* **qui est-ce que?**	Whom?/Whose?
Pour **qui** travailles-tu?*	or *Pour* **qui est-ce que** tu travailles?*	For whom are you working?

EXAMPLES: *Avec* **qui** *joues-tu au tennis?*
With whom do you play tennis?

Chez **qui est-ce que** *vous avez passé le week-end?*
At whose house did you spend the weekend?

b) **Questions about <u>things</u>** → *Que, Qu'est-ce que, Qu'est-ce qui, Quoi?*

<u>Subject of a verb</u>

Qu'est-ce qui?	What?
Qu'est-ce qui fait ce bruit?	What is making this noise?

Direct object of a verb

Que?	or *Qu'est-ce que?*	What?
Que lisez-vous?	or *Qu'est-ce que vous lisez?*	What are you reading?

After a preposition

*(Preposition) **quoi?***	or *(Preposition) **quoi est-ce que?***	What?
*Avec **quoi** a-t-il fait ce gâteau?*	or *Avec **quoi est-ce qu**'il a fait ce gâteau?*	With what did he make this cake?

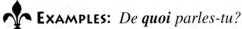 **EXAMPLES:** *De **quoi** parles-tu?*
What are you talking about?

*Sur **quoi est-ce que** tu dors?*
What are you sleeping on?

c) **Interrogative pronouns used to distinguish one thing from another**

	SINGULAR	PLURAL
MASCULINE	*Lequel . . . ?*	*Lesquels . . . ?*
FEMININE	*Laquelle . . . ?*	*Lesquelles . . . ?*

 **EXAMPLES:** *Voici mes deux nouvelles chemises. **Laquelle** préfères-tu?*
Here are my two new shirts. Which one do you prefer?

*Je ne comprends pas un de ces exercices de math. –**Lequel** est-ce que tu ne comprends pas? Je vais t'aider à le faire.*
I don't understand one of these math exercises. –Which one don't you understand? I am going to help you do it.

When the pronoun is preceded by "à" or "de," you must make the usual contractions:

À	SINGULAR	PLURAL
MASCULINE	*auquel*	*auxquels*
FEMININE	*à laquelle*	*auxquelles*

DE	SINGULAR	PLURAL
MASCULINE	*duquel*	*desquels*
FEMININE	*de laquelle*	*desquelles*

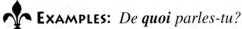 **EXAMPLES:** *Je viens de téléphoner à mon oncle. –Ah oui . . . **auquel**?*
I just called my uncle. –Oh yeah . . . which one?

*Nous n'aimons pas les étudiants à côté **desquels** tu es assis.*
We don't like the students next to whom you are seated.

*Les filles **auxquelles** tu parles sont mes sœurs.*
The girls to whom you are talking are my sisters.

2 Interrogative adjectives

	SINGULAR	PLURAL
MASCULINE	*Quel . . . ?*	*Quels . . . ?*
FEMININE	*Quelle . . . ?*	*Quelles . . . ?*

⚜ EXAMPLES: *Quelle est ta couleur préférée?*
What is your favorite color?

Quel film est-ce que vous avez vu hier soir?
What movie did you see last night?

De quels professeurs as-tu peur?
Which teachers are you afraid of?

3 Interrogative adverbs

Combien de? → How many?/How much?		*Où?* → Where?
Comment? → How?/What?		*Pourquoi?* → Why?
D'où? → From where?		*Quand?* → When?

⚜ EXAMPLES: *Quand est-ce que tu pourras partir en vacances?*
When will you be able to go on vacation?

Combien coûte ce nouveau CD?
How much does this new CD cost?

Où se trouve la Maison Blanche?
Where is the White House (located)?

"Comment?" can be used to mean "What?" when you have not heard what someone has said, or you don't know what something means.

⚜ EXAMPLE:
–*Jean étudie la numismatique.* –John is studying numismatics.
–*Comment?* –What?
–*La numismatique.* –Numismatics.

HERE ARE SOME OTHER GOOD THINGS TO KNOW ABOUT INTERROGATIVES

◆ **Questions seeking a definition**
The following interrogative expressions are very common:

> *Qu'est que c'est qu'un dinosaure?* → What is a dinosaur?
> *Qu'est-ce qu'un "camembert"?* → What is "camembert"?
> *Qu'est-ce que c'est que ça?* → What is this?

◆ **Additional interrogatives**
There are a number of common ways of asking questions in French that do not translate literally into English.

The following are some examples:

> *Comment vous appelez-vous?* → What is your name?
> *Comment s'appelle ton frère?* → What is your brother's name?
> *Quel âge avez-vous?* → How old are you?
> *Quel âge a ta sœur?* → How old is your sister?
> *Comment allez-vous?* → How are you?
> *Quel temps fait-il?* → What is the weather like?
> *Quelle heure est-il?* → What time is it?
> *De quelle couleur est votre voiture?* → What color is your car?

 # EXERCICES

1. Complete the sentences with interrogative pronouns, adjectives, or adverbs:

a. _____ est-ce que tu achètes ta glace préférée? –Au supermarché.

b. _____ étudies-tu le français? –Parce que j'ai envie de voyager dans les pays francophones d'Afrique.

c. _____ heure est-il?

d. _____ d'étudiants est-ce qu'il y a dans la classe? –Il y en a vingt.

e. _____ est-ce que tu as eu cet accident? –En conduisant trop vite.

f. _____ fait ce bruit? –La machine à laver.

g. _____ est le professeur le plus ennuyeux?

h. _____ nous allons faire demain soir? –Nous allons danser!

i. _____ t'a dit cette bonne nouvelle? –Marie-Antoinette.

j. Avec _____ veux-tu jouer du piano?

2. **There are three errors in the following dialogue. Underline and correct them:**

–Combien est-ce que tu es allé aux Jeux Olympiques

de Vancouver?

–J'y suis allé parce que c'est là que sont les meilleurs

athlètes du monde.

–Qui est-ce que tu as voyagé et où est-ce que tu as logé?

–Je suis allé en avion bien sûr, et nous sommes restés

dans un petit hôtel près des montagnes. C'était bon

marché.

–Qu'est-ce que personnes célèbres est-ce que tu as vues?

–J'ai vu Shaun White ("The Flying Tomato") et Bode

Miller. Au revoir!

3. You are talking to a friend who is rather vague. Ask for clarification:

Example: J'ai vu un bon film samedi. _____ **Lequel** _____ ?

a. J'ai choisi plusieurs disques. _____ ?

b. J'ai écrit à deux de mes amis. _____ ?

c. Je suis allergique à certaines plantes. _____ ?

d. Mon cousin Simon est amoureux
d'une de tes sœurs. _____ ?

e. Arthur se moque toujours de certains _____ ?
de ses camarades trop sérieux.

4. Ask logical questions to the answers provided. The underlined word(s) is the specific answer to the question:

Example: C'est <u>mon père</u> qui a fait le gâteau d'anniversaire.
      Qui est-ce qui a fait le gâteau d'anniversaire?
      OR: Qui a fait le gâteau d'anniversaire?

a. Nous avons joué au foot avec <u>nos voisins</u>.

_____

b. <u>Ces NIKE</u> sont mes chaussures préférées.

_____

c. J'ai réparé <u>ma bicyclette</u> ce matin.

_____

d. Thomas est chez <u>Marie-Louise</u>.

_____

e. Il fait <u>beau</u>.

_____

f. <u>Le directeur</u> invite les élèves chez lui.

_____

5. Translate the following questions:

a. How many girls are in your English class?

_____

b. Why did Thierry Henry decide to play soccer?

_____

c. Which one of your dresses are you going to wear Saturday night?

_____

d. To which ones (of your male friends) did you write?

_____

e. What is a _"camembert"_?

_____

🔑 C) LES CONJONCTIONS

Conjunctions are words that join sentences or parts of sentences. In English they are words such as: "and, or/either, nor/neither, but."

The words in French are:

Conjunctions
_et_ → and
_ou_ → or, either
_ni_ → nor, neither
mais → but

Helpful Tips: **1)** Do not confuse _ou_ (or) with _où_ (where).
2) _"Ni"_ is a negative conjunction and therefore requires _"ne"_ before the verb.

EXAMPLES: *Pour les vacances, les enfants vont à la plage **ou** à la montagne.*
For vacation, the children go either to the beach or to the mountain.

*Il **n'**aime **ni** le café **ni** le thé.*
He doesn't like coffee or tea (He likes neither coffee nor tea).

EXERCICES

1. **Choose one of the following conjunctions for each of the sentences below** *(et, mais, ni, ou)*:

   a. Il a vingt _____ un ans.

   b. Joséphine n'a _____ frères _____ sœurs.

   c. J'adore le jus d'orange _____ je n'aime pas le jus de pamplemousse qui est amer.

   d. Rome est la capitale de l'Italie _____ de l'Espagne?

   e. Tu as aimé ce film, _____ moi je l'ai trouvé ennuyeux.

   f. En hiver, nous jouons au basket _____ au hockey.

   g. Dans la pizza, on met du fromage _____ de la sauce tomate.

2. **There are five errors in the following paragraph. Underline and correct them:**

    Hier, je suis allé à la cafétéria. Je n'ai vu ni Isabelle ou Brigitte.

   D'abord, j'ai acheté trois et quatre bouteilles de Coca. Je voulais les

   partager avec Jacques ni Pierre et ils ne sont pas venus mais j'ai bu toutes

   les bouteilles de Coca-Cola!

D) LES PRONOMS SUJETS

Pronouns are words that take the place of nouns. There are many categories of pronouns. This section will review **subject pronouns**. In English you always use either a noun or a subject pronoun with all verbs (and the same is true in French except in commands, e.g., "Go!").

Here are the subject pronouns in French:

Singular	Plural
je/j'	*nous*
tu	*vous*
il/elle/on	*ils/elles*

They correspond to these pronouns in English:

I	we
you (singular, informal)	you (singular, formal; also, plural, either informal or formal)
he/she/one	they (m./f.)

WHAT IS THE DIFFERENCE BETWEEN "TU" AND "VOUS"?

It is important to understand the difference between *"tu"* and *"vous."*

◆ The *"tu"* form is used among friends and members of a family.

◆ The *"vous"* form is used when greeting a new acquaintance, addressing someone years older than you, or addressing an important person. This form conveys a feeling of formality and respect.

◆ *"Vous"* is also the plural form, used to address a <u>group</u> of people.

> **Helpful Tip:** *"On"* can have the same meaning as *"nous."* For example, *"On y va!"* is translated as "Let's go!".

 EXERCICES

1. Choose *"tu"* or *"vous"* and then conjugate verbs in parentheses:

a. Mesdames, _____ _____ (chanter) très mal.

b. Elisabeth, mon amour, est-ce que _____ m'_____ (aimer)?

c. Mademoiselle, _____ (préférer) -_____ la jupe verte ou la jupe bleue?

d. Maman, est-ce _____ _____ (aimer) ma nouvelle jupe bleue?

e. Thomas! _____ _____ ([ne . . . pas] pouvoir) dormir en classe.

f. Monsieur le Président, qu'est-ce que _____ _____ (penser) de la situation économique de l'Union européenne?

g. Madame, _____ (pouvoir) -_____ me dire si ce bus va à l'aéroport Charles de Gaulle?

h. Monsieur Thiriet, _____ _____ (devoir) faire du sport pour maigrir.

i. Christophe, _____ _____ (être) mon meilleur ami.

j. Les enfants! _____ (se laver) les mains avant de passer à table.

2. **Fill in each blank with the correct subject pronoun:**

a. Robert et moi, _____ allons au petit marché cet après-midi.

b. Combien de stylos bleus est-ce que _____ as?

c. _____ venez chez moi, samedi matin, n'est-ce pas?

d. _____, les étudiants du Lycée français, dînons chaque soir à six heures et demie.

e. Qui va à la fête: la belle Rosie, la jolie Amandine, et Laura, la blonde? Oui,

_____ y vont.

f. Dans le club de l'Alliance Française à Baton Rouge, _____ parle français tout le temps.

g. J'ai vu le film *Twilight* et je suis amoureuse de Robert Pattinson. _____ est tellement mignon!

These two sets of questions use grammatical structures and vocabulary from this lesson. Working with a partner, alternate asking and answering each question. When you get to the bottom of each list, start over at the top, switching roles. As a variation, write out the answers in complete sentences.

A) Est-ce que tu **lis** lentement ou rapidement?

Achètes-tu des vêtements bon marché?

Comment s'**appelle** ton professeur?

Ton professeur **est**-il **ennuyeux**, **sérieux** ou **modeste**?

Est-ce que ton ami **parle italien**?

Est-ce que tu **cours** le marathon de Boston chaque année?

Pourquoi **fais**-tu cette tête-là?

B) **Quelle** heure **est-il** à Paris?

Comment s'appelle le président français?

Qui est Zinédine Zidane?

Quand est-ce que tu pars pour la Corse?

Où est-ce que tu préfères aller pour les vacances?

Combien de filets mignons peux-tu manger en un fois?

Pourquoi es-tu aussi sérieuse?

EXERCICES DE RÉVISION

A) LE PRÉSENT DE L'INDICATIF

1. Translate these three verbs and then conjugate them in the present tense:

écouter	jeter	s'habiller
(to _____)	(to _____)	(to _____)

_____ _____ _____

_____ _____ _____

_____ _____ _____

_____ _____ _____

_____ _____ _____

2. Write the correct present indicative form of the infinitive in parentheses:

a. Chaque soir Scrooge _____ son argent. (compter)

b. Mon petit chien _____ sous la vieille chaise. (dormir)

c. Le père _____ une maison de poupée pour sa fille. (construire)

d. _____ -vous assez d'argent pour sortir ce soir? (Avoir)

e. L'équipe de basket _____ chaque après-midi. (courir)

f. À quelle heure _____ le match de football américain? (commencer)

g. Joséphine _____ aller sur la Côte d'Azur pour les vacances. (vouloir)

h. Nous sommes très contents quand il _____ beaucoup et qu'il n'y a pas de classes. (neiger)

i. Ils _____ le matin ou le soir? (lire)

j. Le 31 décembre je _____ avec mes amis au réveillon du Nouvel An à Baton Rouge. (aller)

3. There are six errors in the following paragraph. Underline and correct them:

Je suis vraiment amoureux de Marie, même si je ne la connais pas personnellement. Elle es dans ma classe d'histoire, et c'est une très bonne élève. Je ne comprends pas grand-chose dans cette classe; je ne me rapele ni les dates ni les villes, et j'oublie toujours la succession des rois! Ça m'et égal, parce que pendant la classe je pense à Marie. Je voudrais bien sortir avec elle, mais je ne sait pas si elle veule être ma petite amie. Dans la classe, quand nous travaillons ensemble par groupes de deux, elle ne faise jamais attention à moi.

B) LES QUESTIONS

1. Write the appropriate interrogative in the blank:

a. _____ était le premier Président des États-Unis?

b. _____ est ton numéro de téléphone?

c. _____ commence l'année scolaire?

d. _____ dit-on "zebra" en français? -Zèbre.

e. J'ai demandé au météorologiste: _____ est-ce qu'il va faire beau?

f. _____ matchs de rugby y a-t-il cette semaine?

g. Je ne me souviens pas _____ j'ai laissé mes lunettes de soleil.

h. _____ boisson préfères-tu: l'Orangina ou Snapple?

i. _____ qu'un "zèbre"?

j. Je ne comprends pas _____ tu attends toujours le dernier moment pour faire tes devoirs.

2. **There are four errors in the following dialogue. Underline and correct them:**

—Bonjour. Je voudrais réserver une table pour ce soir.

—Très bien, mademoiselle. Pour quand de personnes?

—Pour deux personnes.

—Laquelle salle préférez-vous?

—La petite, s'il vous plaît.

—À quelle temps voulez-vous dîner?

—À huit heures.

—Non, je suis désolé, il n'y a plus de place à cette heure-là.

—Pour quoi?

—Nous sommes vendredi et le vendredi soir il y a beaucoup

de monde.

3. What are the logical questions to the answers provided?

a. Je vais bien merci.

_____

b. Un éléphant est un énorme animal gris.

_____

c. Il fait trop froid.

_____

d. Paul est parti parce qu'il s'ennuyait.

_____

e. Nos amis habitent Orléans.

_____

C) LES CONJONCTIONS

Choose one of the following conjunctions for each of the sentences below (et, mais, ni, ou)**:**

a. Tu préfères la glace à la vanille _____ au chocolat?

b. Cette petite fille est très mignonne, _____ elle n'est pas polie.

c. Jean-Paul Duval est accusé d'un crime mais il n'est _____ coupable _____ responsable.

d. _____ tu arrêtes de chanter avec cette voix aiguë _____ je pars!

e. Ils sont paresseux, _____ quand ils s'amusent ils ont beaucoup d'énergie pour s'amuser!

f. Mais non, toutes les Américaines ne sont pas belles _____ blondes!

g. L'avion pour Montréal est déjà parti _____ l'avion pour Paris est encore ici.

h. Je ne parle _____ russe _____ japonais.

D) LES PRONOMS SUJETS

Fill in each blank with the correct subject pronoun:

a. Mon meilleur ami et moi, _____ vivons dans le même appartement.

b. Est-ce que _____ savez parler français?

c. Albert répond toujours correctement aux questions; _____ est très doué.

d. _____ ne voulons pas commencer l'école au mois d'août.

e. Comment s'appelle-t-il? — _____ s'appelle Matthieu et il est très mignon!

f. Ces jupes étaient très chères; _____ m'ont coûté trois cents dollars.

g. _____ aime écouter la radio quand je travaille.

h. _____ as faim? Si on allait manger?

i. _____ parles de Jean et Lisa? Oui, c'est vrai . . .

j. _____ ai beaucoup de devoirs, mais je n'ai pas envie de les faire parce que je veux regarder le dernier épisode de *American Idol*.

LE QUÉBEC

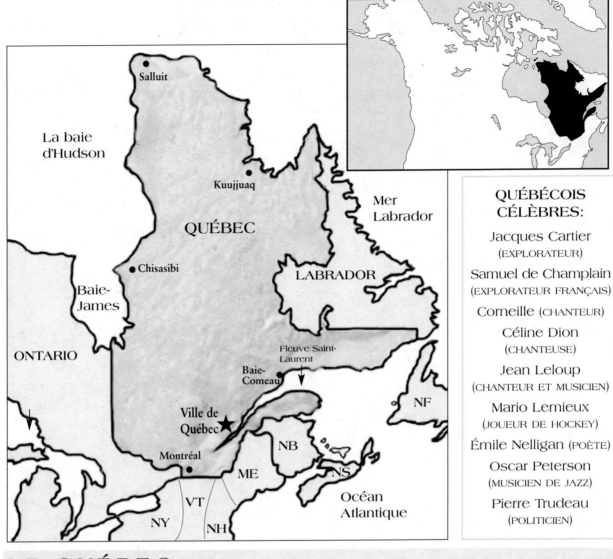

QUÉBÉCOIS CÉLÈBRES:

Jacques Cartier (EXPLORATEUR)

Samuel de Champlain (EXPLORATEUR FRANÇAIS)

Corneille (CHANTEUR)

Céline Dion (CHANTEUSE)

Jean Leloup (CHANTEUR ET MUSICIEN)

Mario Lemieux (JOUEUR DE HOCKEY)

Émile Nelligan (POÈTE)

Oscar Peterson (MUSICIEN DE JAZZ)

Pierre Trudeau (POLITICIEN)

LE QUÉBEC

Capitale:	Ville de Québec
Population:	7.900.000
Gouvernement:	Province du Canada (Confédération Parlementaire Démocratique)
Chef d'état:	Premier Ministre Jean Charest
Monnaie:	Dollar canadien
Langue:	Français
Ressources:	Aéronautique, forêts, haute couture, hydroélectricité, mines, pêche, télécommunications
Musique/Danse:	Clog, folk rock, folklorique, jazz, reel
Principales richesses touristiques:	Château Frontenac, Île de Bonaventure (réserve d'oiseaux), Île d'Orléans, Îles-de-la-Madeleine, Parc du Mont Tremblant, Péninsule de Gaspé, Région de l'Érable, Vieux Montréal, Vieux Québec
Cuisine:	Bière, cidre, crabes et langoustes, crêpes, creton du Québec, fromages, poisson, poisson fumé, pot-en-pot, poutine, ragoût de boulettes, sirop d'érable, soupe de petits pois verts, tartes au sucre, tourtière (tarte à la viande)

VOCABULAIRE LEÇON DEUX

ADJECTIFS

amusant/amusante	amusing	*jeune*	young
aveugle	blind	*juif/juive*	Jewish
blessé/blessée	injured	*malade*	sick
carré/carrée	square	*moyen/moyenne*	average
catholique	Catholic	*muet/muette*	mute
chauve	bald	*obligatoire*	necessary, required
délicieux/ délicieuse	delicious		
dernier/dernière	last, past	*pauvre*	poor
doux/douce	sweet, soft	*plat/plate*	flat
dur/dure	hard	*plein/pleine*	full
énorme	enormous	*prêt/prête*	ready
entier/entière	entire	*privé/privée*	private
étrange	strange	*protestant/ protestante*	Protestant
froid/froide	cold	*quotidien/ quotidienne*	daily
gauche	left	*récent/récente*	recent
gentil/gentille	nice, kind	*sage*	wise, intelligent
grand/grande	big, tall		
gratuit/gratuite	free of charge	*surpris/surprise*	surprised
grave	serious	*sympa*	nice, attractive (as a person)
gros/grosse	fat, big		
incroyable	unbelievable, incredible	*tranquille*	calm, quiet
		trempé/trempée	soaked

LEÇON DEUX

KEY GRAMMAR CONCEPTS

A) LE PASSÉ COMPOSÉ → *The past tense*

B) L'IMPARFAIT → *The imperfect tense*

C) LE PASSÉ COMPOSÉ ET L'IMPARFAIT → *The past tense and the imperfect tense*

D) LES PRONOMS ACCENTUÉS → *Stressed pronouns*

A) LE PASSÉ COMPOSÉ

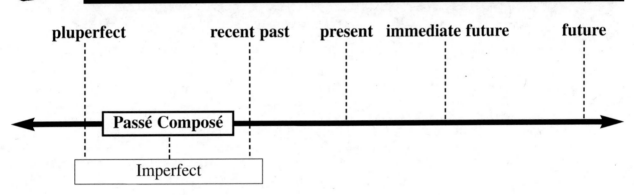

The *passé composé* is a verbal tense used to report **completed actions** — events that took place in the past.

EXAMPLES: *Elles **ont gagné** le grand prix.*
They won the big prize.

*Nous **avons cassé** la fenêtre avec le ballon.*
We broke the window with the ball.

*Hier soir j'**ai parlé** avec ma mère pendant trente minutes.*
Last night I talked with my mother for thirty minutes.

Helpful Tip: Whenever you tell how long something lasted, you must use the *passé composé* because you are conveying an ending point.

Verbs in the *passé composé* are made up of two parts: the auxiliary or "helping verb," and the past participle. The auxiliary verb is either *"avoir"* or *"être"* conjugated in the present tense and followed by the past participle.

1) LES VERBES CONJUGUÉS AVEC "AVOIR"

For most verbs in French, the *passé composé* is formed with the present tense of the auxiliary verb *"avoir"* and the past participle.

Here is the formula for constructing the *passé composé*:

Subject	+	*Avoir*	+	Past Participle
J'		*ai*		
Tu		*as*		
Il/Elle	+	*a*	+	*mangé (écrit, pris, etc.)*
Nous		*avons*		
Vous		*avez*		
Ils/Elles		*ont*		

Here are three model verbs in the *passé composé*:

PARLER		FINIR		ENTENDRE	
j'ai parlé	nous avons parlé	j'ai fini	nous avons fini	j'ai entendu	nous avons entendu
tu as parlé	vous avez parlé	tu as fini	vous avez fini	tu as entendu	vous avez entendu
il a parlé	ils ont parlé	elle a fini	ils ont fini	il a entendu	ils ont entendu

Here is a list of some common verbs with irregular past participles:

asseoir → **assis**	*croire* → **cru**	*lire* → **lu**	*recevoir* → **reçu**
avoir → **eu**	*dire* → **dit**	*mettre* → **mis**	*savoir* → **su**
boire → **bu**	*écrire* → **écrit**	*offrir* → **offert**	*suivre* → **suivi**
connaître → **connu**	*être* → **été**	*pouvoir* → **pu**	*voir* → **vu**
courir → **couru**	*faire* → **fait**	*prendre* → **pris**	*vouloir* → **voulu**

2) L'ACCORD DU PARTICIPE PASSÉ

With verbs conjugated with *"avoir,"* the past participle must agree in gender and number with the direct object (pronoun) **if, and only if**, it precedes the auxiliary.

Let's take a look at a model sentence: *J'ai mangé le sandwich.* There is no preceding direct object. What if we replace "the sandwich" with "it"? Then we write: *Je l'ai mangé.* In this example, the preceding direct object is masculine, singular, so no changes are needed.

Let's examine some others where changes <u>are</u> needed.

⚜ **EXAMPLES:** *J'ai payé **la baguette** mais il l'a **prise**.*
    I paid for the baguette, but he took it.

*Il aime **les photos** que j'ai **prises**.*
    He likes the photos I took.

*Combien de **gâteaux** est-ce que tu as **achetés**?*
How many cakes did you buy?

Direct Object after *"avoir"*	Direct Object (pronoun) before *"avoir"*
Il a mis les pulls. →	*Il **les** a mis.* (m. pl.)
J'ai cassé la chaise. →	*Je **l'**ai cassée.* (f. s.)
Nous avons vendu les places. →	*Nous **les** avons vendues.* (f. pl.)
Tu as connu ce monsieur. →	*Tu **l'**as connu.* (m. s.)
Vous avez écrit les devoirs. →	*Vous **les** avez écrits.* (m. pl.)

ATTENTION! The past participle <u>never</u> agrees with an <u>indirect</u> object. *J'ai parlé à Claire hier.* → *Je lui ai parlé.*

3) LES VERBES CONJUGUÉS AVEC "ÊTRE"

There are sixteen "motion" and "existential" verbs that use *"être"* rather than *"avoir"* as the auxiliary verb in compound tenses such as the *passé composé*. With *"être"* as the auxiliary, the past participle must always agree with the subject.

Set 1: Coming/Going			
aller	to go	*rentrer*	to return
arriver	to arrive	*sortir*	to go out
entrer	to go in, to enter	*venir*	to come
partir	to go away		
Set 2: Up/Down/Stay/Fall			
descendre	to go down	*rester*	to stay
monter	to go up	*tomber*	to fall
Set 3: Returning/Passing			
passer	to pass, to go by	*revenir*	to come back
retourner	to return		
Set 4: "Birth"/"Death"			
devenir	to become	*naître*	to be born
mourir	to die		

Some of these "motion" verbs have irregular past participles:

devenir → ***devenu***	*revenir* → ***revenu***
mourir → ***mort***	*venir* → ***venu***
naître → ***né***	

ATTENTION! *Monter, descendre, passer, rentrer, retourner* and *sortir* can use both *"avoir"* and *"être"* as auxiliary verbs. If the verb is transitive (i.e., if the verb takes a direct object), you need to use *"avoir."* If the verb is intransitive (no direct object), use *"être."*

Transitive: ***J'ai monté*** *la valise de ma mère.*
I carried my mother's suitcase upstairs.

Intransitive: ***Je suis montée*** *dans ma chambre pour écouter de la musique.*
I went up to my room to listen to some music.

Transitive: ***J'ai descendu*** *mes devoirs et je les ai montrés à mes parents.*
I brought my homework downstairs, and I showed it to my parents.

Intransitive: ***Je suis descendue*** *pour parler avec mes amis.*
I came downstairs to talk with my friends.

4) LES VERBES RÉFLÉCHIS

All reflexive verbs use "*être*" as the auxiliary verb in the *passé composé*.

s'asseoir	
je me suis assis(e)	*nous nous sommes assis(e)s*
tu t'es assis(e)	*vous vous êtes assis(e)(s)*
il s'est assis	*ils se sont assis*
elle s'est assise	*elles se sont assises*

Helpful Tips: **1)** You may have noticed the agreement of the past participle with the reflexive pronoun *(elle s'est assise)*. The plural is *elles se sont assises*.
2) Don't forget the agreement of the past participle with the subject when verbs are conjugated with *être!*

5) LE PASSÉ COMPOSÉ NÉGATIF

Negative sentences in the *passé composé* follow this pattern:

> **Subject + *Ne* + Auxiliary + *Pas* + Past Participle**
> (*avoir, être* conjugated
> in the present tense)

⚜ **EXAMPLES:** *Il **n'a pas vu** ce film avec Catherine Deneuve.*
He didn't see that movie with Catherine Deneuve.

*Nous **n'avons pas reçu** votre carte.*
We didn't receive your letter.

*Elle **n'est pas allée** au concert avec Jules.*
She didn't go to the concert with Jules.

EXERCICES

1. Conjugate these verbs in the *passé composé*:

marcher   finir

_____   _____

_____   _____

_____   _____

_____   _____

_____   _____

vendre (ne . . . pas)   **se reposer**

_____   _____

_____   _____

_____   _____

_____   _____

_____   _____

2. Complete the following sentences with the correct form of the *passé composé*:

a. Hier nous _____ des exercices ennuyeux au tableau noir. (écrire)

b. Je _____ à Montréal au Québec. (naître)

c. Le pauvre garçon _____ chanter une seule note dans la chanson. ([ne . . . pas] pouvoir)

d. Vous _____ au Labrador l'année dernière. ([ne . . . pas] aller)

e. Je _____ ma Renault chez René-Lévesque, le gentil monsieur qui habite au coin du boulevard. (conduire)

f. Elles _____ deux pièces de Shakespeare. (lire)

g. Mon cousin, qui est aveugle et muet, _____ un accident hier soir. (avoir)

h. M. Gervais me _____ une excellente glace au chocolat. (vendre)

i. Caroline _____ à côté de Julien la semaine dernière. ([ne . . . pas] s'asseoir).

j. Ma sœur _____ trop vite et elle _____. (descender/tomber)

k. Ma copine et moi, nous _____ aux Tuileries pour regarder les écureuils. (se promener)

3. There are six errors in the following paragraph. Underline and correct them:

Cet été j'ai allé à la mer avec ma famille. Nous avons passé deux semaines entières dans une jolie maison. Pendant le voyage ma mère ait conduit notre nouvelle voiture et mon père a conduit la vieille. Ma grand-mère ne pouvait pas nous accompagner cette année parce qu'elle était malade. Quand nous avon arrivés, je suis allé au magasin de photo du quartier et je me suis achetés une pellicule pour mon appareil-photo. J'ai prise beaucoup de photos de ma famille. Après, mes parents se sont couché. Moi, je suis allé à la discothèque pour retrouver des amis.

4. Put the following sentences into the *passé composé*:

a. Je pars. _____

b. Il ne me parle pas. _____

c. Tu nous écris. _____

d. Elle vous téléphone. _____

e. Vous la croyez. _____

f. Elle s'habille. _____

g. Je ne l'attends pas. _____

h. Tu la comprends. _____

i. Vous les recevez. _____

j. Je ne vais pas à la plage. _____

k. Je reviens à minuit. _____

l. Ils ne s'amusent pas. _____

5. Complete the following sentences with the correct form of the *passé composé*. Make the past participle agree when necessary:

a. Je ne trouve plus les nouveaux disques de Kanye West que je

_____ hier. (acheter)

b. Est-ce que tu _____ Louise ce matin? (voir) –Oui, je

_____ boulevard Saint Michel. (voir)

c. Arthur, où est votre composition d'anglais? –Monsieur, mon chien

la _____. (manger)

d. Quels DVD est-ce que tu _____ pendant
le week-end? (regarder)

e. Est-ce que vous _____ ma lettre? (recevoir) –Oui, je

la _____ hier. (lire)

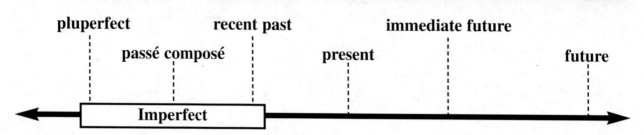

The **imperfect** is another past tense. It is used to describe ongoing actions, to make descriptions, to tell time, and to describe habits in the past.

WHEN DO YOU USE THE IMPERFECT?

1 **to express an ongoing (incomplete) action in the past**

> **EXAMPLES:** *Quand Louise est arrivée chez moi, je **regardais** Glee.*
> When Louise arrived at my house, I was watching *Glee*.
>
> *Il **pleuvait** donc nous ne sommes pas allés à la piscine.*
> It was raining, so we did not go to the pool.

2 **to describe a state of mind or a physical state in the past**

> **EXAMPLES:** *Napoléon **était** petit, mais il n'**était** pas tellement plus petit que la moyenne de l'époque.*
> Napoleon was short, but he was not that much shorter than the average at that time.
>
> *Je suis allé chez le dentiste parce que j'**avais** mal aux dents.*
> I went to the dentist because I had a toothache.

3 **to express time in the past**

> **EXAMPLE:** *Quand le voleur est entré, il **était** onze heures.*
> When the thief broke in, it was 11 o'clock.

4 **to express an action which used to take place or was done repeatedly (habit) in the past**

> **EXAMPLES:** *Quand j'étais jeune, je **jouais** au baseball dans le jardin.*
> When I was young, I used to play baseball in the yard.

*Il y a cinq ans, j'**habitais** à Québec et j'**achetais** du pain frais tous les matins.*

> Five years ago, I lived in Quebec, and I used to buy fresh bread every morning.

1) LES VERBES RÉGULIERS

With the exception of the verb *"être,"* all verbs in the imperfect are regular. For this reason,
the imperfect is often a favorite tense of French students.

The formation of the imperfect is quite simple:

◆ Start with the *"nous"* form of the present indicative
◆ Take off the *"-ons"*
◆ Replace it with the following endings:

-ais	-ions
-ais	-iez
-ait	-aient

In the three model verbs below, notice the *"nous"* form of the present indicative in parentheses; the ending *"-ons"* is crossed out so that you are left with the stem of the imperfect.

Here are three model verbs fully conjugated in the imperfect:

THE IMPERFECT (e.g., I was speaking, I used to speak, etc.)		
PARLER	**FINIR**	**ENTENDRE**
(nous parl~~ons~~)	(nous finiss~~ons~~)	(nous entend~~ons~~)
je parl**ais**	je finiss**ais**	j'entend**ais**
tu parl**ais**	tu finiss**ais**	tu entend**ais**
il parl**ait**	elle finiss**ait**	il entend**ait**
nous parl**ions**	nous finiss**ions**	nous entend**ions**
vous parl**iez**	vous finiss**iez**	vous entend**iez**
ils parl**aient**	elles finiss**aient**	ils entend**aient**

2) "ÊTRE"

"Être" is the <u>only</u> irregular verb in the imperfect tense!

ÊTRE	
j'étais	nous étions
tu étais	vous étiez
il était	elles étaient

3) Les verbes pronominaux

There are no special rules for reflexive verbs. The formation of the imperfect is the same as for regular verbs.

se demander → nous nous demand~~ons~~	
je me demandais	*nous nous demandions*
tu te demandais	*vous vous demandiez*
elle se demandait	*elles se demandaient*

4) Verbes à changements orthographiques

◆ Verbs like *"manger"* need to keep the *"j"* sound in the imperfect. Consequently, you must add an *"e"* before *a, o,* or *u,* just as in the present *"nous"* form.

je mangeais	*nous mangions*
tu mangeais	*vous mangiez*
elle mangeait	*elles mangeaient*

◆ Verbs like *"commencer"* need to keep the *"s"* sound. Therefore, there is a *"ç"* (cedille) before *a, o,* or *u,* just as in the present *"nous"* form, *"commençons."*

je commençais	*nous commencions*
tu commençais	*vous commenciez*
elle commençait	*elles commençaient*

EXERCICES ▶

1. Change these verbs to the correct form of the imperfect:

a. je conduis   → _____

b. tu vas   → _____

c. nous voyons   → _____

d. elles se parlent → _____

e. ils voyagent   → _____

f. elle court   → _____

g. vous vous rasez → _____

h. j'entends → _____

i. tu choisis → _____

j. elle avance → _____

2. Use the correct form of the imperfect in these sentences:

a. Il _____ une heure du matin quand mes parents sont rentrés. (être)

b. Le sofa ne _____ pas confortable, alors je ne l'ai pas acheté. (paraître)

c. A chaque fois que mon pere rentrait du bureau le soir, le chien _____ (aboyer)

d. Quand elle était jeune, ma tante _____ souvent à la piscine municipale d'Ajaccio. (nager)

e. L'année dernière, les cours de maths _____ à 8 heures. (commencer)

3. There are four errors in the following paragraph. Underline and correct them:

Quand j'étais enfant je ne veulais jamais aller à l'école. En général je me cacheait sous les couvertures pendant que le réveil sonnait. Un jour ma mère a commencé à me réveiller à six heures du matin. Je n'ai pas du tout fait attention. Mais quand elle m'a renversé un verre d'eau froide sur la tête, j'ai crié comme un fou; j'étais trempé comme une soupe!

(correction above line: j'étais)

Understanding the difference between the *passé composé* and the *imparfait* is a sign of a good French speaker. With practice, you'll become more comfortable choosing which tense to use.

WHAT IS THE IMPERFECT TENSE USED FOR?

1 an habitual action in the past

> **EXAMPLE:** *Quand j'étais petit, j'**allais** chez ma grand-mère tous les dimanches.*
> When I was young, I used to go to my grandmother's every Sunday.

2 an action or a situation which begins in the past and is continuing at the time of a second past action

> **EXAMPLES:** *Le ciel **était** bleu quand je suis sortie.*
> The sky was blue when I went out.
> (It had been blue for a while before I went out.)
>
> *Les enfants **dansaient** et **criaient** quand le bibliothécaire s'est mis en colère parce qu'il y avait trop de bruit.*
> The children were dancing and screaming when the librarian became angry because there was too much noise.

As you can see, in order to decide which tense to choose, you need to pay close attention to the story — the context. Remember that any verb can be in either tense . . . it just depends how it relates to the other verbs in the story. To be in the imperfect, the action does not need to be long, only longer than another action in the same context.

◆ Notice the contrast provided by choosing the imperfect and then the *passé composé* in these two sentences.

> **EXAMPLES:** *Le bébé **pleurait** quand sa mère est entrée.*
> The baby was crying when his mother came in.
>
> *Le bébé a **pleuré** quand le monstre est arrivé.*
> The baby cried when the monster came in.

◆ On the other hand, a series of separate past actions will all be in the *passé composé*.

> **EXAMPLE:** *Le joueur de basket **a lancé** le ballon à son ami qui l'**a mis** dans le panier.*
> The basketball player threw the ball to his friend, who put it in the basket.

3 Very often (but not always) *croire, devoir, être, penser, pouvoir, savoir* and *vouloir* call for the imperfect because they are used to . . .

◆ **describe**

> *Le film **était** intéressant, mais l'intrigue **était** ennuyeuse.*
> The film was interesting, but the plot was boring.

◆ **express a state of mind**

> *Elle **voulait** aller Chez Panisse parce qu'elle **avait** faim.*
> She wanted to go to Chez Panisse because she was hungry.

◆ **express a continuing obligation**

> *Elle n'est pas venue avec nous parce qu'elle **devait** étudier pour un examen.*
> She didn't come with us because she had to study for an exam.

◆ **express a form of knowledge or awareness**

> *Est-ce que tu **savais** que Baton Rouge **était** un nom français?*
> Did you know that Baton Rouge was a French name?

ATTENTION! If you know when the state of mind, obligation, or knowledge started or ended, or if you know exactly how long it lasted, use the *passé composé.*

⚜ **EXAMPLES:** *Hier il **a plu** toute la journée et Bernard **a été** de mauvaise humeur du martin jusqu'au soir.*
> Yesterday it rained, and Bernard was in a bad mood all day.

*Soudain la voiture **a commencé** à faire des bruits étranges et j'**ai dû** la conduire au garage.*
> Suddenly the car started making strange noises, and I had to take it to the garage.

*Quand j'**ai vu** l'énorme chien, j'**ai été** surpris.*
> When I saw the enormous dog, I was surprised.

EXERCICES

1. The following paragraphs will help you practice using the *passé composé* or the *imparfait*. Choose the tense which best captures the spirit of the narrative:

Passage 1

Le vingt-neuf août c'est mon anniversaire. Quand je _____

(être) petit, je _____ (aimer) beaucoup ce jour. Mes

parents me _____ (acheter) toujours des cadeaux

intéressants: une fois je _____ (recevoir) une collection

de timbres et une autre année ils me _____ (donner) une

table de pique-nique. Je leur _____ (dire) toujours, "Merci

beaucoup." Une fois mon oncle me _____ (surprendre). Il

_____ (arriver) avec des cheveux blancs et une grande

chemise noire. Je _____ ([ne . . . pas] le reconnaître).

Quand enfin je _____ (voir) que ce _____

(être) mon oncle, je _____ (être) très content.

Passage 2

Il _____ (être) deux heures de l'après-midi quand

l'examen _____ (commencer) dans la grande salle. Les

étudiants _____ (être) calmes et _____

(tailler) leurs crayons. Ils _____ (écouter) attentivement

les questions orales. Après un quart d'heure, il _____ (se

passer) quelque chose de bizarre. Un oiseau blessé _____

(entrer) par la fenêtre. Il _____ (voler) d'un bout à l'autre

de la classe. Personne ne _____ (faire attention) à l'exam-

en. Enfin tous les élèves _____ (devoir) sortir de la salle

pour chercher un endroit plus tranquille pour passer l'examen. Quelle horreur,

l'examen _____ (être) déjà assez dur sans distractions!

Passage 3

L'année dernière, ma famille et moi, nous _____

(passer) quelques jours dans la ville de Québec. Nous _____

(visiter) les musées, le Château Frontenac et aussi nous _____

(aller) au Parlement. Le jour où nous sommes allés au Parlement, je me

souviens que nous _____ (se réveiller) de très bonne

heure. D'abord nous _____ (prendre) le petit déjeuner et

après nous _____ (partir) en autobus. Il _____

(être) sept heures du matin, mais il _____ (faire) chaud

parce que ce _____ (être) l'été. Quand nous

_____ (arriver) au Parlement, nous _____

(être) surpris de voir la quantité de gens qu'il y _____

(avoir) à l'entrée. Il y avait déjà beaucoup de monde, et nous

_____ (devoir) faire la queue pendant plus de cinquante

minutes.

D) LES PRONOMS ACCENTUÉS

The following words are **"stressed" pronouns**. They refer only to people.

moi	→ me	*nous*	→ us
toi	→ you	*vous*	→ you
lui, elle	→ him, her	*eux, elles*	→ them
soi	→ oneself in general		

STRESSED PRONOUNS ARE USED IN MANY CIRCUMSTANCES:

1 after the prepositions and prepositional phrases listed here

à	→ at, in	*devant*	→ in front of
à côté de	→ next to	*entre*	→ between
à travers	→ across	*jusqu'à*	→ until
après	→ after	*parmi*	→ among
au-dessous de	→ below	*pour*	→ for
au-dessus de	→ above	*près de*	→ near
avec	→ with	*sans*	→ without
contre	→ against	*sous*	→ under
dans	→ in	*sur*	→ on
de	→ from	*vers*	→ toward
derrière	→ behind		

EXAMPLES: *Marie pense toujours à moi.*
Marie always thinks about me.

J'ai acheté la chemise pour lui, pas pour toi.
I bought the shirt for him, not for you.

À l'examen, on travaille chacun pour soi.
During the exam, one works for oneself.

ATTENTION! *Chez* is a special preposition that means "at the place of." It is used only with people.

EXAMPLE: *Je passe toujours Noël chez eux.*
I always spend Christmas at their place.

2 after *ce + être (c'est/ce sont)*

EXAMPLES: *Qui a dit cela? –C'est elle; ce n'est pas moi.*
Who said that? –It's her; it's not me.

C'est nous qui avons lavé la voiture.
We are the ones who washed the car.

Ce sont eux!
It's them!

3 **in comparisons**

aussi . . . que (qu') → as . . . as *autant . . . que (qu')* → as much as	*moins . . . que (qu')* → less . . . than *plus . . . que (qu')* → more . . . than

EXAMPLES: *Antoine est **plus** grand que **moi**.*
Antoine is taller than me.

*Monsieur Fontaine est **aussi** chauve que **toi**.*
Mr. Fontaine is as bald as you.

4 **when you want to stress who the subject is**

EXAMPLE: ***Moi**, je suis gentille, **toi**, tu es méchant.*
I am nice, <u>you</u> are mean!

5 **when the pronoun stands alone** (the verb is implied, but not expressed)

EXAMPLE: *Qui a fait cela? –**Moi**.*
Who did that? –Me (I did).

A FINAL NOTE

You will often see the French word *"-même"* placed after the stressed pronoun for added emphasis.

EXAMPLES: *J'ai fait ces crêpes **moi-même**.*
I made these crepes myself.

*Le Premier Ministre **lui-même** a parlé au champion, toujours souriant de sa récente victoire sportive.*
The Prime Minister himself talked to the champion, still smiling from his recent sports victory.

EXERCICES

1. Complete with the appropriate stressed pronoun:

a. J'ai fait cette statue _moi_ -même.

b. C'est _lui_ qui a résolu le problème. Il est intelligent!

c. Et _nous_ , nous allons au cinéma ce soir. Elle aime les mêmes films que _moi_ .

d. Paul et Antoine sont sympa. J'aime bavarder [to chatter/gossip] avec _eux_ .

e. J'ai téléphoné à mes cousines. Elles ne sont pas chez _elles_ parce qu'on ne répond pas.

f. Est-ce que c'est _toi_ ~~lui~~ qui as fait ce délicieux gâteau?

g. Qui a dit ça? _moi_ et je sais que j'ai raison.

h. Paul a dit la même chose. _lui_ aussi il pense que ce livre est trop long.

i. Pour les vacances, _lui_ ~~après~~ il va à la Réunion, _eux_ ils vont aux îles de la Madeleine et _moi_ je reste chez ~~moi~~ _moi_.

j. C'est grâce à _lui_ que l'équipe a gagné. Vous avez très bien joué.

2. Answer these questions with the stressed pronoun that corresponds to the word in parentheses:

a. Qui a emprunté [to borrow] mon pull jaune? (Thomas) _lui, il l'a emprunté_

b. Qui a fait la vaisselle [crockery] ce matin? (Ma sœur et moi) _Nous nous l'a fait_

c. Qui a réparé les bicyclettes? (Anne et Catherine) _Elles Elles les ont réparé_

d. Qui a réussi à l'examen? (Tu) _Toi tu y l'a réussi._

e. Qui est prêt à partir? (Je) _moi je suis prêt à partir._

3. There are four errors in the following paragraph. Underline and correct them:

Dimanche prochain, je pensais aller faire un pique-nique au bord [seaside]

de la mer avec ~~tu~~ [TOI] *et les enfants. Mais si ~~me~~ tu ne veux pas venir* [avec]

je peux y aller seule avec ~~leur~~ [eux]*. Les enfants ne sont plus des bébés. Elsa,*

qui est encore petite, ne pourra pas porter de sac, mais Pierre, ~~toi~~, [lui]

est [ratmer] *assez grand pour m'aider.* [Thus] *Ainsi tu peux choisir en toute liberté ce que*

tu veux faire.

4. Translate the following phrases:

a. with my friend	avec mon ami
b. under the bed	sous le lit
c. in the tunnel	dans le tunnel
d. next to the house	à côté de la maison
~~**e.**~~ across the globe (world)	à travers ~~la globe~~ le monde
f. in front of the book	devant le livre
g. after the game	après la joue
h. against the wall	contre le mur
i. until 8 o'clock	jusqu'à huit heures
j. behind the barn	derrière la grange

PRATIQUE DE L'ORAL
QUESTIONS PAR DEUX

These two sets of questions use grammatical structures and vocabulary from this lesson. Working with a partner, alternate asking and answering each question. When you get to the bottom of each list, start over at the top, switching roles. As a variation, write out the answers in complete sentences.

A) Quelle heure **était**-il lorsque tu **es revenu(e)** de Montréal?

Es-tu **allé(e)** au Canada parce que tu **avais** besoin de vacances?

Pourquoi **mangeais**-tu de la tourtière quand je **suis arrivé(e)**?

Commençait-il à pleuvoir quand tu **as quitté** l'école?

Ton ami **pleurait**-il parce qu'il **avait perdu** son match de hockey?

Étudiais-tu quand je t'ai **téléphoné**?

Pourquoi **était**-il aussi étrange quand je l'**ai rencontré**?

B) Penses-tu souvent **à moi**?

Ton père est-il **plus** grand **que toi**?

Pourquoi es-tu parti **sans lui**?

Est-ce vous qui avez cassé ma fenêtre?

As-tu cuisiné cette délicieuse tarte **toi-même**?

Ton frère est-il **aussi** amusant **que toi**?

Aimes-tu aller au cinéma **avec lui**?

Exercices De Révision

A) Le passé composé

1. Complete the following sentences with the correct form of the *passé composé*:

a. Pauline et Marguerite _____ dans la cuisine et leurs parents leur ont dit que toute la famille allait faire un voyage. (entrer)

b. Nous _____ tout Victor Hugo en un mois. (lire)

c. Tu _____ le premier à donner le devoir au professeur. ([ne . . . pas] être)

d. Quand j'étais à l'hôpital, mes amis me _____ un énorme bouquet de fleurs. (envoyer)

e. Le facteur _____ distribuer le courrier parce que le chien le menaçait. ([ne . . . pas] pouvoir)

f. Comme projet, notre classe _____ le livre de la Genèse d'anglais en français. (traduire)

g. Tout le monde _____ pendant le Festival "Juste Pour Rire" à Québec. (rire)

h. Personne ne _____ dans l'accident de voiture. (mourir)

i. Elle _____ la télévision à huit heures. (allumer)

j. Est-ce que tu _____ le nouveau numéro de Mademoiselle? (voir)

2. There are five errors in the following paragraph. Underline and correct them:

Hier pendant le cours de français, nous avons dû écrire de petits dialogues. Malheureusement, je n'ai pas pouvu travailler avec Marie.

Oui, c'est parce qu'elle a choisie de travailler avec Luc. Luc est le meilleur joueur de football américain de l'école. En plus, il parle très bien français, parce qu'il ait passé un an en Normandie avec sa famille. Je n'aime pas trop Luc; il n'est pas très sympa. Pendant la classe, Marie et Luc ont beaucoup ri. Leur dialogue étais bien écrit et très drôle. Moi, j'ai travaillé avec Stéphanie, la fille la plus ennuyeuse de la classe. Notre dialogue était nul, avec beaucoup de fautes de grammaire et seulement deux nouveaux mots de vocabulaire. J'était déçu parce que je voulais travailler avec Marie, la fille la plus douce du monde.

B) L'IMPARFAIT

1. **Complete the following sentences with the correct form of the imperfect:**

   a. Qu'est-ce que tu _____ hier soir pendant que je

   _____? (faire/téléphoner)

   b. J'ai pensé qu'il _____, alors je ne suis pas allé à la plage d'Oka. (pleuvoir)

   c. Quand je _____ petit, je déjeunais chez ma grand-mère tous les dimanches. (être)

   d. Madonna _____ toujours dans un miroir avant d'entrer en scène. (se regarder)

   e. Hier soir j'ai rêvé que nous _____ dans un grand incendie. (mourir)

f. Justin Bieber et Miley Cyrus _____ depuis trois heures, quand le journaliste les a vues. (bavarder)

g. Nous _____ quand vous êtes arrivés. (se reposer)

h. Pendant que je _____ au Parc Jean-Drapeau, je

_____ le concert de Kanye West. (courir/écouter)

i. Mon petit frère _____ tellement peur du monstre que nous avons dû partir avant la fin du film. (avoir)

j. Est-ce que vous _____ marcher après votre accident? (pouvoir)

2. There are five errors in the following paragraph. Underline and correct them:

Un soir, je dormai quand soudain le téléphone a sonné. Je pensais que je rêvais parce qu'en général il n'y ont personne qui appelle après dix heures du soir. Comme le téléphone continuais à sonner, je savais que ce n'était pas un rêve. Ni mon père ni ma mère n'étions à la maison. Le téléphone a continué à sonner. Je me suis levé et j'ai répondu. Il n'y avais personne au bout du fil.

C) LE PASSÉ COMPOSÉ ET L'IMPARFAIT

Complete this paragraph with either the *passé composé* or the *imparfait*. Choose the tense that you believe best captures the feeling of the narrative:

Quand elle _____ (être) petite, ma sœur Julie

_____ (être) sûre de pouvoir devenir une joueuse de

baseball célèbre. Tous les samedis elle _____ (s'entraîner)

dans le jardin parce qu'elle _____ (vouloir) être acceptée

dans l'équipe de l'école primaire. Pendant que Julie _____

(frapper) la balle, l'oncle Bernard _____ (rire) et

_____ (se moquer) d'elle. Julie _____

(être) agacée mais, elle _____ (continuer) à s'entraîner. Un

jour, Julie _____ (se réveiller) de bonne heure. Elle

_____ (s'habiller) très vite et elle _____

(descendre) à la cuisine parce qu'elle _____ (avoir) faim. À

sept heures elle _____ (regarder) par la fenêtre et elle

_____ (voir) Chris qui _____ (passer)

dans la rue. Julie _____ (appeler) et Chris

_____ (inviter) Julie à venir avec lui. Quand ils

_____ (arriver) au terrain de baseball, ils

_____ (voir) qu'un des joueurs _____

(manquer). Julie _____ (demander) si elle

_____ (pouvoir) prendre sa place. L'entraîneur

_____ (accepter). Julie _____ (jouer)

magnifiquement bien qu'elle _____ (devenir) la meilleure

joueuse de l'équipe. Ce soir-là, quand elle _____ (rentrer)

chez nous, elle _____ (raconter) toute l'histoire à la famille.

L'oncle Bernard _____ (être) très étonné.

D) LES PRONOMS ACCENTUÉS

1. There are three errors in the following paragraph. Underline and correct them:

Il y a eu un grand drame en classe ce matin. Le professeur a pensé que je trichais. J'étais assis entre Philippe et Thomas. Thomas, elle, est un excellent élève et il ne triche jamais. Mais Philippe qui était aussi à côté de toi ne fait jamais rien et il copie toujours sur des autres. C'est vraiment lui qui a triché, mais malheureusement le professeur a pensé que c'était vous. Je ne sais pas quoi faire. Mes parents vont être furieux. Qu'est-ce que tu en penses?

2. Fill in each blank with a stressed pronoun:

a. Est-ce qu'elle t'a invité chez _____?

b. Thomas va arriver dans dix minutes. _____ et _____, nous voulons répéter notre rôle pour la pièce.

c. C'est _____ qui avons gagné le match.

d. Peter Gammons . . . oui, c'était _____ qui présentait les sports hier soir.

e. Paul et Marc sont au premier rang. Nous sommes assis derrière _____.

f. _____ aussi, vous devez parler plus souvent en classe.

g. Est-ce que c'est _____ qui as téléphoné hier soir?

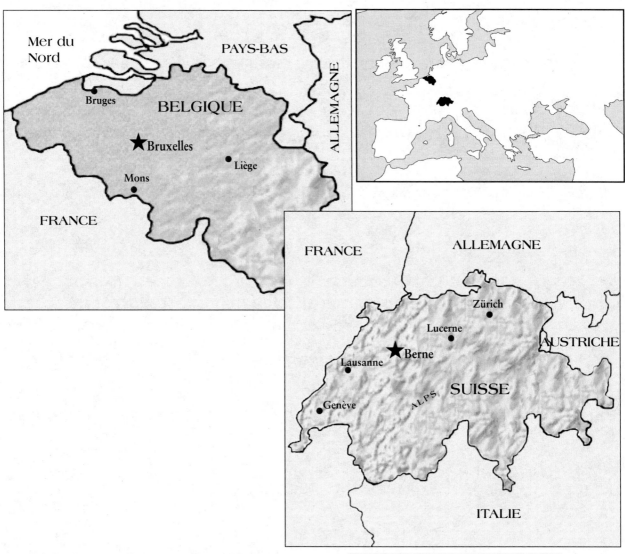

Mer du Nord

PAYS-BAS

ALLEMAGNE

● Bruges

BELGIQUE

★ Bruxelles

● Liège

● Mons

FRANCE

FRANCE   ALLEMAGNE

● Zürich

● Lucerne

★ Berne

AUSTRICHE

● Lausanne

SUISSE

ALPS

● Genève

ITALIE

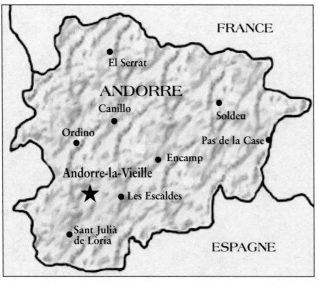

FRANCE

● El Serrat

ANDORRE

● Canillo

● Soldeu

● Ordino

Pas de la Case ●

● Encamp

Andorre-la-Vieille

★

● Les Escaldes

● Sant Julià de Lòria

ESPAGNE

ANDORRANS
CÉLÈBRES

Éric Bataille
(CHAMPION DE MOTO)

Luis Claret
(VIOLONCELLISTE)

Juli Minoves Triquell
(MINISTRE, DIPLOMATE, ÉCRIVAIN)

Antoni Morell
(ÉCRIVAIN)

Ricard Fiter Vilajoana
(ÉCRIVAIN, AVOCAT, MÉDIATEUR DE
LA PRINCIPAUTÉ D'ANDORRE
DEPUIS 1998)

L'EUROPE FRANCOPHONE:
LA BELGIQUE, LA SUISSE & ANDORRE

LA BELGIQUE

Capitale:	Bruxelles (également capitale de l'Union européenne)
Population:	10.400.000
Gouvernement:	Monarchie constitutionnelle
Chef d'état:	Le Roi Albert II Premier Ministre Yves Leterme
Monnaie:	Euro
Langues:	Français (sud), néerlandais (nord), allemand (sud-est)
Ressources:	Betteraves, bière, chocolat, métaux, produits chimiques, produits maraîchers (endives, asperges), sucre, sucrières, taille de diamants
Musique:	César Franck, classique
Principales richesses touristiques:	Béguinage de Bruges, Cathédrale de Gand, Foire du midi (Bruxelles), Forêt d'Ardenne, Grand Place de Bruxelles, Manneken Piss (Bruxelles)
Cuisine:	Bières, chocolat, cuisine française, frites, gaufres, moules marinières, plats régionaux, tomates aux crevettes

LA SUISSE

Capitale:	Berne
Population:	7.600.000
Gouvernement:	République fédérale
Chef d'état:	Président Micheline Calmy-Rey
Monnaie:	Franc suisse (CHF)
Langues:	Allemand, français, italien, romanche
Ressources:	Banques, chocolat, couteaux, fromages, horlogerie, produits pharmaceutiques
Musique:	Alphorn, chant yodlé, jazz
Principales richesses touristiques:	Les Alpes, Lac Léman, Lac des Quatre Cantons, Jungfraujoch (chemin de fer), vieille ville de Genève, Zurich
Cuisine:	Bière, fondues (fromage, bœuf, chocolat, charcuterie), gugelhopf (gâteau), kirsch, muesli (céréales), vin

LA PRINCIPAUTÉ D'ANDORRE

Capitale:	Andorre-la-Vieille
Population:	85.000
Gouvernement:	Gouverné par le président français (Nicolas Sarkozy) et l'évêque espagnol d'Urgel (Joan Enric Vives)
Chef d'état:	Premier Ministre Jaume Bartumen
Monnaie:	Euro
Langues:	Catalan (langue officielle), français, espagnol
Ressources:	Bœuf, pommes de terre, minéraux, tabac
Musique/Danse:	Jazz, musique classique et andalouse, opéra
Principales richesses touristiques:	Colonies de vacances de ski, Encamp, Les Escalades (spa à Engordany), paysages pittoresques, El Serrat
Cuisine:	Catalan-Français, cunillo (lapin), escudella (soupe), fromages et saucisses, truites de carreroles

BELGES CÉLÈBRES

Pieter Breugel (PEINTRE)

Kim Clijsters (JOUEUSE DE TENNIS)

Paul Delvaux (SURRÉALISTE)

Justine Henin (JOUEUSE DE TENNIS)

Maurice Maeterlinck (ÉCRIVAIN)

René Magritte (SURRÉALISTE)

Josquin des Prés (COMPOSITEUR)

Georges Rémi (Hergé) (AUTEUR DE TINTIN)

Pieter Paul Rubens (PEINTRE)

Georges Simenon (ÉCRIVAIN, CRÉATEUR DU PERSONNAGE DE MAIGRET)

Marguerite Yourcenar (ÉCRIVAIN)

SUISSES CÉLÈBRES

Friedrich Dürrenmatt (DRAMATURGE)

Roger Federer (JOUEUR DE TENNIS)

Max Frisch (ÉCRIVAIN DE ROMANS)

Albert Giacometti (SCULPTEUR)

Carl Jung (PSYCHANALYSTE)

Paul Klee (PEINTRE)

Carl Spitteler (AUTEUR ET LAURÉAT DU PRIX NOBEL)

VOCABULAIRE
LEÇON TROIS

ADJECTIFS

actuel/actuelle	current	*japonais/japonaise*	Japanese
anglais/anglaise	English	*jeune*	young
attentif/attentive	attentive	*laid/laide*	ugly
bouclé/bouclée	curly, buckled	*léger/légère*	light
caché/cachée	hidden	*lourd/lourde*	heavy
canadien/ canadienne	Canadian	*moche*	ugly, lousy, shoddy
cher/chère	expensive	*mort/morte*	dead
chrétien/ chrétienne	Christian	*mou/molle*	soft, mushy
confus/confuse	embarrassed	*nécessaire*	necessary
crevé/crevée	burst, exhausted	*occupé/occupée*	busy
		plusieurs	several, many
déchiré/déchirée	torn, ripped	*premier/première*	first
drôle	funny	*prochain/ prochaine*	next
éclaté/éclatée	burst		
étroit/étroite	narrow, tight	*prudent/prudente*	prudent, careful
fatigué/fatiguée	tired	*raide*	stiff
fidèle	faithful	*sans goût*	tasteless, without taste
fier/fière	proud		
gâté/gâtée	spoiled	*satisfait/satisfaite*	satisfied
imprimé/ imprimée	printed	*sec/sèche*	dry
		sourd/sourde	deaf
		têtu/têtue	stubborn
inutile	useless		

LEÇON TROIS

KEY GRAMMAR CONCEPTS 	**A) L'IMPÉRATIF** → *The imperative*
	B) LES ARTICLES DÉFINS, INDÉFINS ET PARTITIF → *Definite, indefinite and partitive articles*
	C) LE PASSÉ RÉCENT → *The recent past*
	D) LE PLUS-QUE-PARFAIT → *The pluperfect*

A) L'IMPÉRATIF

When you ask someone to do something or not to do something you use the **imperative**. In French, these commands have different forms depending on the person being addressed. There are imperative forms for "*tu*," "*nous*," and "*vous*."

1) LES IMPÉRATIFS AFFIRMATIFS (GIVING AFFIRMATIVE COMMANDS)——

For **-IR** verbs and for **-RE** verbs, the imperative forms are the same as in the corresponding forms of the present tense!

	Finir		*Courir*		*Prendre*	
(tu)	*Finis!*	Finish!	*Cours!*	Run!	*Prends!*	Take!
(nous)	*Finissons!*	Let's finish!	*Courons!*	Let's run!	*Prenons!*	Let's take!
(vous)	*Finissez!*	Finish!	*Courez!*	Run!	*Prenez!*	Take!

For **-ER** verbs, the only difference is that the "*tu*" form drops the final "*s*."

	Manger	
(tu)	*Mange!*	Eat!
(nous)	*Mangeons!*	Let's eat!
(vous)	*Mangez!*	Eat!

Helpful Tip: In French you never use a subject pronoun when delivering a command.

2) LES IMPÉRATIFS NÉGATIFS (GIVING NEGATIVE COMMANDS)

Negative imperatives in French are also simple. Just place a *"ne"* before the positive command form and a *"pas"* after it. *Voilà!* — you have formed a negative command.

⚜ **EXAMPLES:**   *Ne mange **pas**!*   Don't eat!
 *N'ouvrez **pas** la porte!*   Don't open the door!

3) L'IMPÉRATIF AVEC LES VERBES RÉFLÉCHIS

To form a positive command with a reflexive verb, simply add a hyphen and the following reflexive pronouns after the verb: *"toi," "nous,"* and *"vous."*

⚜ **EXAMPLES:**   *Lève-**toi**!*   Get up!
 *Asseyons-**nous**!*   Let's sit down!
 *Dépêchez-**vous**, les filles!*   Hurry up, girls!

Negative commands are a bit different. Here's the pattern:

◆ Start with *"ne"*
◆ Add a reflexive pronoun *("te," "nous," "vous")*
◆ End with the imperative verb form followed by *"pas,"* etc.

⚜ **EXAMPLES:**   ***Ne te** lève pas!*   Don't get up!
 ***Ne nous** asseyons pas!*   Let's not sit down!
 ***Ne vous** dépêchez pas!*   Don't hurry!

4) L'IMPÉRATIF DES VERBES ÊTRE, AVOIR, ALLER ET SAVOIR

Aller, avoir, être, and *savoir* are the only French verbs with irregular imperatives.

Here are the forms of the only verbs that are irregular in the imperative:

	Aller	*Avoir*	*Être*	*Savoir*
(tu)	*Va!*	*Aie!*	*Sois!*	*Sache!*
(nous)	*Allons!*	*Ayons!*	*Soyons!*	*Sachons!*
(vous)	*Allez!*	*Ayez!*	*Soyez!*	*Sachez!*

⚜ **EXAMPLES:**   ***Va** chercher le pain!*   Go get some bread!
 ***Ayez** confiance en moi!*   Trust me!
 ***Sois** sage!*   Be good! (Behave!)
 ***Sachez** que vous êtes très agaçants!*   Know that you are very annoying!

EXERCICES

1. Write the command form of the following verbs:

	tu	nous	vous
a. appeler	_____	_____	_____
b. dormir	_____	_____	_____
c. offrir (ne . . . pas)	_____	_____	_____
d. avoir (ne . . . pas)	_____	_____	_____
e. courir	_____	_____	_____
f. se raser	_____	_____	_____
g. venir (ne . . . pas)	_____	_____	_____
h. sauter	_____	_____	_____
i. essayer (ne . . . pas)	_____	_____	_____
j. aller	_____	_____	_____
k. s'habiller (ne . . . pas)	_____	_____	_____

2. There are eight errors in the following paragraph. Underline and correct them:

Mes chers amis, je suis très content de vous parler aujourd'hui.

Asseyiez-vous tous et n'avez pas peur. Je suis votre chef, votre

inspiration. Avez confiance en moi et ensemble nous résoudrons tous

les problèmes du monde. Etes tranquilles . . . je suis ici pour vous aider.

Mais, avant de continuer, mets s'il vous plaît vingt dollars dans

la casquette qu'on va passer parmi vous tout de suite. (Marc, passes

la casquette verte, s'il te plaît. Es prudent et vérifie bien que tout

le monde contribue.) À propos, mes chers amis, j'accepte la carte Visa et

MasterCard. Inscrivez simplement le numéro de votre carte sur une feuille

de papier et n'oublie pas d'inscrire la date d'expiration.

B) LES ARTICLES DÉFINIS, INDÉFINIS ET PARTITIFS

1) LES ARTICLES DÉFINIS

The **definite article** is used to indicate a <u>specific</u> person or thing.

EXAMPLE: *Le chat a mangé la souris.*
The cat ate the mouse.

Definite Articles		
	SINGULAR	PLURAL
MASCULINE	*le crayon, l'avion*	*les crayons, les avions*
FEMININE	*la voiture, l'école*	*les voitures, les écoles*

The article *l'* is used before any singular noun (masculine or feminine) beginning with a vowel, and in front of nouns beginning with a silent *"h."*

l'argent (m.)	→	the money	*l'usine* (f.)	→	the factory
l'homme (m.)	→	the man	*l'humidité* (f.)	→	the humidity

Note: There are, however, exceptions to this rule with *"h"*: e.g., *le haricot, le héros, la honte.*

When definite articles follow *à* and *de*, contractions are formed:

à/de + article		Contraction	Examples
à + le	→	*au*	*Nous allons au cinéma.*
à + les	→	*aux*	*Donnons les bonbons aux enfants.*
de + le	→	*du*	*Elle vient du gymnase.*
de + les	→	*des*	*Je vais vous parler des acteurs de ce film comique.*

ATTENTION! Remember, there is <u>no</u> contraction formed with either *l'* or *la*.

EXAMPLES: *Je vais à l'école dans le centre de Bruxelles.*
I am going to school in the center of Brussels.

Tu vas à la piscine.
You are going to the pool.

À quelle heure est-il revenu de la Foire du Midi?
At what time did he come back from the *"Foire du Midi"*?

Elle a téléphoné de l'hôpital.
She called from the hospital.

1 to designate nouns in an abstract or general sense

> **EXAMPLES:** *Le fer est plus dur que le coton.*
> Iron is harder than cotton.
>
> *L'argent ne fait pas le bonheur.*
> Money does not bring happiness.

2 before titles (except when directly addressing a person)

> **EXAMPLES:** *J'ai vu le président à la télé.*
> I saw the president on TV.
>
> **BUT:** *Bonne nuit, docteur Jekyl!*
> Good night, Doctor Jekyl!

3 before a language (except after *"en"*)

> **EXAMPLES:** *Nous apprenons le français.*
> We are learning French.

> **ATTENTION!** Do not add a definite article after *"en."*
>
> *Elle a écrit ce poème en zulu.*
> She wrote that poem in Zulu.

4 before days of the week when an action regularly happens on that day

> **EXAMPLES:** *Nous n'allons pas à l'école le dimanche.*
> We don't go to school on Sundays.
>
> *Mes parents vont souvent au cinéma le samedi.*
> My parents often go to the movies on Saturdays.
>
> **BUT:** *Thomas et Louise se marient dimanche.*
> Thomas and Louise are getting married on Sunday.

5 **to designate names of countries, continents, states, mountains, and rivers**

⚜ **EXAMPLE:** *La Belgique est plus petite que les États-Unis.*
Belgium is smaller than the United States.

6 **often with parts of the body (in place of a possessive adjective as in English)**

⚜ **EXAMPLES:** *Je me suis brossé les dents.*
I brushed my teeth.

Levez la main!
Raise your hand!

7 **with names of seasons and colors** (except after *"en"* or *"au"*... e.g., *en hiver, en été, en automne, au printemps*)

⚜ **EXAMPLES:** *J'aime l'hiver parce que je joue au squash.*
I like winter because I play squash.

Le gris est une couleur sombre.
Gray is a gloomy color.

8 **with dates**

⚜ **EXAMPLES:** *On est le 14 juillet.*
Today is July 14th.

Nous nous marierons le 6 septembre.
We will get married on September 6th.

9 **before nouns of weight and measure**

⚜ **EXAMPLES:** *Ces pommes coûtent quatre dollars le kilo.*
These apples cost four dollars a kilo.

Il a payé ces œufs biologiques trois dollars la douzaine.
He paid three dollars a dozen for those organic eggs.

10 **with certain expressions of time**

le matin →	in the morning
l'après-midi →	in the afternoon
le soir →	in the evening
la semaine prochaine (dernière) →	next week (last week)
le mois prochain (dernier) →	next month (last month)
l'année prochaine (dernière/passée) →	next year (last year)

EXAMPLES: *Le docteur Paul Farmer va à l'hôpital **le matin**.*
Doctor Paul Farmer goes to the hospital in the mornings.

*Nous regardons la télévision **le soir**.*
We watch television in the evenings.

***L'année prochaine** tu iras à l'université à Bruxelles.*
Next year you will go to college in Brussels.

2) LES ARTICLES INDÉFINIS ET LE PARTITIF

The **indefinite article** refers to nouns in a <u>general</u> way, without identifying a specific object or person.

EXAMPLES: *J'ai vu **une** souris dans le placard.*
I saw a mouse in the closet.

*Hier soir nous avons vu **un** bon film du cinéaste Jean-Luc Goddard.*
Last night we saw a good film of the cinematographer Jean-Luc Goddard.

Indefinite Articles		
	SINGULAR	PLURAL
MASCULINE	*un*	*des*
FEMININE	*une*	*des*

Des means "some" or "any" and is often not translated at all in English.

EXAMPLES: *Je connais un magasin qui vend **des** disques de rap en plusieurs langues.*
I know a shop that sells rap CDs in several languages.

*Avez-vous encore **des** billets pour le "Super Bowl"?*
Do you still have (any) tickets for the Super Bowl?

WHEN DO YOU USE THE PARTITIVE ARTICLE?

In French, whenever you are referring to "a part" of something—often referred to as "any" or "some" in English—you must use a partitive article. Keep in mind that while the French partitive means "part," "some," or "any," sometimes none of these words are used in English.

⚜ **EXAMPLES:** *Le matin il boit **du** jus d'orange.*
In the morning he drinks (some) orange juice.

*Est-ce que vous avez **du** temps?*
Do you have (any) free time?

Here are the four forms of the partitive:

> ***du*** — Masculine, singular
>
> ***de la*** — Feminine, singular
>
> ***de l'*** — Masculine/feminine, singular (before a vowel)
>
> ***des*** — All plural nouns

⚜ **EXAMPLES:** *Est-ce que vous voulez **du** lait dans votre café?*
Do you want (some) milk in your coffee?

*Il a acheté **de l'**essence à la station service.*
He bought gas at the gas station.

WHAT SITUATIONS CALL FOR THE USE OF DE (D')?

"De (d')" replaces the indefinite articles *"un, une, des"* and the partitive articles *"du, de la, de l', des"* in the following two situations:

1 **in negative sentences**

⚜ **EXAMPLES:** *Tu as de la chance, mais moi je n'ai pas **de** chance.*
You are lucky, but I am not lucky.

*Est-ce que vous avez **des** fraises? –Non. Je n'ai pas **de** fraises aujourd'hui.*
Do you have (any) strawberries? –No, I don't have (any) strawberries today.

*Pierre a un chien, mais moi, je n'ai pas **de** chien.*
Pierre has a dog, but I don't have a dog.

2 after expressions of quantity

Common adverbs of quantity:

assez de	→ enough	*trop de*	→ too much
beaucoup de	→ a lot of	*un peu de*	→ a little
combien de?	→ how much?/how many?		

Common nouns of quantity:

une boîte de	→ a box of	*un sac de*	→ a bag of
une bouteille de	→ a bottle of	*une tasse de*	→ a cup of
un morceau de	→ a piece of	*un verre de*	→ a glass of

⚜ **EXAMPLES:** ***Combien de** joueurs est-ce qu'il y a dans une équipe de basketball?*
How many players are there on a basketball team?

*Je voudrais **une bouteille d'**Orangina, s'il vous plaît.*
I would like a bottle of Orangina, please.

ATTENTION! The adjective *"plusieurs"* (several) is always followed directly by a plural noun.

⚜ **EXAMPLE:** *Je vais téléphoner à **plusieurs** amis ce soir.*
I will call several friends tonight.

ATTENTION! *"La plupart"* (most of) is followed by *"de"* + definite article.

⚜ **EXAMPLES:** ***La plupart des** enfants aiment les bonbons.*
Most children like candy.

***La plupart des** élèves n'aiment pas les devoirs.*
Most students don't like homework.

3 before plural nouns

"Des" also becomes *"de"* or *"d'"* in front of plural nouns that are preceded by an adjective.

⚜ **EXAMPLES:** *Elle a des problèmes.*
She has problems.

*Elle a **d'**énormes problèmes.*
She has huge problems.

BUT: *Elle a des problèmes intéressants.*
She has interesting problems.

*Nous avons vu **des** éléphants au Congo.*
We saw elephants in the Congo.

*Nous avons vu **de** gros éléphants au Congo.*
We saw fat elephants in the Congo.

BUT: *Nous avons vu **des** éléphants élégants au Congo.*
We saw elegant elephants in the Congo.

 EXERCICES ▶

1. **Write the appropriate article in front of the nouns, making any necessary contractions:**

   a. _____ enfants fatigués n'aiment pas aller à _____ musée.

   b. Est-ce que tu as envoyé _____ lettre à _____ mère de ton ami?

   c. Je vous attends à _____ arrêt d'autobus dans la banlieue de Lausanne.

   d. Mon père revient de _____ bureau à 7 heures.

   e. Est-ce que tu connais _____ homme qui est debout à côté

   de _____ magasin de vélos?

2. **Fill in the spaces with *"le, la, l', les, en, au, aux,"* or leave blank:**

   a. Ma sœur s'est cassé _____ jambe, en jouant au foot. C'est

   _____ docteur Picpus qui l'a soignée.

b. Est-ce que tu t'es lavé _____ mains?

c. J'apprends l'espagnol à l'école et je comprends très bien _____ japonais.

d. J'ai même écrit deux nouvelles _____ espagnol _____ semaine dernière.

e. Mon ami roux aime _____ carottes.

f. D'habitude je fais du sport _____ samedi.

g. _____ Sénégal est _____ Afrique de l'ouest.

h. Mon vieux chien Fido est mort _____ mardi dernier.

i. Quelle langue est-ce qu'on parle _____ Mexique? –On parle

_____ espagnol.

j. C'est une surprise: fermez _____ yeux!

3. **Make a list of supplies for a picnic in the Alps.** ATTENTION! **Use the partitive!**

Example: tomates   <u>**des tomates**</u>

a. pain _____ **f.** ketchup _____

b. eau minérale _____ **g.** glace _____

c. jambon _____ **h.** beaux verres _____

d. fruits _____ **i.** fromage _____

e. assiettes en papier **j.** glace à la vanille

_____ _____

4. Fill in the blanks with the appropriate article (definite, indefinite, partitive), *"de"* or nothing:

    a. Pour faire une tarte il faut _____ fruits, _____ farine et un

       peu _____ sucre et beaucoup _____ beurre; si tu oublies

       quelque chose, tu auras une tarte sans goût.

    b. Est-ce que tu as assez _____ argent pour passer plusieurs _____

       jours à Lausanne?

    c. Non, je n'ai pas _____ argent, mais j'ai ma carte Visa.

    d. Jules a les muscles mous parce qu'il ne fait pas _____ sport.

    e. Est-ce que vous avez lu _____ bons livres récemment?

    f. Anne est tellement têtue qu'elle n'a pas voulu prendre _____ photos

       pendant ses vacances dans les Alpes.

    g. Pour le petit déjeuner nous prenons une tasse _____ thé, _____

       croissants et _____ céréales.

    h. Je ne mets jamais _____ sucre dans mon café parce que je n'aime

       pas _____ sucre.

    i. Apporte une boîte _____ chocolats belges à ta tante suisse.

    j. Combien _____ temps reste-t-il avant le départ de l'avion?

    k. Est-ce que tu aimes _____ ketchup? –Non, je n'aime pas _____

       ketchup. Je ne mets jamais _____ ketchup sur mes hamburgers.

    l. Il y a _____ belles chambres dans cet hôtel de Genève.

    m. La plupart _____ temps, Anatole dort en classe.

    n. Ma sœur met toujours _____ sucre et _____ crème dans son café.

    o. Tu as _____ frères intelligents et dynamiques.

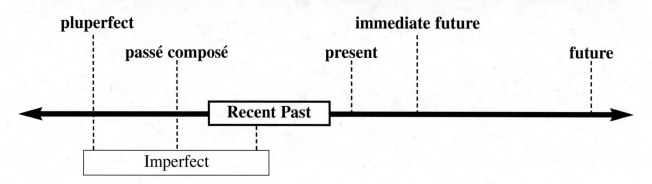

The **recent past tense** is used to describe an action that took place in the very recent past (e.g., I just ate).

The formation of the recent past is simple:

- ◆ Start with the present tense of *"venir"*
- ◆ Add the preposition *"de"*
- ◆ End with an infinitive

Je viens	*Nous venons*			
Tu viens	*Vous venez*	**+** ***De*** **+**	**Infinitive of the Verb**	
Elle vient	*Ils viennent*			

EXAMPLES: *Nous **venons de voir** un film nul.*
We have just seen a lousy film.

*Pierre et Angélie **viennent de manger** du chocolat.*
Pierre and Angélie just ate some chocolate.

Complete the sentence in English and then translate the entire sentence into French:

Example: Phil Mickelson just __won another tournament__

 __Phil Mickelson vient de gagner un autre tournoi.__

a. My three best friends just _____

_____

b. I just _____ five minutes ago.

_____

c. Bill Gates and Steve Jobs just announced _____

_____

d. Colin Firth has just _____

_____

e. "Madame Delvaux, did you just decide to _____

_____

f. Did _____ just win _____

_____

D) LE PLUS-QUE-PARFAIT

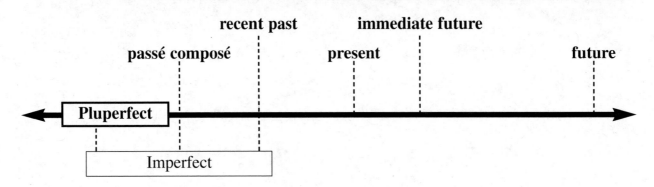

The **pluperfect tense** is used to describe an action that began and ended in the past, <u>before</u> a specific point in time or before another past action began.

HOW DO YOU FORM THE PLUPERFECT?

It's easy. Just use the imperfect of *"avoir"* or *"être"* and add the past participle of the verb.

Here are examples of the pluperfect:

Present	Pluperfect	Translation
Je parle.	***J'avais parlé.***	I had spoken.
Tu choisis.	***Tu avais choisi.***	You had chosen.
Elle part.	***Elle était partie.***	She had left.
Nous nous habillons.	***Nous nous étions habillés.***	We had gotten dressed.
Vous attendez.	***Vous aviez attendu.***	You had waited.
Ils viennent.	***Ils étaient venus.***	They had come.

EXAMPLES: *Hélas, quand vous êtes arrivés, nous **avions** déjà **mangé** toutes les frites!*
Alas, when you arrived, we had already eaten all the french fries!

*Elle **avait appris** à jouer du piano avant de déménager à l'étranger.*
She had learned how to play the piano before moving to a foreign country.

*Elle **avait entendu** parler de toi avant de te rencontrer.*
She had heard about you before meeting you.

*J'**avais réservé** une chambre dans l'hôtel où vous étiez.*
I had reserved a room in the hotel where you were (staying).

EXERCICES

1. Write the correct form of the pluperfect using the given verb:

a. Quand le golfeur Lee Westwood est arrivé à l'aéroport, son avion

_____; le lendemain, il a acheté son propre avion!
(partir)

b. Quand je suis rentré chez moi, ma grand-mère _____

déjà _____ le dîner. (préparer)

c. M. Caravel est arrivé à six heures; trois minutes avant, son fils

_____ et il _____ le bras.
(tomber/se casser)

d. Jusqu' à l'âge de dix ans, je ne _____ rien

_____ d'illégal. (faire)

e. Marc pensait qu'il _____ une nouvelle étoile. (découvrir)

f. Elle _____ sa voiture au garage quand il a
commencé à pleuvoir. (laisser)

g. Quand il m'a offert un morceau de fromage, je _____

déjà _____ les dents. (se brosser)

h. Aussitôt que je suis rentrée chez moi j'ai écouté le disque que

je _____ en ville. (acheter)

i. Paul a refusé de conduire parce qu'il _____ ses lunettes.
([ne . . . pas] prendre)

j. Catherine a sauvé la petite fille qui _____ dans la
piscine. (tomber)

2. There are five errors in the following paragraph. Underline and correct them:

Je connaissais quelques personnes avant de venir dans cette ville. Il y avait Antoine qui m'appelle deux fois au téléphone et Mathieu qui m'avait vue à la plage cet été. Ils sont beaux tous les deux même s'ils ne sont pas très intelligents. J'avais lit dans le journal qu'ils faisaient partie de l'équipe de baseball. Antoine et Mathieu avait voulu sortir avec moi; ils ne m'intéressaient pas, mais je ne connaissais personne. Alors, je suis sortie une fois avec eux. Antoine n'avait jamais sorti avec une fille; Mathieu sortait avec des filles tous les soirs. En fait, je me suis vraiment ennuyée avec eux. Si j'avait su, je serais restée chez moi!

These two sets of questions use grammatical structures and vocabulary from this lesson. Working with a partner, alternate asking and answering each question. When you get to the bottom of each list, start over at the top, switching roles. As a variation, write out the answers in complete sentences.

A) **Viens-tu d'arriver** de Belgique?

Viennent-elles de voir le nouveau film de Steven Spielberg?

Pourquoi **viens-tu de** me **donner** ce chocolat?

Qui **vient de gagner** le Tour de France?

Ta mère **vient-elle de** te **téléphoner**?

Viens-tu tout juste **de déménager**?

Venez-vous de déjeuner?

B) **S'étaient**-ils **brossé** les dents avant d'aller au lit?

Est-ce que Angelina avait déjà **parlé** avec Brad?

Le train **était**-il **parti** lorsque tu es arrivé à la gare?

Avions-nous déjà **lu** ce roman?

Emilie **avait**-elle **terminé** ses devoirs quand elle a allumé la télévision?

Avais-tu déjà **déjeuné** lorsqu'il t'a invité à boire un café?

Étais-tu **parti** voir ton ami quand l'accident a eu lieu?

"Le Hockey a Montréal"

Near the back of the book (p.307), you will find an article about Canada's favorite sport: hockey. Listen to the audio as you read along. Afterwards, answer the comprehension questions (p.309) either aloud or in written form.

EXERCICES DE RÉVISION

A) L'IMPÉRATIF

1. Change the following sentences to commands:

a. Tu manges lentement. → _____

b. Mon petit chien dort bien. → _____

c. Vous vous mettez à table. → _____

Now transform these sentences to negative commands.

a. Nous allons à la fête. _____

b. Vous vous asseyez avec vos amies. _____

2. These people say that either they want to do something or they don't want to do something. Tell them to do as they please:

Example: Je veux partir tout de suite. <u>**Alors, pars tout de suite!**</u>

a. Nous voulons jouer au tennis. _____

b. Je veux aller au cinéma. _____

c. Nous ne voulons pas faire les devoir. _____

d. Je veux rentrer chez moi. _____

e. Nous voulons prendre l'avion. _____

f. Je veux nager dans ce lac. _____

g. Je veux être gardien de but. _____

h. Nous ne voulons pas regarder ce film. _____

i. Nous aimerions aller à la fête ce soir. _____

j. J'ai faim! _____

B) LES ARTICLES ET LE PARTITIF

Fill in the blanks with the appropriate definite, indefinite or partitive article or leave blank:

a. Ces fraises coûtent quatre euros _____ kilo.

b. Au supermarché, j'ai acheté _____ viande, deux litres _____ lait, un sac _____ pommes de terre canadiennes. Et plusieurs _____ gâteaux pour le dessert.

c. La plupart _____ garçons aiment regarder les matchs de football américain.

d. Combien _____ frères et sœurs avez-vous?

e. _____ reine d'Angleterre a une belle couronne.

f. Si tu as mal à _____ tête, prends une aspirine.

g. En général, _____ dimanche après-midi je regarde un match à la télé sur la première chaîne.

h. Michelle a acheté plusieurs _____ disques de rock.

i. Parlez-vous _____ italien? –Non, mais je comprends _____ portugais.

j. Aujourd'hui c'est _____ 17 octobre.

k. J'ai toujours beaucoup _____ travail _____ mardi soir parce que j'ai sept cours _____ mercredi.

l. Mes parents ont fait _____ beaux voyages quand ils étaient jeunes.

C) LE PASSÉ RÉCENT

Translate the following sentences:

a. Roger Federer has just arrived in Neuchâtel.

_____

b. I am exhausted because I have just run twenty-six miles for the marathon.

_____

c. The Chicago Blackhawks have just won a game in Canada.

_____

d. You just told me that *Inception* is your favorite movie.

_____

D) LE PLUS-QUE-PARFAIT

1. Complete these sentences with the correct form of the pluperfect tense:

a. Quand je suis arrivé chez moi, ma famille _____. (partir)

b. Les élèves n'ont pas pu faire l'exercice parce qu'ils _____

_____ ce chapitre. ([ne . . . pas] avoir encore/étudier)

c. Il était cinq heures de l'après-midi et le soleil _____

déjà _____. (se coucher)

d. Avant de voyager en Belgique, Marguerite ne _____

jamais _____ les États-Unis. (quitter)

e. Je pensais qu'elles _____ la vérité, mais pas toute la vérité. (dire)

f. Vous _____ déjà _____ à la charcuterie avant de venir ici? (aller)

g. Elle ne _____ jamais _____ la neige avant son voyage à Zürich en 2010. (voir)

h. Je ne _____ jamais _____ me marier, mais un jour j'ai fait la connaissance d'une jolie fille et j'ai changé d'avis. (penser)

i. J'étais stressée parce que quand tu es arrivé pour dîner je

_____ à faire la cuisine. ([ne . . . pas] commencer)

j. Si tu me _____, je serais allé avec toi au festival de jazz. (appeler)

2. Translate the following sentences:

a. I had never studied a foreign language before attending high school.

_____

_____

b. We had already learned the pluperfect tense two months before the final exam.

_____

_____

c. They told me that they had always had piano lessons at home.

_____

_____

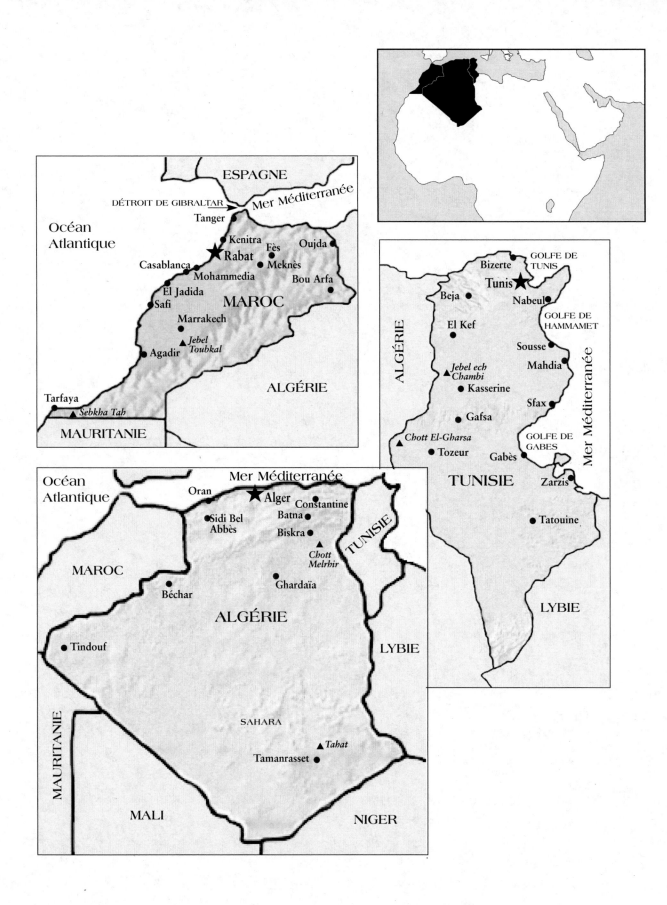

LE MAGHREB:
LE MAROC, L'ALGÉRIE & LA TUNISIE

LE MAROC

Capitale:	Rabat
Population:	31.600.000
Gouvernement:	Monarchie constitutionnelle
Chef d'état:	Le Roi Mohammed VI
Monnaie:	Le dirham marocain (MAD)
Langues:	Arabe (langue officielle), dialectes berbères, français (langue des affaires et du gouvernement)
Ressources:	Céramiques, céréales, fruits, légumes, pêche, tapis, textiles berbères, tourisme
Musique/Danse:	Folk basé sur les contes berbères, souk (fusion de musiques africaine, française, pop et rock)
Principales richesses touristiques:	Chaînes de l'Atlas, Fès, la Kutubiyya (mosquée du 12ème siècle) à Marrakech, le Sahara, souks de Marrakech, villages berbères
Cuisine:	Couscous marocain, kebabs d'agneau et de bœuf, pâtisseries aux amandes (cornes de gazelle), tajines, thé à la menthe

MAROCAINS CÉLÈBRES

Ibn Batuta
(VOYAGEUR ET ÉCRIVAIN DU MOYEN ÂGE)

Tahar Ben Jelloun
(ÉCRIVAIN)

Fatime al Fihria
(ENSEIGNANT, FONDATEUR DE LA PREMIÈRE UNIVERSITÉ DU MONDE)

Abd el-Krim
(BERBER-SAVANT)

L'ALGÉRIE

Capitale:	Alger
Population:	34.600.000
Gouvernement:	République
Chef d'état:	Président Abdelaziz Bouteflika
Monnaie:	Le dinar algérien (DZD)
Langues:	Arabe (langue officielle), français (langue commerciale), dialectes berbères
Ressources:	Agriculture, céréales, gaz naturel, pétrole, raisin
Musique/Danse:	Le raï, traditionnelle
Principales richesses touristiques:	La Côte Turquoise, le Sahara, la ville d'Alger (mosquées, casbahs)
Cuisine:	Couscous, cuisine franco-italienne, poisson

ALGÉRIENS CÉLÈBRES

Jean Amrouche
(ÉCRIVAIN)

Abdelkrim Bahloul
(CINÉASTE)

Mohammed Dib
(ÉCRIVAIN)

Salim Iles
(NAGEUR)

Cheb Khaled
(CHANTEUR)

LA TUNISIE

Capitale:	Tunis
Population:	10.600.000
Gouvernement:	République
Chef d'état:	Président Fouad Mebazaa
Monnaie:	Le dinar tunisien (TND)
Langues:	Arabe (langue officielle), français (langue commerciale)
Ressources:	Céréales, fruits, huile d'olive, minéraux, tapis, vin
Musique/Danse:	Danse du ventre, Malouf (danse traditionnelle)
Principales richesses touristiques:	Carthage (El-Jem), Quartier médiéval de Tunis, le Sahara, sites préhistoriques romains
Cuisine:	Agneau, couscous tunisien, épices exotiques, poisson, tagines, thé à la menthe

TUNISIENS CÉLÈBRES

Férid Boughédir
(CINÉASTE)

Aboul-Qacem Echebbi
(ÉCRIVAIN)

Mohammed Gammoudi
(ATHLÈTE, 5000 M.)

Salah Mehdi
(COMPOSITEUR)

VOCABULAIRE LEÇON QUATRE

ADJECTIFS

agaçant/agaçante	annoying	*gigantesque*	huge
arrogant/arrogante	arrogant	*impatient/ impatiente*	eager
autre	other		
branché/branchée	plugged in, "in" (in the know, connected)	*infini/infinie*	infinite
		ivre	drunk
		jaloux/jalouse	jealous
capable	able	*maigre*	thin
certain/certaine	certain	*maladroit/maladroite*	clumsy
chaud/chaude	hot, warm	*marrant/marrante*	funny
court/courte	short	*marron*	brown
cuit/cuite	cooked	*mortel/mortelle*	lethal
dégoûtant/ dégoûtante	disgusting	*musulman/musulmane*	Muslim
		naïf/naïve	naïve
désolé/désolée	sorry	*peint/peinte*	painted
écrit/écrite	written	*pressé/pressée*	in a hurry
effrayant/effrayante	frightful, frightening	*prudent/prudente*	prudent, careful
enchanté/enchantée	pleased	*puissant/puissante*	powerful
énervé/énervée	fidgety, nerv- ous, exasperated	*rouillé/rouillée*	rusty
		sportif/sportive	athletic, sporty
entretenu/ entretenue	maintained, kept up	*sucré/sucrée*	sweet, sugary
		sûr/sûre	sure, certain
familial/familiale	of the family	*volé/volée*	stolen
fort/forte	strong, loud		
fou/folle	crazy, mad		

LEÇON QUATRE

KEY GRAMMAR
CONCEPTS

A) LE FUTUR → *The future tense*

B) LE FUTUR ANTÉRIEUR → *The future perfect*

C) LES EXPRESSIONS IDIOMATIQUES AVEC "AVOIR" → *Idiomatic expressions with "avoir"*

D) LA NÉGATION → *Negation*

A) LE FUTUR

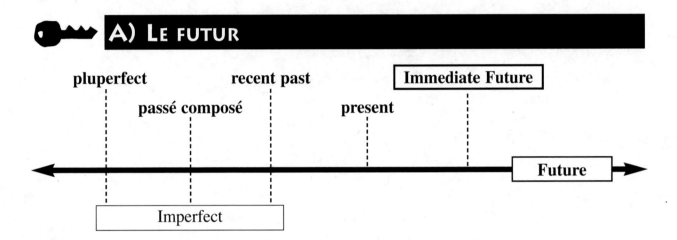

In most situations, the use of the **future tense** is obvious: it is used to describe an action that will take place in the future.

1) THE IMMEDIATE FUTURE

The immediate future normally refers to events that, in the speaker's mind, will occur relatively soon. You simply use the present tense of *"aller"* and an infinitive.

Here is the pattern for the immediate future:

Je vais	*Nous allons*		
Tu vas	*Vous allez*	**+**	**Infinitive**
Elle va	*Ils vont*		

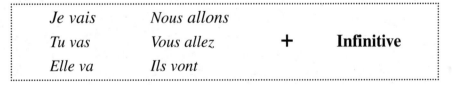 **EXAMPLES:** *Oprah va arriver au Rwanda demain.*
Oprah is going to arrive in Rwanda tomorrow.

Est-ce que nous allons voir The Fighter la semaine prochaine?
Are we going to see *The Fighter* next week?

As with any infinitive construction, just insert *"ne . . . pas"* around the verb *"aller"* to form the negative.

⚜ **EXAMPLE:** *Hillary Clinton **ne** va **pas** voyager avec le Président.*
Hillary Clinton is not going to travel with the President.

2) THE "TRUE" FUTURE OF REGULAR VERBS

The "true" future describes events that may be somewhat further away in the speaker's mind.

The future of regular verbs is quite simple:

◆ For **-ER** and **-IR** verbs, the infinitive form is the stem to which you add the future endings.

◆ For **-RE** verbs, just take off the *"e"* of the infinitive and you are left with the future stem.

Here are the future endings:

-ai	-ons
-as	-ez
-a	-ont

THE FUTURE (e.g., I will speak, etc.)		
PARLER	**FINIR**	**ENTENDRE**
je parler**ai**	je finir**ai**	j' entendr**ai**
tu parler**as**	tu finir**as**	tu entendr**as**
il parler**a**	elle finir**a**	il entendr**a**
nous parler**ons**	nous finir**ons**	nous entendr**ons**
vous parler**ez**	vous finir**ez**	vous entendr**ez**
ils parler**ont**	elles finir**ont**	ils entendr**ont**

⚜ **EXAMPLES:** *Elle **chantera** dans un grand concert pour toute l'école.*
She will sing in a huge concert for the entire school.

*Quand je **serai** en vacances, je **jouerai** au tennis tous les jours.*
When I am on vacation, I will play tennis every day.

3) THE FUTURE OF IRREGULAR VERBS

There are a number of irregular future stems in French. The good news is that you only have to learn these irregular stems once, because all of these verbs share the same stem for both the future and the conditional (which we will study in the next lesson).

Here are the irregular verb stems for the future:

aller → **ir-**	être → **ser-**	pouvoir → **pourr-**	valoir → **vaudr-**
avoir → **aur-**	faire → **fer-**	recevoir → **recevr-**	venir → **viendr-**
courir → **courr-**	falloir → **faudr-**	s'asseoir → **s'assiér-**	voir → **verr-**
devoir → **devr-**	mourir → **mourr-**	savoir → **saur-**	vouloir → **voudr-**
envoyer → **enverr-**	pleuvoir → **pleuvr-**	tenir → **tiendr-**	

EXAMPLES: *Tu **seras** toujours ma meilleure amie.*
You will always be my best friend.

*Vous **aurez** beaucoup de succès si vous travaillez dur.*
You will have a lot of success if you work hard.

*Nous **viendrons** à Pittsburgh cet été pour voir les trois fleuves.*
We will come to Pittsburgh this summer to see the three rivers.

When you talk about events in the future, these words and phrases will come in very handy.

après que → after	*lorsque* → when
aussitôt que → as soon as	*quand* → when
dès que → as soon as	

ATTENTION! In English, we use the present tense after "when" or "as soon as" even though the action refers to the future. It's different in French. You <u>must</u> use the <u>future</u> tense.

EXAMPLES: *Nous dînerons **aussitôt que** vous **arriverez**.*
We will have dinner as soon as you arrive.

***Dès que** j'**arriverai** à Casablanca, je te téléphonerai.*
As soon as I arrive in Casablanca, I will call you.

*Il partira **lorsqu'il sera** prêt.*
He will leave when he's ready.

***Quand** vous **irez** en Algérie, vous visiterez la Côte Turquoise.*
When you go to Algeria, you will visit the Turquoise Coast.

Helpful Tip: With *"après que,"* you will need to use the "future perfect" (see p. 88).

EXAMPLE: *Nous mangerons **après qu'il sera venu**.*
We will eat after he comes.

1. Write the correct form of the future tense using the verb and subject provided:

    a. boire (je)   _____

    b. croire (elles)   _____

    c. être (nous)   _____

    d. faire (il)   _____

    e. jouer (les filles)   _____

    f. aller (elle)   _____

    g. prendre (je)   _____

    h. savoir (il)   _____

2. Change the following verbs from the present tense to the future:

    a. elle finit   → _____

    b. vous regardez   → _____

    c. je me brosse les dents → _____

    d. tu as   → _____

    e. vous êtes   → _____

    f. vous finissez   → _____

    g. nous nous asseyons   → _____

3. Fill in the blanks with the correct form of the given verb:

   a. Quand tu _____ 18 ans tu pourras voter. (avoir)

   b. Nous sortirons quand il _____ beau. (faire)

   c. Je vous téléphonerai aussitôt que je _____. (arriver)

   d. Lorsque ma mère _____ du bureau, je lui demanderai si je peux emprunter la voiture. (revenir)

   e. Quand le chat _____ la souris, il essaiera de l'attraper. (voir)

   f. J'emprunterai la voiture de mes parents dès que je _____ mon permis de conduire. (avoir)

4. Write these verbs in the future tense:

   a. Katie Couric _____ son émission demain. (faire)

   b. Nous _____ les billets de théâtre. ([ne . . . pas] acheter)

   c. Je _____ nos amis à la plage. (conduire)

   d. Je ne veux pas boire ce vin blanc qui me _____ ivre. (rendre)

   e. Mes amis _____ la semaine prochaine. ([ne . . . pas] appeler)

   f. Nous _____ partir quand la cloche sonnera. (pouvoir)

   g. Tu _____ la réponse demain. (savoir)

B) LE FUTUR ANTÉRIEUR

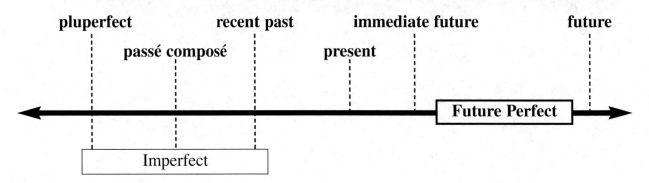

The **future perfect tense** is used to describe a future action that will begin and end <u>before</u> another future event or time (i.e., someone will have gone, studied, fallen asleep, etc.).

EXAMPLES: *Dans deux semaines, tu **auras terminé** ton travail écrit.*
In two weeks, you will have finished your written work.

*Quand tu viendras, nous **aurons dîné**.*
When you come, we will have had dinner.

HOW DO YOU FORM THE FUTURE PERFECT?

1) FOR "AVOIR" VERBS
The formation of the future perfect for *"avoir"* verbs is quite simple:

◆ Start with the future tense of *"avoir"*

◆ Add a past participle

Here is the formula for constructing the future perfect with *"avoir"*:

Subject	+	*Avoir*	+	Past Participle
J'		*aurai*		
Tu		*auras*		
Il/Elle	+	*aura*	+	*mangé (écrit, pris, etc.)*
Nous		*aurons*		
Vous		*aurez*		
Ils/Elles		*auront*		

EXAMPLES: *Quand **tu auras fini** tes devoirs, tu pourras regarder la télé.*
When you finish (have finished) your homework, you will be allowed to watch TV.

*Elle parlera français couramment après qu'elle **aura passé** un an à Genève.*
She will speak French fluently after she has (will have) spent a year in Geneva.

2) FOR "ÊTRE" VERBS

The formation of the future perfect for *"être"* verbs follows the same pattern:

◆ Start with the future tense of *"être."*

◆ Add a past participle.

ATTENTION! Don't forget that the past participle must agree with the subject!

Here is the formula for constructing the future perfect with *"être"*:

Subject	+	Être	+	Past Participle
Je		*serai*		*sorti(e)*
Tu		*seras*		*sorti(e)*
Il/Elle	+	*sera*	+	*sorti/sortie*
Nous		*serons*		*sortis, sorti(e)s*
Vous		*serez*		*sorti(e)(s)*
Ils/Elles		*seront*		*sortis, sorties*

EXAMPLES: *Les enfants seront tristes après que leur grand-mère **sera partie**.*
The children will be sad after their grandmother has left (will have left).

*Aussitôt que le chat **sera parti**, les souris danseront.*
As soon as the cat has left (will have left), the mice will dance.

3) RELEXIVE VERBS

All reflexive verbs, as you know, are conjugated with *"être."* Notice how the past participle agrees with the subject.

Subject	+	Être	+	Past Participle
Je me		*serai*		*assis(e)*
Tu te		*seras*		*assis(e)*
Il/Elle se	+	*sera*	+	*assis/assise*
Nous nous		*serons*		*assis(e)s*
Vous vous		*serez*		*assis(e)(s)*
Ils/Elles se		*seront*		*assis/assises*

EXAMPLES: *Après que nous nous **serons reposés**, nous descendrons du Mont Blanc.*
After we have had a rest, we will come down from Mont Blanc.

*Monsieur et Madame Hanin dîneront quand leur bébé se **sera endormi**.*
Mr. and Mrs. Hanin will have dinner when the baby has gone to sleep.

1. There are five errors in the following paragraph. Underline and correct them:

L'année prochaine, j'allerai à l'université. Je suis impatient de rencontrer mes futurs camarades, mais j'ai peur! Mon camarade de chambre sera peut-être agaçant ou arrogant. J'espère que mes professeurs ne serent pas fous et qu'ils ne me fairont pas trop travailler. Je suierai des cours branchés et marrants. Comme je n'habitrai plus avec mes parents, je pourrai écouter la musique de Lil' Wayne très fort avec mes copains.

2. Complete these sentences with the future or the future perfect tense:

a. Je te prêterai ce livre effrayant quand je le _____. (lire)

b. Elle te téléphonera aussitôt qu'elle _____ à Oran. (arriver)

c. Quand tu auras 20 ans tu _____ à l'université. (être)

d. Dès que l'instituteur _____ le dos tourné, tous les petits enfants feront des bêtises. (avoir)

e. Quand je _____ mon vélo, nous pourrons partir. (réparer)

f. Saïd et Abdullah se réveilleront quand ils _____ le réveil. (entendre)

g. Quand la cloche _____, nous partirons. (sonner)

h. Le voleur, prudent, _____ quand la police arrivera. (s'enfuir)

C) LES EXPRESSIONS IDIOMATIQUES AVEC "AVOIR"

Make sure you are familiar with these *"avoir"* expressions:

avoir . . . ans	→	to be . . . years old
avoir besoin de	→	to need
avoir de la chance	→	to be lucky
avoir chaud	→	to be hot
avoir le droit	→	to be allowed to
avoir envie de	→	to want to
avoir faim	→	to be hungry
avoir froid	→	to be cold
avoir honte (de)	→	to be ashamed
avoir l'habitude de	→	to be accustomed to
avoir l'intention de	→	to plan to
avoir lieu	→	to take place
avoir l'occasion de	→	to have the chance to
avoir mal à	→	to have a . . . –ache
avoir mal à la gorge	→	to have a sore throat
avoir mal à la tête	→	to have a headache
avoir peur (de)	→	to be afraid
avoir raison	→	to be right
avoir soif	→	to be thirsty
avoir sommeil	→	to be sleepy
avoir le temps de	→	to have time to
avoir tort	→	to be wrong

EXAMPLES: *As-tu besoin de ce livre?*
Do you need this book?

J'ai envie de partir en vacances au Sahara.
I want to go on vacation to the Sahara Desert.

Il a honte de sa note en français.
He is ashamed of his French grade.

Il avait l'intention de faire ses devoirs, mais il était trop fatigué pour les faire.
He planned to do his homework, but he was too tired to do it.

Si tu as mal à la tête, prends une aspirine.
If you have a headache, take an aspirin.

De quoi a-t-il peur?
What is he afraid of?

Si elle avait sommeil, elle dormirait.
If she were sleepy, she would sleep.

EXERCICE

Using an *"avoir"* idiom, write logical questions to the answers given:

a. Non, merci, je viens de boire un Sprite.

_____

b. Non, j'ai chaud. Il fait plus de 90 degrés.

_____

c. Oui, j'ai mal à la tête.

_____

d. Non, j'ai bien dormi hier soir.

_____

e. Oui, parce que ce film est effrayant.

_____

f. Je veux sortir avec Mirabelle!

_____

g. Oui, je pourrais manger trois Big Macs bien cuits.

_____

h. Non, je ne peux pas boire d'alcool parce je n'ai pas 21 ans.

_____

i. Non, à la loterie je n'ai jamais rien gagné.

_____

j. J'ai vingt-six ans.

_____

1) NEGATIVE EXPRESSIONS

The following expressions are used to express negation in French:

ne . . . aucun(e)	no	*ne . . . personne*	no one
ne . . . jamais	never	*ne . . . plus*	no longer
ne . . . nulle part	nowhere	*ne . . . que*	only
ne . . . pas	not	*ne . . . rien*	nothing/not . . . anything
ne . . . pas encore	not yet	*ne . . . ni . . . ni*	neither . . . nor . . . nor

ne . . . aucun(e)	*Il **n'a aucune** idée de l'université où il va aller.* He has no idea where he is going to go to college.
ne . . . jamais	*Nous **n'avons jamais** été au Maroc en hiver.* We have never been to Morocco in winter.
ne . . . nulle part	*Est-ce que tu vas quelque part pour les vacances?* *–Non, je **ne** vais **nulle part**.* Are you going somewhere for the vacation? –No, I am not going anywhere.
ne . . . pas	*Elle **ne** va **pas** être contente quand elle apprendra la nouvelle.* She is not going to be happy when she hears the news.
ne . . . pas encore	*Elles **n'ont pas encore** eu l'occasion de lire le roman.* They haven't yet had the chance to read the novel.
ne . . . personne	*Quand je suis entré, j'ai demandé: "Est-ce qu'il y a quelqu'un?" Mon père a répondu, "Non, il **n'y** a **personne**."* When I entered, I asked: "Is anyone home?" My dad answered: "No, there's no one."
ne . . . plus	*Jake Gyllenhaal **ne** sort **plus** avec Taylor Swift.* Jake Gyllenhaal no longer goes out with Taylor Swift.
ne . . . que	*Je **n'ai que** deux dollars sur moi.* I only have two dollars on me.
ne . . . rien	*Malheureusement, je **n'ai rien** à te donner.* Unfortunately, I don't have anything to give you.
ne . . . ni . . . ni	*Mon père **n'aime ni** le thé **ni** le café.* My father likes neither tea nor coffee.

◆ A number of negative expressions can be used without the particle *"ne"* when there is no verb involved.

> *pas* → not   *pas du tout* → not at all   *pas encore* → not yet

⚜ **EXAMPLES:** *Qui peut m'aider? –Pas nous. Nous n'avons pas le temps.*
       Who can help me? –Not us. We don't have time.

       Est-ce que tu as beaucoup travaillé? –Pas du tout.
       Did you study a lot? –Not at all.

       Vous avez vu les photos? –Non, pas encore.
       Have you seen the pictures? –No, not yet.

◆ Now take a look at the following chart that shows some affirmative expressions and their negative counterparts.

Affirmative	Negative
déjà → already	*ne . . . pas encore* → not yet
encore → still, more	*ne . . . plus* → no longer/no more
quelqu'un → someone	*ne . . . personne* → no one
quelque chose → something	*ne . . . rien* → nothing
quelque part → somewhere	*ne . . . nulle part* → nowhere
toujours → always	*ne . . . jamais* → never
un, une → one, a	*ne . . . aucun, aucune* → none, no
ou . . . ou/et . . . et → or . . . or/and . . . and	*ne . . . ni . . . ni* → neither . . . nor

Helpful Tip: For a double negative, the general rule is to follow alphabetical order for negative words.

⚜ **EXAMPLES:** *Je n'ai jamais rien traduit.*
       I have never translated anything.

       Je ne vais plus rien faire avec le groupe.
       I am no longer going to do anything with the group.

       Il ne prend ni sucre ni lait dans son café.
       He takes neither sugar nor milk in his coffee.

2) THE NEGATIVE FORM IN SIMPLE AND COMPOUND TENSES

In simple tenses (the present, imperfect, imperative, future, and conditional), using the negative form is quite simple:

◆ Place the *"ne"* directly <u>before</u> the verb

◆ Place the second half of the negative, (e.g., *jamais, pas, rien*) immediately <u>after</u> the verb.

Simple Tense	Negative
Present	*Je **ne porte pas** de pull.* I am not wearing a (any) sweater.
Imperfect	*Vous **ne regardiez ni** à droite **ni** à gauche.* You were looking neither right nor left.
Imperative	***Ne sautez pas** encore!* Don't jump yet!
Future	*Il **ne se rasera que** le matin.* He will shave only in the morning.
Conditional	*Nous **ne mangerions plus** si nous **n'avions pas** faim.* We would not eat anymore if we were not hungry.

For compound tenses (*passé composé*, pluperfect, future perfect, and conditional perfect):

◆ Place the *"ne"* <u>before</u> the auxiliary verb

◆ Place the second half of the negative (e.g., *jamais, pas, rien*) <u>after</u> the auxiliary.

Compound Tense	Negative
Past	*Je **n'ai jamais** porté ce pull.* I have never worn this sweater.
Pluperfect	*Vous **n'aviez rien** vu.* You hadn't seen anything.
Future Perfect	*Je **n'aurai eu aucune** difficulté.* I won't have had any problems.
Conditional Perfect	*Nous **n'aurions pas** mangé.* We wouldn't have eaten.

ATTENTION! With the expressions *ne . . . personne, ne . . . ni . . . ni* and *ne . . . que,* the second part of the negative follows the past participle.

EXAMPLES: *Je **n'ai** rencontré **personne** au supermarché!*
I met no one at the supermarket!

*Marie **n'a** invité **ni** Marc **ni** Kareem.*
Marie invited neither Marc nor Kareem.

*Tu **n'as** lu **que** deux pages.*
You only read two pages.

3) THE NEGATIVE FORM WITH REFLEXIVE VERBS

Now let's take a quick look at reflexive verbs.

◆ You will see that the reflexive pronoun always follows the *"ne."*

◆ Just like regular verbs, the negative surrounds the verb in simple tenses and surrounds the auxiliary verb in compound tenses.

Simple Tense	Negative
Present Indicative	*Je **ne me** coiffe **pas**.* (I don't comb my hair.)
Present Conditional	*Nous **ne nous** inquiéterions **pas**.* (We wouldn't worry.)
Compound Tense	**Negative**
Pluperfect	*Vous **ne vous** étiez **pas** levé.* (You had not gotten up.)
Future Perfect	*Elle **ne se** sera **pas** maquillée.* (She will not have put on any make-up.)

With imperatives, the negative surrounds the entire reflexive command (e.g., ***Ne te coupe pas**!* or ***Ne vous asseyez jamais** ici!*).

4) THE USE OF "DE"

In this section, we will see how the indefinite articles and partitives are replaced by *"de"* in French in the negative form.

◆ First, recall that the indefinite articles are *un, une* and *des* and the partitive articles are *du, de la, de l'* and *des*.

◆ Second, change these articles to *"de"* in any negative.

Un, une, du, de la, de l', and *des* become ***"de"*** after a negative:

⚜ EXAMPLES:

Nous avons un verre.	We have a glass.
*Nous n'avons pas **de** verre.*	We don't have a glass.
Tu as eu une copine.	You had a girlfriend.
*Tu n'as pas eu **de** copine.*	You didn't have a girlfriend.
J'ai acheté du fromage.	I bought some cheese.
*Je n'ai pas acheté **de** fromage.*	I didn't buy any cheese.
Tu as mangé des fraises.	You ate strawberries.
*Tu n'as jamais mangé **de** fraises.*	You never ate strawberries.

ATTENTION! This rule does not apply to definite articles *(le, la, l', les)*!

⚜ EXAMPLES:

J'ai visité le musée.	I visited the museum.
*Je n'ai pas visité **le** musée.*	I didn't visit the museum.
J'ai compté l'argent.	I counted the money.
*Je n'ai pas compté **l'**argent.*	I didn't count the money.

5) THE NEGATIVE FORM WITH INFINITIVES

If you are going to use a negative expression before an infinitive, both negative words precede the infinitive.

 **EXAMPLES:** *Mes grands-parents préfèrent **ne plus** voyager.*
My grandparents prefer not to travel any more.

*Être ou **ne pas** être, c'est ça la question.*
To be or not to be, that is the question.

 EXERCICES

1. **Rewrite the following sentences incorporating the negative expression in parentheses. Make the necessary changes so that the sentences make sense.**

a. Je veux aller au match ce soir. (ne . . . pas)

_____

b. Vous avez faim! (ne . . . plus)

_____

c. J'emporte beaucoup de choses chez moi le soir. (ne . . . rien)

_____

d. Monsieur Apple mange des pommes. (ne . . . pas)

_____

e. Nous avons des places pour voir le match des Celtics. (ne . . . aucun)

_____

f. Ma sœur regarde *30 Rock* et *Grey's Anatomy*. (ne . . . ni . . . ni)

_____

g. J'ai rendu visite à mon cousin de Tunis. (ne . . . jamais)

_____

h. Il est encore énervé après son examen. (ne . . . plus)

_____

2. Rewrite these sentences using a variety of negative expressions; use _ne . . . pas_ only twice.

a. Il est déjà allé en Tunisie.

_____

b. Quelqu'un a pris mon pull vert.

_____

c. Monsieur Lepic est encore au bureau.

_____

d. Francine a acheté quelque chose à J.Crew.

_____

e. Beaucoup de garçons portent des cravates.

_____

f. Nous allons quelque part ce week-end.

_____

g. Pierre et Antoinette sont allés à la fête.

_____

h. Les personnes arrogantes sont toujours populaires.

_____

i. L'agent de police a arrêté quelqu'un près de la banque.

_____

j. Mon petit frère aime beaucoup les épinards.

_____

These two sets of questions use grammatical structures and vocabulary from this lesson. Working with a partner, alternate asking and answering each question. When you get to the bottom of each list, start over at the top, switching roles. As a variation, write out the answers in complete sentences.

A) **Vas**-tu **arriver** à Tunis demain?

Vont-ils **aller** au cinéma pour voir Harry Potter?

Cheb Kaleb **chantera**-t-il à Alger l'année prochaine?

Finiras-tu ton travail à temps pour aller au cinéma?

M'attendras-tu à l'aéroport ou à la gare?

Prendrez-vous des cours de français ou d'arabe?

Croiras-tu au Père Noël lorsque tu auras vingt ans?

B) Pourras-tu venir me voir quand tu **auras fini** ton travail?

S'achètera-t-elle une voiture quand elle **aura passé** son permis?

Seras-tu déjà **parti** pour la Tunisie lorsque je reviendrai de voyage?

Vous **serez**-vous **endormis** si nous revenons à minuit?

Pourras-tu me prêter ton roman de Jean Amrouche quand tu l'**auras lu**?

Auras-tu **terminé** tes devoirs dans une heure?

Irons-nous sur la Côte Turquoise dès que tu **seras arrivé**?

EXERCICES DE RÉVISION

A) LE FUTUR

1. Complete these sentences using the future tense:

a. Lequel de mes amis me _____ ce soir? (téléphoner)

b. Est-ce que nous _____ voir un match de football en France cet été? (pouvoir)

c. Mon frère _____ un dîner de couscous et de brochettes d'agneau samedi soir pour sa copine. (préparer)

d. Tu _____ travailler pour le bac. (devoir)

e. Cet été, quand je serai en Algérie, est-ce que tu m' _____? (écrire)

f. _____ –vous assez de temps pour terminer l'examen, ou est-ce qu'il y a trop de questions? (Avoir)

g. L'avion de Jet Blue _____ dans dix minutes. (partir)

2. There are four errors in the following paragraph. Underline and correct them:

Ce week-end ma soeur et moi allons rendrai visite à mes grands-parents dans le Vermont. On adore y aller parce qu'on peut faire du ski et boire du chocolat chaud. Nous y passerions deux jours. Il y a toujours beaucoup de choses à faire. À la radio ils disent qu'il va neiger vendredi soir. S'il neige nous allez faire du ski samedi. Et je crois que samedi soir il neigerat encore quelques centimètres. Dimanche, nous irons déjeuner à

la Woodstock Inn avec des amis.

3. Fill in the blanks with the future of the verbs in parentheses.

Quand je _____ (avoir) 25 ans, je _____ (être)

très beau et très fort. Je _____ (vivre) en Californie. Je

_____ (pouvoir) nager tous les jours. Je _____

(courir) sur la plage et je _____ (envoyer) des photos à

mes amis de Philadelphie pour leur montrer mon magnifique bronzage. Je ne

_____ (aller) jamais à New York en hiver. Quand il

_____ (pleuvoir) en Californie, il _____

(falloir) aller en Floride. Tous mes amis _____ (vouloir)

être comme moi et ils _____ (venir) me rendre visite.

Quand ils _____ (devoir) rentrer chez eux en Nouvelle

Angleterre, ils _____ (être) désolés. Je _____

(mourir) à l'âge de 110 ans et je _____ (devenir)

immédiatement un ange au paradis.

B) LE FUTUR ANTÉRIEUR

Change the following verbs from the present to the *futur antérieur*:

a. tu écris   → _____

b. ils pleurent   → _____

c. vous vous souvenez → _____

d. elle téléphone   → _____

e. nous nous habillons → _____

f. vous allumez   → _____

g. j'habite   → _____

A & B) LE FUTUR ET LE FUTUR ANTÉRIEUR

Choose the best tense (future, present, immediate future or the future perfect) to complete the following sentences:

a. En 2016 les Jeux Olympiques _____ à Brésil. (avoir lieu)

b. Tu _____ tes devoirs avant de dîner, ou alors tu ne vas pas manger. (aller faire)

c. Excusez-moi. Est-ce que vous _____ me dire où est le café Starbucks le plus proche? (pouvoir)

d. Les garçons paresseux _____ peut-être dans trois ans. (travailler)

e. Ma mère me _____ le premier jour de l'école. (accompagner)

f. Brett Favre vient d'annoncer qu'il _____ sa retraite l'année prochaine. (prendre)

g. Ma mère sera enchantée quand je _____ ma chambre. (ranger)

C) Les expressions idiomatiques avec "avoir"

Fill in the blanks with the appropriate "*avoir*" expression:

a. Je n'ai pas _____ parce que je viens de dîner.

b. Le professeur a toujours _____ mais les élèves ont toujours tort.

c. Je suis sûr que tu as _____ d'avoir eu de si mauvaises notes.

d. Ces enfants ont _____ des réunions familiales. Ils en ont tous les dimanches.

e. Je n'ai pas _____ de parler français parce que tous mes amis font de l'arabe.

f. Séraphin n'a pas eu _____ de te parler parce qu'il était en retard pour à rendez-vous de dentiste.

g. Des accidents mortels ont toujours _____ à cet endroit précis de la route.

D) Les négations

Write an appropriate negative response to the following questions:

a. Tu les as vus quelque part? (ne . . . nulle part)

_____

b. Est-ce que tu as fait quelque chose hier matin? (ne . . . rien)

_____

c. Est-ce que vous avez visité le Maghreb? (ne . . . jamais)

_____

d. Est-ce que tu veux une boisson chaude? (ne . . . pas)

_____

e. Qui a reçu une bonne note à l'examen? (ne . . . personne)

_____

f. Est-ce que tu aimes toujours jouer au golf? (ne . . . plus)

_____

g. Est-ce que vous êtes déjà allé à Graceland? (ne . . . pas encore)

_____

h. Est-ce tu parles français et arabe? (ne . . . que)

_____

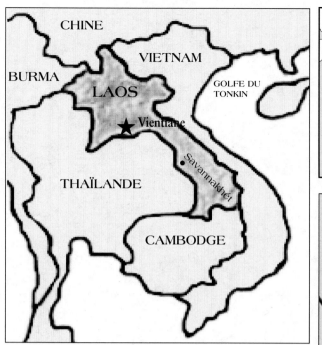

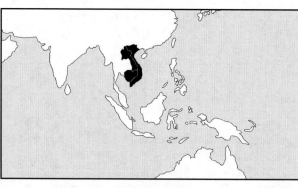

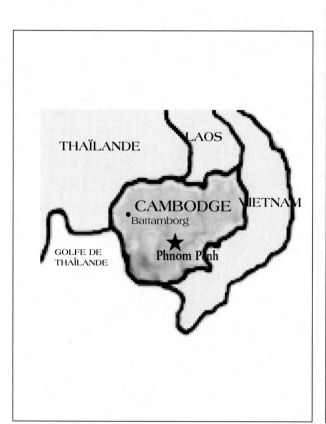

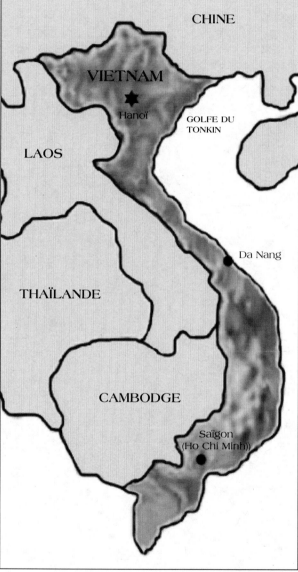

L'ASIE FRANCOPHONE:
LE VIETNAM, LE CAMBODGE & LE LAOS

LE VIETNAM

Capitale:	Hanoï
Population:	89.600.000
Gouvernement:	République socialiste
Chef d'état:	Président Nguyen Minh Triet
Monnaie:	New Dong (VND)
Langues:	Vietnamien (langue officielle), anglais, français
Ressources:	Café, caoutchouc, minéraux, riz, sucre, thé
Musique/ Danse:	Fêtes bouddhistes, cai long (comédie musicale), mua roi nuoc (marionnettes sur eau), opéra chinois
Principales richesses touristiques:	Baie de Halong, fleuve Mekong, Quartier français à Hanoï, Hoi An, Île de Cat Ba, lac Hoan Kiem, marchés flottants, Temple de Jade, ville de Ho Chi Minh
Cuisine:	Baguettes, bière, nem (viande, légumes, nouilles emballées dans du papier de riz), nuoc cham (sauce de chilis), nuoc mam (sauce de poisson), Pho (soupe), poisson, porc, sauce de cacahuètes, thé de riz, thé vert

VIETNAMIENS CÉLÈBRES

Tan Da
(POÈTE)

Thich Nhat Hahn
(MOINE ET CANDIDAT POUR LE PRIX NOBEL)

Viet Lam
(SCULPTEUR)

Ho Chi Minh
(LEADER POLITIQUE DU VIETNAM DU NORD)

Trung Trac et Trung Nhi
(SŒURS ET RÉVOLUTIONNAIRES)

Tue Tinh
(MÉDECIN VIETNAMIEN)

LE CAMBODGE

Capitale:	Phnom Penh
Population:	14.500.000
Gouvernement:	Monarchie constitutionnelle, HoS: King Norodom Sihamoni
Chef d'état:	Roi Norodom Sihamoni, Premier Ministre Hun Sen
Monnaie:	New Riel (KHR)
Langues:	Khmer (langue officielle), français, anglais
Ressources:	Agriculture (bananes, cassaves, sucre, riz), argent, bois, mines, pierres précieuses
Danse:	Danse traditionelle
Principales richesses touristiques:	Temple d'Angkor (le bâtiment religieux le plus grand du monde), Palais Royal et la Pagode d'Argent (Phnom Penh)
Cuisine:	Fruits, légumes, mangues, poisson, porc, riz

CAMBODGIENS CÉLÈBRES

Meng Keo Pichenda
(CHANTEUSE)

Fan Shih-man
(FONDATEUR DE L'EMPIRE FUNAN)

LE LAOS

Capitale:	Vientiane
Population:	6.300.000
Gouvernement:	République Démocratique Populaire Lao
Chef d'état:	Président Lt. Gen. Choummali Saignason
Monnaie:	Lao Kip (LAK)
Langues:	Lao (langue officielle), français (première langue étrangère d'enseignement)
Ressources:	Café, maïs, minéraux, noix moulues, riz, tabac
Musique/ Danse:	Fêtes bouddhistes, khène (flûte de bambou), lamvong (danse traditionnelle), théâtre d'ombres
Principales richesses touristiques:	Fleuve Mekong, Luang Prabang (Palais Royal), Monument aux Morts (Vientiane), Xien Khuang (Plaine des Jarres)
Cuisine:	Baguettes, bananes, bière, croissants, lao lao (alcool de riz), noix de coco, poisson, riz

LAOTIENS CÉLÈBRES

Dia Cha
(AUTEUR)

Mai Neng Moua
(AUTEUR)

Fa Ngum
(FONDATEUR DU ROYAUME LAN XANG)

Sarah Vongmary
(CHANTEUSE)

VOCABULAIRE
LEÇON CINQ

LES NOMS

l' *affection* (f.)	affection	le *droit*	right, law, privilege
l' *âge* (m.)	age		
l' *amant/ amante* (m./f.)	lover	l' *employé/ employée* (m./f.)	employee
l' *amitié* (f.)	friendship	l' *enfance* (f.)	childhood
l' *autorité* (f.)	authority	l' *entraînement* (m.)	training, practice
l' *autoroute* (f.)	freeway, highway	l' *entrevue* (f.)	interview
la *bague*	ring	la *fatigue*	tiredness
la *banque*	bank	la *frontière*	border
le *billet*	ticket	le *goût*	taste
la *bourse*	scholarship	le *grand magasin*	department store
la *campagne*	campaign, countryside	l' *inscription* (f.)	registration
le *commerce*	business	le *mariage*	wedding
la *confiance*	confidence	le *peignoir*	bathrobe
le *conseil*	advice	le *plateau*	tray
le *courrier*	mail	la *plume*	feather
le *départ*	departure	le *quartier*	neighborhood, section, quarter
le *dessin*	drawing		
le *détail*	detail	la *révision*	review
les *devoirs* (m.)	homework	le *salaire*	salary
la *douleur*	pain, grief	les *vacances* (f.)	vacation
le *drapeau*	flag		

LEÇON CINQ

KEY GRAMMAR CONCEPTS 	**A) LE CONDITIONNEL** → *The conditional tense*
	B) LE CONDITIONNEL PASSÉ → *The conditional perfect tense*
	C) LES PHRASES AVEC "SI" → *Sentences with "if"*
	D) LES NOMS FÉMININS → *The feminine form of nouns*

 A) LE CONDITIONNEL

◆ The **conditional tense** is used to explain what would happen in a hypothetical situation.

> **EXAMPLES:** *J'irais au théâtre si j'avais le temps.*
> I would go to the theater if I had time.
>
> *Nous achèterions ces fraises si elles étaient mûres.*
> We would buy these strawberries if they were ripe.

◆ The conditional is also commonly used to describe an action that occurs subsequent to another past action or to a time in the past. In the same way that the present and future can be linked *(Je dis qu'il pleuvra demain),* so, too, can the past and conditional *(Hier, j'ai dit qu'il pleuvrait aujourd'hui).*

> **EXAMPLES:** *Mes amis m'ont dit qu'ils achèteraient la tente plus tard.*
> My friends told me that they would buy the tent later.
>
> *Sophie m'a dit, hier soir, qu'elle arriverait à trois heures aujourd'hui.*
> Sophie told me last night that she would arrive at 3:00 today.

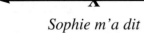

X	X	X	X
Sophie m'a dit hier soir	*qu'elle arriverait à trois heures*	présent (when I am speaking)	*qu'elle arriverait à trois heures.*

Let's look at the timeline above — Last night Sophie told me that she would be arriving in the future (at three o'clock today). Three o'clock can be either before or after the moment when I'm speaking.

◆ The conditional is also used to make a softened or polite request, such as in a restaurant, on the telephone, or when expressing a wish.

◆ **EXAMPLES:** *J'aimerais* parler à l'homme au dentier.
I would like to speak to the man with false teeth.

Je voudrais une salade composée et deux crêpes.
I would like a mixed salad and two crepes.

Pourriez–vous me dire à quelle heure est le prochain avion pour Hanoï?
Could you tell me when the next plane leaves for Hanoi?

HOW DO YOU FORM THE CONDITIONAL?

To conjugate verbs in the conditional, this simple rule works for <u>all</u> verbs. There are <u>no</u> exceptions.

◆ Start with the "future stem" of the verb (see p. 84).
◆ Then add the "imperfect endings" (see p. 37).

Here are three regular verbs in the present conditional:

THE PRESENT CONDITIONAL (e.g., I would speak, etc.)		
PARLER	**OBÉIR**	**PRENDRE**
je parler**ais**	j'obéir**ais**	je prendr**ais**
tu parler**ais**	tu obéir**ais**	tu prendr**ais**
elle parler**ait**	il obéir**ait**	elle prendr**ait**
nous parler**ions**	nous obéir**ions**	nous prendr**ions**
vous parler**iez**	vous obéir**iez**	vous prendr**iez**
ils parler**aient**	elles obéir**aient**	ils prendr**aient**

Note: **-ER**, **-IR**, and **-RE** verbs all have the same endings.

IRREGULAR VERBS

These verbs are the same ones that are irregular in the future tense. Simply use the same irregular future stem and add imperfect endings.

The following verbs have irregular forms:

VOULOIR		ALLER	
je voudrais	nous voudrions	j'irais	nous irions
tu voudrais	vous voudriez	tu irais	vous iriez
elle voudrait	ils voudraient	il irait	ils iraient

Once you have learned the *"je"* form of these irregular conditionals, you can figure out all the other forms. The irregularity stays constant in all forms, just as in the future.

aller → **j'irais**	*pouvoir* → **je pourrais**
avoir → **j'aurais**	*recevoir* → **je recevrais**
courir → **je courrais**	*s'asseoir* → **je m'assiérais**
devoir → **je devrais**	*savoir* → **je saurais**
envoyer → **j'enverrais**	*tenir* → **je tiendrais**
être → **je serais**	*valoir* → **je vaudrais**
faire → **je ferais**	*venir* → **je viendrais**
mourir → **je mourrais**	*voir* → **je verrais**
	vouloir → **je voudrais**

 Falloir and pleuvoir are only used in 3rd person singular: il faudrait, il pleuvrait.

Helpful Tip: Remember, the conditional stem and the future stem are <u>always</u> identical!

 B) LE CONDITIONNEL PASSÉ

The **conditional perfect tense** refers to the past and describes an event that would have taken place if something else had happened prior to that event.

EXAMPLES: *Nous **aurions compris** la leçon de grammaire si nous avions travaillé plus sérieusement.*
We would have understood the grammar lesson if we had studied more seriously.

J'aurais mangé les biscuits si j'avais acheté du lait.
I would have eaten the cookies if I had bought milk.

HOW DO YOU FORM THE CONDITIONAL PERFECT?

It's easy. Use the conditional of *"avoir"* or *"être"* along with a past participle. Let's look at an example of an *"avoir"* and an *"être"* verb in the conditional perfect.

THE CONDITIONAL PERFECT (e.g., I would have spoken, etc.)			
J'aurais	*Nous aurions*		***parlé***
Tu aurais	*Vous auriez*	**+**	***compris***
Elle aurait	*Ils auraient*		***entendu***
Je serais	*Nous serions*		***allé(e)s***
Tu serais	*Vous seriez*	**+**	***parti(e)(s)***
Elle serait	*Ils seraient*		***mort(e)(s)***

1. Write the correct form of the present conditional using the verb and subject provided:

a. (avoir) Ils _____

b. (aller) Nous _____

c. (manger) Elle _____

d. (savoir) On _____

e. (être) Je _____

f. (attendre) Tu _____

g. (jouer) On _____

h. (parler) Nous _____

i. (écrire) Vous _____

j. (aimer) Ils _____

2. Write the correct form of the conditional perfect using the verb and subject provided:

a. (sortir) Tu _____

b. (prendre) Nous _____

c. (lire) Vous _____

d. (naître) Il _____

e. (savoir) Je _____

f. (se dépêcher) Elles _____

 C) LES PHRASES AVEC "SI"

We are going to examine different types of sentences that contain an **"if clause."** It is useful to think of these "if clauses" in pairs.

Take a careful look at the following chart:

"Si" Clause	**Result Clause**
Present	Present
Present	Future
Present	Imperative
Imperfect	Present Conditional
Pluperfect	Conditional Perfect
Pluperfect	Present Conditional

◆ The chart shows that if you use the present tense in the "if clause," you have three choices for the "result clause": the present, the future, or the imperative.

EXAMPLES: *Si le professeur te* **pose** *une question, tu* **réponds**. (present/present)
If the teacher asks you a question, you answer.

Si le professeur te **pose** *une question, tu* **répondras**. (present/future)
If the teacher asks you a question, you will answer.

Si le professeur te **pose** *une question,* **réponds***!* (present/imperative)
If the teacher asks you a question, answer!

◆ When you use the imperfect in the "if clause," you must use the present conditional in the "result clause."

EXAMPLE: *Si le professeur te* **posait** *une question, tu* **répondrais**. (imperfect/conditional)
If the teacher asked you a question, you would answer.

ATTENTION! Keep in mind that the order of the sentence can be reversed.

EXAMPLE: *Tu* **répondrais** *si le professeur te* **posait** *une question.*
You would answer if the teacher asked you a question.

◆ When you use the pluperfect in the "if clause," you can use the conditional perfect or the present conditional in the "result clause" depending on the meaning and the time frame you want to convey.

EXAMPLES: *Si le professeur t'avait posé une question, tu* **aurais répondu**. (pluperfect/ conditional perfect)
If the teacher had asked you a question, you would have answered.

Si tu avais lu le livre (hier), tu **pourrais** *répondre au professeur (maintenant).* (pluperfect/present conditional)
If you had read the book (yesterday), you would be able to answer the question (now).

1. **Complete the following sentences with the correct form of the verb given:**

   a. Si tu venais me voir ce soir, nous _____ ensemble. (chanter)

   b. Si ma mère me téléphone, je lui _____ toujours des conseils. (demander)

   c. Si tu avais été gentille, je _____ avec toi. (sortir)

   d. Achète une maison dans le quartier français de Hanoï si tu le

   _____. (aimer)

   e. Si on n'a pas de passeport, on ne _____ pas passer la frontière. (pouvoir)

   f. Vous _____ super contents si vous aviez des billets pour le match des San José Sharks! (être)

   g. Si tu veux voir *American Idol,* _____ la télé tout de suite. (allumer)

   h. Si tu avais donné de l'argent à la campagne du président, tu

   _____ moins d'impôts. (payer)

   i. _____ chez le dentiste si tu as mal aux dents. (aller)

   j. Si Suzanne m'avait donné son numéro de téléphone, je lui _____ maintenant. (téléphoner)

2. There are five errors in the following letter. Underline and correct them:

 Chère Gudule,

J'aurai dû t'écrire il y a très longtemps. Si je l'avais fait,

je t'écris des horreurs parce que j'étais encore très en colère. Je

voulerais que tu comprennes mon indignation quand j'ai découvert

que tu m'avais volé mon amant. Est-ce que je pourrais continuer à

vivre si Jojo n'avait plus été près de moi? Si tu l'aimes, gardez-le,

mais tu as perdu mon affection et ma confiance pour toujours.

Ton ancienne amie,

Valentine

 # D) LES NOMS FÉMININS

Some nouns that refer to people or animals have unpredictable feminine forms that need to be learned. Fortunately, many of these nouns are derived from the masculine form.

1 **The great majority of feminine nouns are formed by adding an "*e*" to the masculine.**

EXAMPLES: *un enseignant → une enseignante* a teacher
un villageois → une villageoise a person living in a village
un Américain → une Américaine an American man/woman

2 **If the masculine noun already ends in an "e," usually nothing changes.**

⚜ **EXAMPLES:** *un fonctionnaire →*
une fonctionnaire   a government employee
un avare → une avare   a miser
un analyste → une analyste   an analyst
un journaliste → une journaliste   a journalist

ATTENTION! A very small number of masculine nouns do not follow this rule, and the feminine ending becomes "*-esse.*"

⚜ **EXAMPLES:** *un hôte → une hôtesse*   a host – a hostess
un tigre → une tigresse   a tiger – a tigress
un maître → une maîtresse   a master – a mistress

3 **Masculine nouns ending in "*-eur*" have two possible endings in the feminine.**

a) **If they end in "*-teur,*" they will <u>usually</u> (not always) end in "*-trice*" in the feminine.**

⚜ **EXAMPLES:** *le directeur → la directrice*   the headmaster/headmistress (director)
le moniteur → la monitrice   the coach
un acteur → une actrice   an actor – an actress

As many more women enter professions where men traditionally worked, language evolves to reflect changes in society. It is now correct to say:

⚜ **EXAMPLES:** *le sénateur → la sénatrice*   the senator
le facteur → la factrice   the mailman – the mailwoman
(the letter carrier)

b) **In other cases, masculine nouns will end in "*-euse*" in the feminine.**

⚜ **EXAMPLES:** *le coiffeur → la coiffeuse*   the hairdresser
le menteur → la menteuse   the liar
le vendeur → la vendeuse   the salesman – the saleswoman

4 **Masculine nouns ending in "*-ien*" will double the "*n*" and add an "*e*."**

⚜ **EXAMPLES:** *un comédien → une comédienne*   an actor – an actress
un politicien → une politicienne   a politician

5 Most masculine nouns ending with a consonant will double the consonant and add an *"e"* in the feminine. This is particularly the case with female animals.

⚜ **EXAMPLES:**

le chat → *la cha**tte***	the cat
le chien → *la chie**nne***	the dog
le lion → *la lio**nne***	the lion
le patron → *la patro**nne***	the boss
le paysan → *la paysa**nne***	the peasant

ATTENTION! Some female animal nouns are not based on the male nouns. Here are some common ones:

⚜ **EXAMPLES:**

le coq → *la poule*	the rooster → the hen
le taureau → *la vache*	the bull → the cow
le cheval → *la jument*	the horse → the mare
le bouc → *la chèvre*	the billy goat → the goat
le mouton → *la brebis*	the sheep → the ewe

6 Masculine nouns ending in *"-er"* do <u>not</u> double the consonant for the feminine form. Instead, they acquire an accent (`) on the *"e"* and add an additional *"e."*

⚜ **EXAMPLES:**

*le boulang**er*** → *la boulang**ère***	the baker
*un cuisini**er*** → *une cuisini**ère***	a cook
*un étrang**er*** → *une étrang**ère***	a foreigner
*un infirmi**er*** → *une infirmi**ère***	a nurse
*un ouvri**er*** → *une ouvri**ère***	a workman – a female worker

7 Some nouns have no feminine counterpart and only exist in the masculine form. In other words, you use the same form for men and women. The articles do not change, either.

⚜ **EXAMPLES:**

un assassin	a murderer
un auteur	an author
un médecin	a doctor (The word *"la médecine"* means "science")
un professeur	a professor
un témoin	a witness

⚜ **EXAMPLES:** *Cette femme est **un assassin**!*
This woman is a murderer!

*Charlotte Brontë est **l'auteur** de <u>Jane Eyre</u>.*
Charlotte Brontë is the author of <u>Jane Eyre</u>.

8 **Similarly, there are also nouns that exist only in the feminine form:**

⚜ EXAMPLES: *une personne*   a person
               une victime   a victim
               une star   a star (a famous person)

*Ton ami Georges est **une personne** charmante.*
   Your friend Georges is a charming person.

*Les enfants sont souvent **les malheureuses victimes** d'accidents.*
   Children are often the unfortunate victims of accidents.

*Brad Pitt est **une grande star** du cinéma américain.*
   Brad Pitt is a big star of American movies.

ATTENTION! Remember to make adjectives agree with the gender of the <u>noun</u> with which it is associated. In the first sentence, for example, George is a man, but *"charmante"* is in the feminine form because it agrees with *"personne."*

9 **Some nouns change meaning depending on their gender. Here are some of the more common ones to learn:**

⚜ EXAMPLES: ***un** livre*   a book
               ***une** livre*   a pound (half a kilo)

               ***un** manche*   a handle
               ***une** manche* a sleeve

               ***un** poste*   an employment position
               ***une** poste*   a post office

               ***le** physique*   the physical appearance
               ***la** physique*   physics

               ***un** tour*   a tour
               ***une** tour*   a tower

EXERCICES

1. Pair the following nouns with their corresponding feminine counterparts:

a. un pharmacien → _____

b. un chien → _____

c. un pâtissier → _____

d. un coq → _____

e. un assistant → _____

f. un instituteur → _____

g. un infirmier → _____

h. un élève → _____

i. un tricheur → _____

2. Write an article (definite or indefinite) to indicate the gender of the following noun:

a. _____ politique est un sujet de conversation dangereux!

b. Est-ce que tu connais _____ victime du crime? –Oui, je crois que c'est

_____ frère de _____ assassin.

c. _____ étudiant est _____ personne qui va à l'université. Si

vous allez à l'école, vous êtes _____ élève.

d. Ma mère est _____ médecin que beaucoup de mes amis vont voir.

e. J'aime beaucoup _____ vendeuse qui travaille le samedi au marché
flottant de Da Nang!

f. _____ gymnaste qui a gagné aux Jeux Olympiques est un garçon

remarquable. C'est _____ star dans son pays!

g. _____ conductrice de la voiture n° 26 a eu un accident, pourtant

c'est _____ professionnelle.

h. _____ trapéziste porte une jolie robe rose.

i. Avez-vous vu _____ conducteur de l'autre voiture? Il est fou!

j. _____ garagiste qui travaille chez Gulf est l'ami de ma sœur.

These two sets of questions use grammatical structures and vocabulary from this lesson. Working with a partner, alternate asking and answering each question. When you get to the bottom of each list, start over at the top, switching roles. As a variation, write out the answers in complete sentences.

A) **Aurions**-nous **pris** des vacances si nous avions beaucoup travaillé?

Aurais-tu **été** jalouse si j'étais allé dîner au restaurant avec ton ami?

Aurais-tu **passé** l'examen de français si tu avais étudié?

Auriez-vous **mangé** le steak s'il avait été trop cuit?

Aurais-tu **pu** gagner cette bourse si tu avais voulu?

M'aurais-tu **téléphoné** si je t'avais donné mon numéro?

M'aurais-tu **aidé** si j'avais eu des problèmes?

B) Si je t'**invite** à manger chez moi, **viens**-tu?

Si je t'**invite** à manger chez moi, **viendras**-tu?

Si je t'**invitais** à manger chez moi, **viendrais**-tu?

Viendrais-tu si je t'**invitais** à manger chez moi?

Si je t'**avais invité** à manger chez moi, **serais**-tu venu?

Aurais-tu **partagé** ton argent avec moi si tu **avais gagné** à la loterie?

Si je te **disais** que je suis champion mondial de tennis, me **croirais**-tu?

EXERCICES DE RÉVISION

A) LE CONDITIONNEL

Change these verbs to the corresponding form of the present conditional:

   a. je peux   → _____

   b. vous finissez   → _____

   c. elles perdent   → _____

   d. tu vois   → _____

   e. nous nous souvenons → _____

   f. il mange   → _____

B) LE CONDITIONNEL PASSÉ

Write the correct form of the conditional perfect using the verb and subject provided:

   a. descendre (elle)   → _____

   b. danser (vous)   → _____

   c. être (tu)   → _____

   d. ne pas mourir (il) → _____

   e. se dépêcher (elles) → _____

   f. voir (je)   → _____

   g. rester (ils)   → _____

   h. vivre (elle)   → _____

C) LES PHRASES AVEC "SI"

1. Fill in each blank with the correct form of the infinitive in parentheses:

a. Si tu avais confiance en moi, tu me _____ tous tes secrets. (dire)

b. Ils _____ le match s'ils avaient fait plus d'efforts à l'entraînement. (gagner)

c. Si tu as encore cette douleur aiguë, _____ voir le médecin. (aller)

d. S'il finit son portrait avant midi, il _____ le montrer au prof de dessin. (pouvoir)

e. S'il te _____ une bague, tu sauras qu'il t'aime. (donner)

f. Si le plateau était tombé, les verres _____. (se casser)

g. Comme nous serions contents si nous _____ en vacances à Angkor pour voir les temples! (partir)

h. _____ tes devoirs si tu veux aller au cinéma avec tes copains. (Faire)

i. J'aurais acheté un beau chapeau avec des plumes si Geneviève me

_____ à son bal costumé. (inviter)

j. Si elle n' _____ pas votre amitié, elle serait bien triste. (avoir)

k. Si le commerce électronique continue à se developper, est-ce que les magasins

_____ encore? (exister)

l. Je ne sais pas ce que je _____ si la banque avait été fermée. (faire)

m. Si les oiseaux n'avaient pas de plumes, ils _____ froid! (avoir)

n. Si l'entrevue s'était bien passée, on le _____ pour ce poste. (prendre)

o. Si tu _____ l'examen hier, _____ plus la prochaine fois! (rater/travailler)

2. There are five errors in the following paragraph. Underline and correct them:

Nicolas est allé à une entrevue pour entrer à l'université. Je pense que s'il n'aurait pas été si intimidé, il aurait fait meilleure impression.

La prochaine fois, il devait porter des vêtements plus confortables. S'il étaient plus à l'aise, il ne penserait pas que ses chaussures lui font mal.

Ses parents n'auront pas dû l'accompagner. S'il m'avais demandé mon avis, je lui aurais donné de bons conseils.

D) LES NOMS FÉMININS

1. Pair the following nouns with the corresponding feminine form (noun):

a. un africain   → _____

b. un conducteur   → _____

c. un prince   → _____

d. un sorcier   → _____

e. un skieur   → _____

f. un avare   → _____

g. un ambassadeur → _____

h. un acrobate → _____

i. un auteur → _____

j. un mouton → _____

2. **Translate the following sentences:**

a. My cousin Paul is a charming person, but he is not a very good student!

_____

_____

b. A goat is a stubborn animal who eats everything!

_____

_____

c. My brother would like to be a star!

_____

_____

d. I saw the Mekong River when I went to Vietnam.

_____

_____

e. I study physics, and my friend Naomi studies politics.

_____

_____

f. My sister wants to become an electrician!

_____

_____

g. The first person who arrived at my party was your brother.

_____

_____

h. My sweater has long sleeves, but it is not purple!

_____

_____

i. The postal service is very quick in France.

_____

_____

j. Eggs come from hens, but milk comes from cows!

_____

_____

3. **Write an article _(le, la, un, une)_ to indicate the gender of the following noun:**

   a. Ces belles pommes sur le plateau coûtent 2 euros _____ livre.

   b. Madame Antibiotik est _____ médecin de la famille Durand.

   c. Helen Fielding est _____ auteur anglais qui vient d'écrire un roman très amusant.

   d. _____ patron du nouveau restaurant vietnamien près de chez nous est

   _____ personne très désagréable.

e. Allons tous au zoo voir _____ lionne qui vient d'avoir trois bébés lionceaux.

f. _____ Tour de Pise risque de tomber sur la tête de ces touristes imprudents!

g. Gérard Depardieu est _____ star du cinéma français.

h. Va vite changer de chemise parce que _____ manche gauche est sale.

i. Je n'aime pas aller dans cette boutique parce que _____ vendeur n'est pas très aimable.

j. Cet employé n'aime pas son travail au Cambodge et il va chercher _____ autre poste.

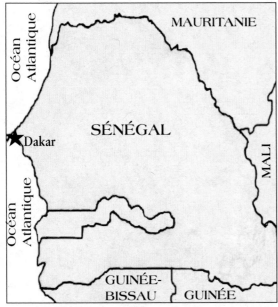

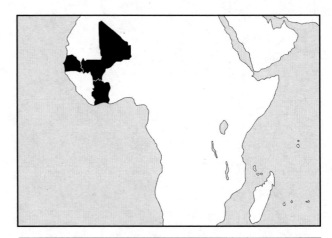

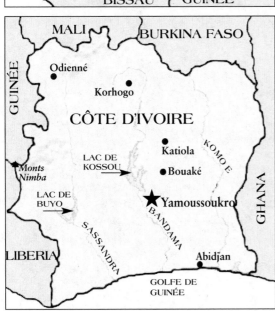

LA CÔTE D'IVOIRE

Capitale: Yamoussoukro (capitale officielle), Abidjan (capitale commerciale et administrative)

Population: 21.000.000

Gouvernement: République

Chef d'état: Président Alassane Ouattara

Monnaie: Franc CFA (XOF)

Langues: Français (langue officielle), dioula, d'autres langues africaines

Ressources: Cuivre, diamants, gaz naturel, minéraux, pétrole

Musique/Danse: Griots (chanteurs qui accompagnent tous les événements de la vie — naissance, mariages, enterrements), instruments musicaux — gourdis, djembe, kpalago, shekere, kora

Principales richesses touristiques: Carnaval de Bouaké, Fête du Dipri, Fêtes des Masques

Cuisine: Attieke (manioc râpé), kedjenou (poulet), soupe aux avocats

IVOIRIENS CÉLÈBRES

Gadji Céla
(CHANTEUR)

Djimmy Danger
(ACTEUR)

Didier Drogba
(JOUEUR DE FOOT)

Aïcha Koné
(CHANTEUSE)

Ahmadou Kourouma
(ÉCRIVAIN)

Masta
(HUMORISTE)

Véronique Tadjo
(ÉCRIVAIN ET PEINTRE)

LE SÉNÉGAL, LE MALI &
LA CÔTE D'IVOIRE

LE SÉNÉGAL

Capitale: Dakar

Population: 12.300.000

Gouvernement: République constitutionnelle

Chef d'état: Président Abdoulaye Wade

Monnaie: Franc CFA (XOF)

Langues: Français (langue officielle), le wolof et d'autres langues africaines

Ressources: Minéraux, phosphates, poissons

Musique/ Danse: Mbalax (musique traditionnelle), rap, wango (danse traditionnelle)

Principales richesses touristiques: Casamance (forêt tropicale), Île de la Madeleine, parcs nationaux, pêche et chasse, sanctuaires d'oiseaux, sports nautiques

Cuisine: Aubergines diakhatou, bœuf et agneau, céréales, choux, gombo, mangues vertes, manioc, melons, navets, oranges, papayes, thiof et autres poissons grillés

SÉNÉGALAIS CÉLÈBRES

Kiné Lam
(CHANTEUSE)

Youssou N'Dour
(CHANTEUR DE MBALAX)

Omar-Père
(AUTEUR-COMPOSITEUR)

Ousmane Sembene
(CINÉASTE, ÉCRIVAIN)

Léopold Sédar Senghor
(PREMIER PRÉSIDENT, POÈTE, AUTEUR ET COMPOSITEUR DE L'HYMNE NATIONAL)

LE MALI

Capitale: Bamako

Population: 13.800.000

Gouvernement: République constitutionnelle

Chef d'état: Président Amadou Toumani Toure
Premier Ministre Modibo Sidibe

Monnaie: Franc CFA (XOF)

Langues: Français (langue officielle), bambara et d'autres langues africaines

Ressources: Agriculture, phosphates, mines d'or

Musique/Danse: Bambara, Bobo, Senufo pop (musiques traditionnelles), Wassoulou

Principales richesses touristiques: Djenné (patrimoine mondial de L'UNESCO), Mopti (la Venise du Mali), Pays Dogon, Tombouctou

Cuisine: Le capitaine (gros poisson du fleuve Niger), cuisine à base de riz et de mil souvent accompagné de poisson, le foutou (couscous vert et très fin accompagné d'une sauce liquide et de haricots blancs), mouton, poulet, le tô (gâteau au mil malaxé avec de la sauce au gombo) et de nombreux fruits (mangues, ananas, papayes)

MALIENS CÉLÈBRES

Amadou Hampâté Bâ
(ÉCRIVAIN)

Amadou et Mariam
(CHANTEURS)

Souleymane Cissé
(CINÉASTE)

Ali Farka Fouré
(CHANTEUR)

Oumou Sangaré
(CHANTEUSE)

Fily Dabo Sissoko
(HOMME POLITIQUE ET ÉCRIVAIN)

VOCABULAIRE
LEÇON SIX

LES NOMS

l' *aube* (f.)	dawn	la *légende*	legend
l' *autorisation* (f.)	permission	le *manque*	lack
la *bataille*	fight, battle	le *miracle*	miracle
le *bonheur*	happiness	le *morceau*	piece, bit, selection
la *carotte*	carrot		
le *cintre*	hanger	le *mystère*	mystery
les *ciseaux* (m.)	scissors	l' *ongle* (m.)	fingernail, toenail
le *contrôle*	quiz		
le *destin*	destiny, fate	la *peinture*	painting
la *dette*	debt	la *plainte*	complaint
l' *église* (f.)	church	le *poison*	poison
l' *entrée* (f.)	entrance, first course	la *poussière*	dust
		la *presse*	press
la *fin*	end	le *rapport*	report
la *flamme*	flame	le *retard*	lateness
le *futur*	future	la *sécurité*	security, certainty
le *genre*	kind, sort		
le *gérant*	manager	la *sortie*	exit
le *geste*	gesture	le *témoin*	witness
la *goutte*	drop	le *ticket*	ticket (métro, bus)
l' *image* (f.)	picture		
la *jeunesse*	youth	le *troupeau*	herd
		la *valise*	suitcase

LEÇON SIX

KEY GRAMMAR CONCEPTS

A) LE PRÉSENT DU SUBJONCTIF → *The present subjunctive*

B) LES PRONOMS OBJETS ET LE CAS DE "Y" ET "EN" → *Object pronouns*

C) LES COMPARAISONS ÉGALES ET INÉGALES → *Equal and unequal comparisons*

A) LE PRÉSENT DU SUBJONCTIF

The **subjunctive** mood is used frequently in French. While the subjunctive is used occasionally in English, most of us are not really aware of it. (e.g., God bless you! I require that he study his algebra; They insist we be here early).

This lesson will consider the use of the subjunctive after verbs of volition, expressing wishes and commands.

1) THE CONJUGATION OF THE SUBJUNCTIVE

To form the subjunctive of most verbs:

◆ Start with the 3rd person plural *(ils/elles)* of the present tense of the verb.
◆ Take off the *"-ent."*
◆ Replace it with the following endings:

-e	*-ions*
-es	*-iez*
-e	*-ent*

Helpful Tip: *"Que"* always precedes the subjunctive form.

PARLER		
Take the stem from the present indicative	Add these endings:	Present subjunctive
ils parle̶n̶t̶	*e*	*que je parle*
	es	*que tu parles*
	e	*qu'elle parle*
	ions	*que nous parlions*
	iez	*que vous parliez*
	ent	*qu'ils parlent*

Some verbs in the subjunctive use the imperfect for the *"nous"* and *"vous"* form.

BOIRE
Present subjunctive
que je **boive**   *que tu* **boives**   *qu'elle* **boive**   *que nous* **buvions**   *que vous* **buviez**   *qu'ils* **boivent**

A few verbs are irregular in the subjunctive. Because they are very common, you must memorize them:

ALLER	AVOIR	ÊTRE
que j'aille que tu ailles qu'elle aille que nous allions que vous alliez qu'ils aillent	que j'aie que tu aies qu'elle ait que nous ayons que vous ayez qu'ils aient	que je sois que tu sois qu'il soit que nous soyons que vous soyez qu'elles soient
FAIRE	**POUVOIR**	**SAVOIR**
que je fasse que tu fasses qu'il fasse que nous fassions que vous fassiez qu'elles fassent	que je puisse que tu puisses qu'elle puisse que nous puissions que vous puissiez qu'ils puissent	que je sache que tu saches qu'il sache que nous sachions que vous sachiez qu'elles sachent
VOULOIR	**FALLOIR***	**PLEUVOIR***
que je veuille que tu veuilles qu'il veuille que nous voulions que vous vouliez qu'elles veuillent	qu'il faille	qu'il pleuve

*These two verbs are only conjugated in the 3RD person singular.

2) USE OF THE SUBJUNCTIVE AFTER VERBS EXPRESSING WISHES OR COMMANDS

The following verbs take the subjunctive:

aimer → to like		
aimer mieux → to prefer		
commander → to order		
demander → to ask		
empêcher → to prevent		
exiger → to require, to demand	**+ que +**	**Subjunctive**
insister → to insist		
interdire → to forbid		
ordonner → to order		
préférer → to prefer		
vouloir → to want		

EXAMPLES: *Mes parents ne **veulent** pas que ma petite sœur **aille** à cette fête.*
My parents don't want my little sister to go to that party.

*J'**aimerais** que vous m'**aidiez** à faire mon devoir de math.*
I would like you to help me do my math homework.

*Il **interdit** que nous **jouions** avec sa nouvelle raquette.*
He forbids us to play with his new racquet.

Helpful Tip: Surprisingly, *espérer* never takes the subjunctive.

EXAMPLE: *J'**espère** que tu **viendras** dîner ce soir.*
I hope you will come to dinner tonight.

3) USE OF THE INFINITIVE INSTEAD OF THE SUBJUNCTIVE

When the subject of both verbs is the same, the second verb is in the infinitive.

EXAMPLES: *Mes parents ne veulent pas **aller** à la fête.*
My parents don't want to go to the party.

*Je veux te **voir** ce soir.*
I want to see you this evening.

*J'aimerais t'**aider** à faire ton devoir.*
I would like to help you do your homework.

1. Conjugate these verbs fully in the present subjunctive. ATTENTION! **Remember the** *que!*

finir   **prendre**

_____   _____

_____   _____

_____   _____

_____   _____

_____   _____

_____   _____

avoir   **se souvenir**

_____   _____

_____   _____

_____   _____

_____   _____

_____   _____

_____   _____

2. Choose the appropriate verb form. Most will be in the subjunctive. However, some may be in the indicative or the infinitive.

a. Le général interdit que vous _____ du chewing gum pendant la bataille. (mâcher)

b. L'agent de police demande que tu lui _____ ton permis de conduire. (montrer)

c. J'espère que tu _____ assister au match de foot demain. (pouvoir)

d. Je n'aime pas _____ la nuit. (conduire)

e. Mon père aimerait que je lui _____ une mousse au chocolat pour son anniversaire. (faire)

f. Mais moi, je préfère _____ *30 Rock*. (regarder)

g. Le directeur du zoo interdit que les poissons _____ de l'eau. (sortir)

h. Le professeur exige que nous _____ toute la pièce de Shakespeare pour demain. (lire)

i. Le gérant de l'immeuble demande que vous _____ le loyer. (payer)

j. Je ne veux pas _____ au cinéma parce que j'ai l'entraînement de natation. (aller)

k. Anatole est content que Claire _____ la vérité. (savoir)

l. Claire est contente de _____ la vérité. (savoir)

3. There are nine errors in the following letter. Underline and correct them:

 Cher Elvis,

Comment vas-tu? J'espère que tu ailles bien. Je veux te dis des choses importantes alors je te demande d'aller dans un endroit tranquille. Je veux que tu lis cette lettre attentivement. Je t'adore mais je ne peux pas sortir avec toi ce soir. Ma mère refuse que nous nous voyons. Elle ne veut pas que je fais la connaissance de tes amis célèbres. Elle ne veut pas que je sorte avec une idole du Rock 'n Roll. Elle exige que je fais mes devoirs de français et que je reste à la maison. Je ne veux plus fais mes

devoirs! Je veux te voir! Je t'assure que mes parents ne peuvent pas

empêcher que je sors avec toi. À minuit ce soir, je voudrais que tu

viennes sous la fenêtre de ma chambre avec ta guitare et ta voiture. Nous

partirons ensemble. A bientôt mon amour! J'espère que tu viennes ce soir.

Tendres baisers,

Sidonie

B) LES PRONOMS OBJETS ET LE CAS DE "Y" ET "EN"

You already know the subject pronouns, so we will use them as a point of reference.
Here is a chart of the corresponding object pronouns and their uses:

For people and things		For people only	
subject	direct object	indirect object pronouns	object of other prepositions
je	*me (m')*	*me (m')*	*moi*
tu	*te (t')*	*te (t')*	*toi*
il	*le (l')*	*lui*	*lui*
elle	*la (l')*	*lui*	*elle*
nous	*nous*	*nous*	*nous*
vous	*vous*	*vous*	*vous*
ils	*les*	*leur*	*eux*
elles	*les*	*leur*	*elles*

EXAMPLES: *Nous voyons la fille.*
    We see the girl.

    *Nous **la** voyons.*
    We see her.

L'enfant écrit au Père Noël.
    The child writes to Santa Claus.
*L'enfant **lui** écrit.*
    The child writes to him.

Est-ce que tu téléphones souvent à ta mère?
    Do you call your mother often?
*Est-ce que tu **lui** téléphones souvent?*
    Do you call her often?

Vous allez jouer au tennis avec Suzie et Paul.
    You are going to play tennis with Suzie and Paul.
*Vous allez jouer au tennis avec **eux**.*
    You are going to play tennis with them.

In the case of a compound tense, such as the *passé composé,* the pronoun comes right before the auxiliary verb.

EXAMPLES: *Si j'avais regardé* The Da Vinci Code, *je connaîtrais Audrey Tautou.*
    If I had watched *The Da Vinci Code*, I would know Audrey Tautou.
*Si je l'avais regardé, je **la** connaîtrais.*
    If I had watched it, I would know her.

Nous voulons trouver la sortie.
    We want to find the exit.
*Nous voulons **la** trouver.*
    We want to find it.

Let's look now at the object pronouns *"y"* and *"en"* which are used as follows:

Y	1. object of *à* for things only
	2. places
EN	1. object of *de* for things only
	2. quantities for things and people

1) Y

"Y" can stand for places or things. You will notice that *"y"* (as well as *"en"*) is placed right before the verb of which it is the complement.

Est-ce que tu as pensé à ce problème?
Did you think of this problem?

–Oui, j'y ai pensé.
   –Yes, I thought of it.

Ils vont au centre commercial le dimanche.
   They go to the mall on Sundays.
Ils y vont le dimanche.
   They go there on Sundays.

Il n'a pas cru au miracle.
   He did not believe in the miracle.
Il n'y a pas cru.
   He did not believe in it.

2) EN

"En" refers to people and things in expressions of quantity. It can replace a *"de"* object phrase when things are involved.

♣ EXAMPLES: *J'ai besoin de ciseaux pour me couper les ongles.*
   I need scissors to cut my nails.

J'en ai besoin pour les couper.
   I need them to cut them.

Tu prends du sucre dans ton café? –Oui, j'en prends.
   Do you take sugar with your coffee? –Yes, I do.

*As-tu beaucoup de travail? –Oui, j'en ai **beaucoup**.*
   Do you have a lot of work? –Yes, I have a lot (of it).

Nous avons trop de travail.
   We have too much work.
*Nous en avons **trop**.*
   We have too much (of it).

Nous n'avons pas assez d'argent.
   We don't have enough money.
*Nous n'en avons pas **assez**.*
   We don't have enough (of it).

When you replace a noun preceded by a quantity, you need to repeat the quantity.

♣ EXAMPLES: *Vous avez deux chiens? –Oui, j'en ai **deux**.*
   You have two dogs? –Yes, I have two (of them).

 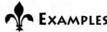

*Combien de frères avez-vous? –J'en ai **trois**.*
How many brothers do you have? –I have three (of them).

*Est-ce qu'il a pris une valise? –Oui, il **en** a pris **une**.*
Did he take a suitcase? –Yes, he took one.

"Un" and *"une"* are always considered a quantity, never an article, as illustrated in the following example.

⚜ **EXAMPLE:** *Vous avez fait **une** erreur? –Oui, malheureusement, j'en ai fait **une**.*
You made a mistake? –Yes, unfortunately, I did (make one).

At times, you may need two object pronouns in a sentence. In that case, always follow this pattern:

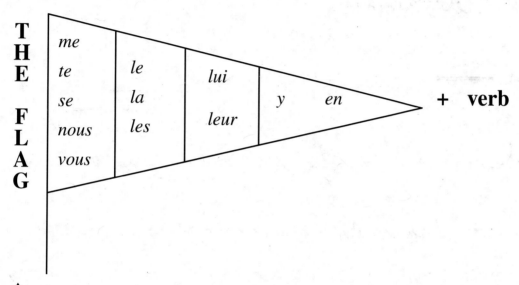

THE FLAG

| me te se nous vous | le la les | lui leur | y en | **+ verb** |

⚜ **EXAMPLES:** *Elle a laissé sa valise sur l'autoroute.*
She left her suitcase on the highway.
*Elle **l'y** a laissée.*
She left it there.

Sophie me parle de ses problèmes.
Sophie speaks to me about her problems.
*Sophie **m'en** parle.*
Sophie speaks to me about them.

Les grands-parents n'ont pas raconté cette légende terrifiante aux petits enfants.
The grandparents did not tell that terrifying legend to the little children.
*Ils ne **la leur** ont pas racontée.*
They did not tell it to them.

ATTENTION! Remember: In sentences with a verb in the *passé composé* conjugated with *"avoir,"* the past participle must agree with the direct object if it is preceding the auxiliary *"avoir."*

Rewrite the following sentences, replacing the underlined nouns with pronouns. ⚠ATTENTION! **Be careful of their placement!**

a. J'aime beaucoup <u>la peinture de Picasso</u>.

Je l'aime beaucoup

b. <u>Thomas</u> a donné <u>sa photo</u> à <u>sa petite amie</u>.
la lui

Il la lui a donnée

c. <u>Le juge</u> a discuté avec <u>les témoins</u>.
leur

Il ~~leur~~ a discuté avec eux.

d. <u>Le gérant</u> est sorti <u>de l'immeuble</u> sans répondre <u>aux questions</u>. ~~les~~ ~~eux~~ y

Il en est sorti sans y répondre.

e. Je voudrais rembourser <u>ma dette</u>.
la

Je voudrais la rembourser.

f. <u>Marc</u> aimerait voir <u>les photos de ta jeunesse</u>.
les

Il aimerait les voir.

g. <u>La vache</u> est entrée <u>dans l'église</u> sans <u>son propriétaire</u>.
y lui

Elle y est entrée sans lui.

h. J'ai pris trois <u>cintres</u> <u>dans ton placard</u>.
en y

J'y en ~~ai~~ ai pris trois.

i. <u>Le professeur</u> expliquera <u>le futur</u> <u>aux élèves</u>.
le Il leur

Il ~~le leur~~ expliquera.

j. Il n'aurait pas perdu <u>les billets</u> s'il les avait mis <u>sur la table</u>.
les y

Il ne les ~~y~~ aurait pas perdu s'il les y avait mis.

3. THE PLACEMENT OF PRONOUNS IN AFFIRMATIVE AND NEGATIVE COMMANDS

When giving affirmative (not negative) orders, the pronouns *"me"* and *"te"* become *"moi"* and *"toi."* Note that all object pronouns <u>follow</u> these affirmative commands:

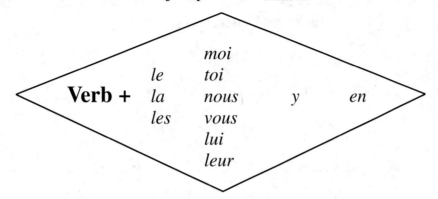

EXAMPLES:

*Donne-**les-moi**!*	Give them to me!
*Envoie-**nous-en**!*	Send us some!
*Vas-**y**!*	Go!
*Montre-**le-lui**!*	Show it to her!

When *"moi"* is followed by *"en"* it becomes *"m'en."*

*Donne-**m'en**!*	Give me some!

However, in negative commands, the word order changes:

*Ne **me les** donne pas!*	Don't give them to me!
*Ne **nous en** envoie pas!*	Don't send us any!

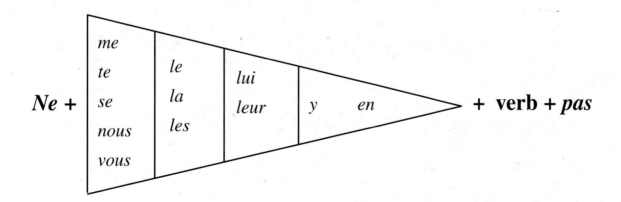

1. **Rewrite the following sentences, replacing the underlined nouns with pronouns.** ATTENTION! **Be careful of their placement!**

   a. Tu apportes <u>des fleurs</u> <u>à ta petite amie</u>.

   Tu lui en apportes.

   b. Ne donne pas <u>cette affreuse photo</u> <u>à ces garçons</u>.
                  le   *leur*

   Ne la leur donne pas.

   c. Mets <u>ces morceaux de carottes</u> <u>dans la soupe</u>.
                                     y

   Mets-les-y.

   d. <u>Mon frère</u> a acheté <u>des chaussettes bleues</u>.
                                   en

   ~~a acheté~~ *Il en a acheté.*

   e. Elle dansera toute la nuit <u>dans ses bras</u>.
                                y

   Elle y dansera toute la nuit.
                             le

   ✗ **f.** Le petit garçon s'est caché derrière <u>son père</u>.   [after prep]

   Il ~~se~~ s'est caché derrière lui.
           la   *en*   [en + quantity]

   ✗ **g.** J'ai rencontré <u>un ange</u> qui descendait <u>du ciel</u>!

   Je l'~~ai en~~ rencontré un qui en descendait.
                           la   [infinitive]

   ✗ **h.** Il n'a pas voulu voir <u>la fin de *Pink Panther 2*</u>.

   Il n'a~~ la~~ pas voulu la voir.

2. **Translate these sentences:**

   ✗ **a.** Give it to me.
             le

   Donne-~~la~~-moi.

   ✗ **b.** The police did not find it there.

   ~~Ne Trouve-t-il pas~~
                      y

   la police ne l'y a pas trouvé(e)

c. Don't send me [any of them.]

ne m'en envoie pas.

N'Envoyez - les - moi pas.

d. Why didn't she bring them to him?

D.O.   I.O.

Ø Pourquoi elle ne les lui a pas apportés?

e. Does he like us?

Est ce qu'il nous aime?

f. They saw you with her.

Ils t'ont vu avec elle.

3. There are seven errors in the following story. Underline and correct them:

L'histoire du Petit Chaperon Rouge, vous la connaissez? Non? Je

la

vais vous ~~me~~ raconter. Il était une fois une petite fille qui portait un

petit manteau rouge. Sa mère lui a dit d'aller chez sa grand-mère et de ~~la~~ *lui*

apporter

~~apporer~~ un petit pot de beurre et des galettes. Elle y est allée en traversant

par la forêt. Elle ~~en~~ a rencontré un loup qui lui a demandé où elle allait.

elle

Il a proposé de faire une course avec ~~eux~~. Le loup a gagné. Il est arrivé

chez la grand-mère et l'a dévorée. Quand le Petit Chaperon Rouge est

la

arrivée, elle a dit "Ouvre-moi la porte; ouvre-~~toi~~ vite!" Elle a été surprise

en avait

de voir le loup dans le lit de la grand-mère. Il ~~avait~~ de grandes dents, et

bags adj

en

il ~~y~~ avait beaucoup . . . pour elle manger!!!

Often in speech, a person compares one thing or person to another. There are two types of comparative sentences: those that express equality, and those that express inequality.

1) EQUAL COMPARISONS

The words compared may be **nouns**, **adjectives/adverbs**, or **verbs**.

a) Nouns

These sentences use the adverb *"autant de"* before a noun and use *"que"* after it.

 EXAMPLES: *J'ai **autant** d'amis **que** toi.*
I have as many friends as you do.

*Nous avons acheté **autant de** fleurs **qu'**elle.*
We have bought as many flowers as she has.

b) Adjectives/Adverbs

These sentences use the adverb *"aussi"* before adjectives and adverbs and *"que"* after them.

 EXAMPLES: *Je suis **aussi** grande **qu'**elle.*
I am as tall as she is.

Le film Wedding Crashers *est **aussi** drôle **que** Meet the Parents.*
The movie *Wedding Crashers* is as funny as *Meet the Parents*.

*Nous courons **aussi** vite **que** Franck Ribéry.*
We run as quickly as Franck Ribéry.

c) Verbs

These sentences use the expression *"autant que."*

 EXAMPLES: *Nous dansons **autant qu'**eux.*
We dance as much as they do.

*Je mange **autant qu'**elle.*
I eat as much as she does.

*J'ai dormi **autant que** ma sœur.*
I have slept as much as my sister.

2) UNEQUAL COMPARISONS

The key words for all unequal comparisons are *"plus"* or *"moins"* and *"que."* These words are used when comparing **nouns**, **adjectives/adverbs**, and **verbs**.

a) Nouns

⚜ **EXAMPLES:** *J'ai **plus** de raquettes de tennis **qu'**un professionel.*
I have more tennis racquets than a professional.

*Elle achète **plus** de maquillage **que** son arrière-grand-mère!*
She buys more make-up than her great-grandmother!

b) Adjectives/Adverbs

⚜ **EXAMPLES:** *Jean-Luc est **plus** rapide **que** Usain Bolt.*
Jean-Luc is faster than Usain Bolt.

*Martine est **moins** travailleuse **que** sa sœur.*
Martine is less industrious than her sister.

*Je lis **plus** lentement **que** mes amis.*
I read more slowly than my friends.

*Je fais le ménage **moins** consciencieusement **que** mon mari.*
I do the housework less scrupulously than my husband.

c) Verbs

⚜ **EXAMPLES:** *Je travaille **plus que** mon frère.*
I work more than my brother.

*Je travaille **moins que** ma sœur.*
I work less than my sister.

SPECIAL NOTES

◆ Should you choose to use a pronoun after *"que,"* you need a stressed pronoun (see p. 44).

⚜ **EXAMPLES:** *Je travaille plus que **lui**.*
I work more than him.

*Tu es moins fatigué que **moi**.*
You are less tired than me.

◆ There are a number of irregular comparative forms that you should memorize:

Adjective	Comparative	Adverb	Comparative
bon → *meilleur*		*bien* → *mieux*	
mauvais → *plus mauvais/ pire*			

 EXAMPLES: *Nicolas m'a raconté une **meilleure** blague que Josette.*
Nicolas told me a better joke than Josette.

*Ton gâteau est **meilleur** que le mien.*
Your cake is better than mine.

*Ton orthographe est **plus mauvaise** (pire) que la mienne!*
Your spelling is worse than mine!

*Arthur est **plus petit** que **moi**.*
Arthur is shorter than I (am).

◆ When a number follows an unequal comparison, *"que"* is replaced by *"de."*

 EXAMPLES: *J'ai plus **de quatre** livres ici.*
I have more than four books here.

*Il y a moins **de trois** mois de vacances.*
There are fewer than three months of vacation.

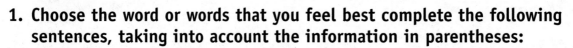

EXERCICES

1. Choose the word or words that you feel best complete the following sentences, taking into account the information in parentheses:

Examples: LeBron James est sportif (+ . . . mon vieil oncle)

LeBron James est plus sportif que mon vieil oncle.

Ton petit frère est exaspérant (= . . . le mien)

Ton petit frère est aussi exaspérant que le mien.

a. Morgan Freeman est un bon acteur (+ . . . George Clooney)

_____

b. Astérix est gros (– . . . Obélix)

_____

c. Les maths sont difficiles (= . . . les sciences)

_____

d. *Vogue* a des réclames (= . . . *Marie-Claire*)

_____

e. Tu es intelligent (– . . . je)

_____

f. La vache court vite (– . . . le cheval)

_____

g. Les jupes courtes sont sexy (+ . . . les jupes longues)

_____

h. Virginie est sympathique (+ . . . tu)

_____

2. Write logical comparisons in complete sentences:

Example: les voitures/les bicyclettes/rapide

> **Les voitures sont plus rapides que les bicyclettes.**
> _OR:_ **Les bicyclettes sont moins rapides que les voitures.**

a. *NCIS / American Idol /* passionnant

_____

b. Les Toyota / les BMW / cher

_____

c. La solitude / la folie / triste

_____

d. La natation / le football / fatigant

_____

e. L'église de mon village / Notre Dame de Paris / grand

_____

f. La jeunesse / la vieillesse / dynamique

_____

These two sets of questions use grammatical structures and vocabulary from this lesson. Working with a partner, alternate asking and answering each question. When you get to the bottom of each list, start over at the top, switching roles. As a variation, write out the answers in complete sentences.

A) Pourquoi tes parents ne veulent-ils pas que tu **ailles** à la fête?

Aimerais-tu que je t'**aide** à faire tes devoirs?

Faut-il que je me **souvienne** de toutes ces conjugaisons?

Est-il interdit de faire du bruit après vingt-deux heures?

Préfères-tu que je **fasse** le travail moi-même?

Ton père exige-t-il que tu **rentres** avant minuit?

Voulez-vous que je vous **laisse** tranquille?

B) Ma voiture vaut-elle **plus** cher **que** la tienne?

Suis-je **moins** intelligent(e) **que** toi?

Dansons-nous **aussi bien que** des professionnels?

Ton père est-il **plus** grand **que** toi?

Son accent est-il **pire que** le mien?

Ton professeur de français est-il **plus** sympathique **que** ton

professeur d'histoire?

La soupe de ta grand-mère est-elle **meilleure que** la soupe de ta mère?

A) LE PRÉSENT DU SUBJONCTIF

1. Conjugate these verbs in the present subjunctive:

être	venir	aller
_____	_____	_____
_____	_____	_____
_____	_____	_____
_____	_____	_____
_____	_____	_____

2. Choose among the infinitive, subjunctive, present or future to best complete these sentences:

a. La loi nous empêche de _____ de l'alcool. (boire)

b. Mes parents veulent que je _____ avant l'aube. (revenir)

c. J'exige que vous _____ la première sortie de l'autoroute. (prendre)

d. J'espère que le héros _____ le bonheur à la fin du film. (trouver)

e. Le président ordonne que les journalistes _____ de son bureau. (sortir)

f. Cristie Kerr aimerait que nous _____ l'entraînement tous ensemble. (commencer)

g. Je pense que le destin _____ un vrai mystère. (être)

h. Est-ce que vous voudriez que nous vous _____ le rapport? (montrer)

i. Je vais _____ une entrée avant le plat principal. (choisir)

j. Mes parents exigent que nous ne _____ pas de retard. (avoir)

3. **There are seven errors in the following letter. Underline and correct them:**

Cher Antoine,

J'aimerais que tu apprends l'anglais, mais je préfère que tu ne faisses pas de projets de voyage avec cette fille américaine. Je pense qu'elle soit bête et rusée. Elle veut apprenne le français seulement pour puisse sortir avec toi. Je préférerais que tu n'ais pas de rendez-vous avec elle. J'espère que tu tiennes compte de mes conseils.

Ta Maman qui t'aime

B) LES PRONOMS OBJET

1. Complete these sentences with the appropriate object pronoun(s):

a. J'aime beaucoup mes chats et je _____ raconte souvent mes problèmes.

b. Ton secret? Je ne _____ dirai à personne.

c. Tu n'as pas besoin de crier, je _____ entends parfaitement bien.

d. Elle est allée à la fête de Benoît et elle _____ est ennuyée.

e. Je sais qu'il y a de la glace dans le réfrigérateur, mais je ne _____ veux pas.

f. Les enfants aiment leur grand-mère et ils _____ téléphonent souvent.

g. Les Béchard partent en Afrique Occidentale, et je pense aller avec _____.

h. Si tu veux voir Valentine, passe chez _____ avant le dîner.

i. On peut voir des troupeaux de zèbres en Afrique. Il y _____ a beaucoup.

2. Change the following statements to affirmative commands:

Example: Tu la lui donnes. **Donne-la-lui!** _____

a. Tu me les présentes. _____

b. Vous lui en parlez. _____

c. Nous y allons avec elle. _____

d. Tu les leur expliques. _____

e. Vous les y mangez. _____

f. Tu m'en donnes. _____

3. Translate the following sentences:

   a. You did not give them to me. _____

   b. He repeats it to her. _____

   c. Send it to us! _____

   d. I saw them there. _____

   e. I want to buy some. _____

   f. Do you work for her? _____

4. There are seven errors in the following paragraph. Underline each error and write the correction above it:

   Je vais toi raconter une histoire assez drôle. Notre ami Gérard avait invité Gwyneth Paltrow chez le sans la connaître, parce qu'il lui trouvait si jolie qu'il leur aimait. Il a été charmant avec elles et il lui a préparé un excellent déjeuner. Elle est tombée amoureuse de sa cuisine et elle ne vous quitte plus!! Est-ce que cette histoire vous surprend?

C) Les comparaisons égales et inégales

1. **Choose the word or words that you feel best complete the following sentences, taking into account the information in parentheses:**

   Example: Mon petit frère est vieux (– . . . mon grand-père)

   **Mon petit frère est moins vieux que mon grand-père.**

   a. Rihanna danse bien (+ . . . je)

   _____

   b. Jacques mange beaucoup de chocolat (= . . . Alain)

   _____

   c. *20/20* est un bon programme de télévision (+ . . . *60 Minutes*)

   _____

   d. Les Français boivent de la bière (– . . . les Allemands)

   _____

   e. Le gâteau que tu as fait est bon (+ . . . le mien)

   _____

   f. Chandler parle le wolof mal (+ . . . le français)

   _____

2. **Complete the following sentences with *que* and/or *de*:**

   a. Je fais autant _____ fautes que toi.

   b. Il a moins _____ chance _____ son frère.

   c. Les poissons nagent mieux _____ les chats.

   d. Les pulls chez Abercrombie & Fitch sont plus jolis _____ aux Galeries Nantaises.

e. Les enfants ont moins _____ problèmes que les adultes.

f. J'aime mieux le français _____ les maths.

g. Il y a plus _____ poussière à la ville _____ à la campagne.

3. There are five errors in the following paragraph. Underline and correct them:

Nous sommes allés aux Galeries Nantaises pour faire quelques courses. Les biscuits y étaient plus chers de ceux de Monoprix mais ils étaient bien mieux et nous en avons acheté plus de vous. Les salades étaient plus fraîches comme les haricots verts. Les Galeries Nantaises sont vraiment les plus bons magasins de ce genre.

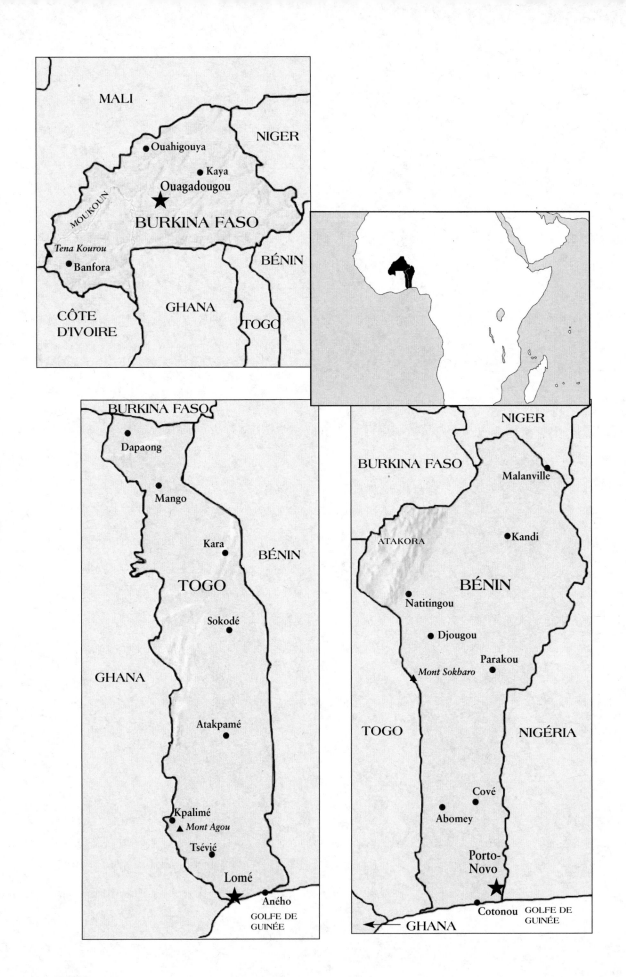

LE BURKINA FASO, LE TOGO & LE BÉNIN

LE BURKINA FASO

Capitale:	Ouagadougou
Population:	16.200.000
Gouvernement:	République parlementaire
Chef d'état:	Président Blaise Compaore
Monnaie:	Franc CFA (XOF)
Langues:	Français (langue officielle) et d'autres langues africaines
Ressources:	Agriculture, arachides, bétail, coton, or
Principales richesses touristiques:	Festival du Film Africain, grand marché de Gorom-Gorom, Grande Mosquée de Bobo-Dioulasso, Le marché artisanal d'Ouagadougou, Musée provincial de Houët (Bobo-Dioulasso), Parc National d'Arli, Réserve de Nazinga, Tiebele
Cuisine:	Bœuf sauce aubergine, mouton sauce tomate, riz gras, sauce de poisson

BURKINABÉS CÉLÈBRES:

Ouedraogo Dim-Dolobsom
(ÉCRIVAIN)

Janusz Mrozowski
(CINÉASTE)

Thomas Sankara
(HOMME POLITIQUE ET RÉVOLUTIONNAIRE)

Maurice Yaméogo
(PREMIER PRÉSIDENT)

LE TOGO

Capitale:	Lomé
Population:	6.600.000
Gouvernement:	République
Chef d'état:	Président Faure Gnassingbe
Monnaie:	Franc CFA (XOF)
Langues:	Français (langue officielle) et d'autres langues africaines
Ressources:	Agriculture, phosphates
Musique/Danse:	Musique traditionnelle, rap, reggae, soukous, "zouk"
Principales richesses touristiques:	Festival de Guin (à Glidji), Maison Royale de Togoville, Marché des Féticheurs, Musée National de Lomé, Parc National de Fazao-Malfacassa, Parc National de Keran, région du Mont-Kabaye
Cuisine:	Aglan (crabe), abodo (escargots en brochettes), koklo meme, lamounou dessi (sauce de poisson), riz sauce arachide

TOGOLAIS CÉLÈBRES:

Sokey Edorh
(PEINTRE)

Kossi Efoui
(ÉCRIVAIN)

Afia Mala
(CHANTEUSE)

Thierry Nkeli-Faha
(CHANTEUR)

Rodrigue Norman
(AUTEUR ET METTEUR EN SCÈNE)

LE BÉNIN

Capitale:	Porto-Novo (officielle), Cotonou (siège du gouvernement)
Population:	9.000.000
Gouvernement:	République
Chef d'état:	Président Thomas Yayi Boni
Monnaie:	Franc CFA (XOF)
Langues:	Français (langue officielle), fon, yoruba et d'autres langues africaines
Ressources:	Bois, coton, marbre, pétrole
Musique/Danse:	Festival de la Gani (danses, musique), jazz, musique traditionnelle, rap, reggae
Principales richesses touristiques:	Grand Marché de Dantokpa, Marché de Bakoumbe, Musée ethnographique de Porto-Novo, Palais de Abomey (site classé pour l'UNESCO), Palais Royal de Fon (Porto-Novo)

BÉNINOIS CÉLÈBRES:

Jean-Marc-Aurèle Afoutou
(POÈTE)

Angélique Kidjo
(CHANTEUSE)

Jean Odoutan
(CINÉASTE)

José Plira
(ÉCRIVAIN)

VOCABULAIRE
LEÇON SEPT

LES NOMS

les **affaires** *(f.)*	things, belongings, business	*la* **racine**	root
l' **affection** *(f.)*	affection	*le* **renseignement**	information
l' **aile** *(f.)*	wing	*le* **résumé**	summary
l' **attitude** *(f.)*	attitude	*le* **rire**	laughter
le **balai**	broom	*le* **risque**	risk
le **but**	aim, goal	*la* **route**	road, route
le **chemin**	path, direction	*la* **saison**	season
la **cloche**	bell	*le* **sentiment**	sentiment, feeling
la **conférence**	lecture	*la* **série**	series
le **contrôle**	quiz, test	*le* **siècle**	century
le **coton**	cotton	*le* **son**	sound
l' **écran** *(m.)*	screen	*le* **succès**	success
l' **endroit** *(m.)*	place	*le* **système**	system
l' **enseignement** *(m.)*	teaching	*la* **tache**	stain
le **morceau**	piece, bit, selection	*la* **tâche**	task
		la **taille**	size, waist
la **paire**	pair	*le* **talent**	talent
le **péché**	sin	*la* **tente**	tent
la **politique**	politics	*le* **toit**	roof
le **portrait**	picture, portrait	*la* **tortue**	turtle

LEÇON SEPT

KEY GRAMMAR CONCEPTS

A) LE SUBJONCTIF APRÈS LES EXPRESSIONS IMPERSONNELLES
→ *The subjunctive after impersonal expressions*

B) LE SUBJONCTIF APRÈS LES ÉMOTIONS ET LES OPINIONS
→ *The subjunctive after expressions of emotion and opinion*

C) LA VOIX PASSIVE → *The passive voice*

 A) LE SUBJONCTIF APRÈS LES EXPRESSIONS IMPERSONNELLES

We saw in *Leçon Six* that the **subjunctive** is used with certain command forms. This lesson will continue the study of the subjunctive.

Impersonal expressions may be used to express either an indirect command (It's necessary that you take out the trash) or an opinion (It's a pity that the Yankees lost last night). The subjunctive often follows these expressions. After a command, the subjunctive reflects the fact that the command might not be followed. After an opinion, the subjective nature expressed by the speaker becomes reflected in the dependent clause.

The expressions in this list will all require the subjunctive in the dependent clause:

Impersonal Expressions
Il est (C'est) dommage que → It is a pity that . . .
Il est (C'est) nécessaire que → It is necessary that . . .
Il est (C'est) normal que → It is normal that . . .
Il est possible (C'est) (impossible) que → It is possible (impossible) that . . .
Il est temps que → It is time that . . .
Il faut que → It is necessary that . . .
Il se peut que → It is possible that . . .
Il semble que → It seems that . . .
Il vaut mieux que → It would be better that . . .
It is better that . . .

EXAMPLES: *Il est dommage que cet enfant ait une attitude si détestable.*
It is a pity that this child has such a horrible attitude.

Il vaut mieux que le Petit Chaperon Rouge obéisse à sa mère.
It would be better that Little Red Riding Hood obey her mother.

Il n'est pas normal que vous ne riiez pas quand vous regardez Saturday Night Live.
It's not normal that you don't laugh when you watch *Saturday Night Live.*

Helpful Tip: With impersonal expressions, the <u>infinitive</u> is used when the subject is not specific, such as in a general statement. In the sentences below, you will notice that there is no *"que"* because there is no subject change.

🔱 **EXAMPLES:** *Il faut travailler pour réussir.*
One must work to succeed.

Il est dangereux de traverser la rue sans regarder.
It is dangerous to cross the street without looking.

ATTENTION! When expressing certainty or likelihood, impersonal expressions <u>do not</u> take the subjunctive:

Il est (C'est) certain que →	It is certain that . . .
Il est (C'est) clair que →	It is clear that . . .
Il est (C'est) évident que →	It is obvious that . . .
Il est (C'est) probable que →	It is likely that . . .
Il est (C'est) vrai que →	It is true that . . .
Il paraît que →	It appears that . . . (Rumor has it . . .)

🔱 **EXAMPLE:** *Il paraît que Marc sort avec Isabelle.*
Rumor has it that Marc is going out with Isabelle.

Note: *"Il est probable"* could take either the indicative or the subjunctive depending on the certainty or doubt the speaker wants to express.

🔱 **EXAMPLE:** *Il est probable que nous aurons (ayons) un contrôle demain.*
It is likely that we will have (may have) a test tomorrow.

In the negative, however, all the above expressions convey a lack of certainty, and, therefore, would take the subjunctive.

🔱 **EXAMPLE:** *Il n'est pas certain que la route soit facile.*
It is not certain that the road will be easy.

ATTENTION! Although the expression *"peut-être que"* (meaning "maybe") suggests some uncertainty, it does <u>not</u> take the subjunctive.

🔱 **EXAMPLE:** *Peut-être que Jules me téléphonera ce soir.*
Maybe Jules will call me tonight.

EXERCICES

1. **Write the appropriate form of the verb in the space provided. Most sentences, but not all, will call for the subjunctive:**

a. Il est possible qu'il _____ cet après-midi. (pleuvoir)

b. Il se peut que la tortue _____ plus vite que le lapin. (aller)

c. Il est probable que je ne _____ pas d'Oscar l'année prochaine. (gagner)

d. C'est dommage que les Islanders _____ tous les matchs cette année. (perdre)

e. C'est normal d'_____ fatigué après un match. (être)

f. Il est clair que ce système _____ mauvais. (être)

g. Il n'est pas évident que le toit de la tente _____ à nous protéger de la tempête. (réussir)

h. Il paraît que ce film _____ beaucoup de succès. (avoir)

i. Il vaut mieux que tu _____ ce soir. ([ne . . . pas] venir)

j. C'est clair que Marie _____ la question. (comprendre)

k. Peut-être que les affaires de Monsieur Legrand _____ mieux l'année prochaine. (aller)

l. Maintenant il est possible d'_____ sur Mars. (aller)

m. Il faut que cet enfant _____ du lait tous les jours. (boire)

n. C'est impossible que Patricia _____ une tortue dans sa chambre. (avoir)

2. There are five errors in the following paragraph. Underline and correct them:

Il paraît que les avions aillent toujours plus vite que les voitures, mais il est évident que Papa soit un cas exceptionnel! Il faut que je vous dites ce qui s'est passé. J'avais demandé à Papa qu'il vienne me chercher. Quand il est arrivé en cinq minutes, je lui ai dit: "Comment est-il possible que tu es arrivé si vite, il est clair que tu ne respectes pas les limites de vitesse. Il vaut mieux que Maman conduit."

B) LE SUBJONCTIF APRÈS LES ÉMOTIONS ET LES OPINIONS

1) ADJECTIVES OF EMOTION

a) Adjectives of emotion used personally

An adjective of emotion used personally in the main clause with *"être"* will introduce a verb in the subjunctive in the dependent clause (after *"que"*).

Here are some common adjectives of emotion:

choqué → shocked		*heureux* → happy	
content → happy		*horrifié* → horrified	
désolé → sorry		*malheureux* → unhappy	
étonné → surprised		*ravi* → delighted	
fâché → angry		*surpris* → surprised	
furieux → furious		*triste* → sad	

Here is the formula for this type of sentence:

```
┌────────── MAIN CLAUSE ──────────┐        ┌────── DEPENDENT CLAUSE ──────┐
1ST SUBJECT + FORM OF ÊTRE + ADJECTIVE + QUE + 2ND SUBJECT + VERB (in subjunctive)
```

 **EXAMPLES:** *Les mariés **sont furieux** que leur portrait **soit** si moche.*
The bride and groom are furious that their portrait is so lousy.

*Ta mère **est triste** que ta chambre **soit** toujours en désordre.*
Your mother is sad that your bedroom is always messy.

*Mélanie **est étonnée** que Paul ne lui **écrive** plus.*
Melanie is surprised that Paul doesn't write to her anymore.

*Le Président **est content** que les journalistes lui **posent** des questions faciles.*
The President is happy that the journalists are asking him easy questions.

b) Adjectives of emotion used impersonally

Adjectives of emotion used impersonally in the main clause can also introduce a subordinate clause in the subjunctive. In this case, the adjective does not modify a personal subject (e.g., "It is necessary that you do your homework now").

 **EXAMPLES:** *C'est triste que cet enfant **soit** toujours seul.*
It is sad that this child is always alone.

*C'est merveilleux que vous vous **entendiez** si bien avec votre belle-mère!*
It is wonderful that you get along so well with your mother-in-law!

*C'est malheureux que ce garçon **perde** toujours ses lunettes avant les examens.*
It is unfortunate that this boy always loses his glasses before exams.

2) VERBS OF EMOTION AND PERSONAL OPINION

The following verbs and expressions in a main clause need the subjunctive in the dependent clause. Once again, these verbs send their feelings beyond the boundaries of the main clause.

avoir peur →	to be afraid
craindre →	to fear
détester →	to hate
douter →	to doubt
regretter →	to regret

EXAMPLES: *Jules **déteste** que son petit frère **vienne** toujours dans sa chambre.*
Jules hates that his little brother always comes in his room.

*Je **crains** que l'aile de l'oiseau **soit** cassée.*
I fear that the wing of the bird is broken.

ATTENTION! Don't forget that in these types of sentences, when the subject of both verbs is the same, the second verb will be in the infinitive.

⚜ EXAMPLES: *Je suis choqué d'**apprendre** que Julie sort avec Thomas.*
　　　　　　I am shocked to learn that Julie is going out with Thomas.

　　　　　*Tu détestes te **lever** tôt.*
　　　　　　You hate getting (to get) up early.

　　　　　*La vieille dame a peur de **traverser** la rue.*
　　　　　　The old lady is afraid to cross the street.

Some verbs and expressions have quite different connotations when they are in the positive, negative or interrogative forms.

⚜ EXAMPLES: *Je suis sûr qu'il **est** malade.*
　　　　　　I am sure that he is sick. (no doubt → certainty!)

　　　　　*Je ne suis pas sûr qu'il **soit** malade.*
　　　　　　I am not sure that he is sick. (negative → doubt)

　　　　　*Es-tu sûr qu'il **soit** malade?*
　　　　　　Are you sure that he is sick? (interrogative → doubt)

Just like *"être sûr que,"* other verbs and expressions trigger the subjunctive in the dependent clause when they are used in the negative or the interrogative form, but <u>not</u> when they are used in the affirmative.

Here are some verbs and expressions in this category:

croire	*être sûr*
être certain	*penser*

⚜ EXAMPLES: *Je **pense** que le 20ème siècle **est** meilleur que le 15ème.*
　　　　　　(positive → no doubt)
　　　　　　I think that the 20th century is better than the 15th.

　　　　　*Je **ne pense pas** que le 20ème siècle **soit** meilleur que le 15ème.*
　　　　　　(negative → doubt)
　　　　　　I don't think that the 20th century is better than the 15th.

　　　　　***Pensez-vous** que le 20ème siècle **soit** meilleur que le 15ème?*
　　　　　　(interrogative → doubt)
　　　　　　Do you think that the 20th century is better than the 15th?

EXERCICES

1. Write the appropriate form of the verb in the space provided. Most sentences, but not all, call for the subjunctive:

a. L'entraîneur craint que son équipe ne _____ pas gagner la coupe du monde. (pouvoir)

b. Pensez-vous que les Français _____ trop de vin? (boire)

c. Les "Packers" sont fiers de _____ le Super Bowl encore une fois. (gagner)

d. Ma mère est ravie que tu _____ ce soir. (venir)

e. Je crois que la cloche _____ dans dix minutes. (sonner)

f. Antoinette est furieuse que Léopold ne _____ pas sortir avec elle. (vouloir)

g. Le Petit Chaperon Rouge a peur d'_____ dans la maison de sa grand-mère. (entrer)

h. Je suis sûre que Leonardo DiCaprio _____ dans *Inception.* (jouer)

i. C'est incroyable que ces enfants _____ si sales. (être)

j. Le public regrette que le pianiste ne _____ pas son morceau. (savoir)

k. Je ne crois pas qu'il _____ mourir pour ses péchés, mais je pense qu'il a eu tort. (devoir)

l. Je suis étonnée que tu _____ avec Paul. (sortir)

m. Penses-tu que mon petit frère _____ encore au Père Noël? (croire)

n. L'entraîneur est fâché que nous _____ si mal. (jouer)

2. Complete the following sentences with a logical ending:

a. Je pense que votre résumé d'histoire _____

b. C'est regrettable que la saison _____

c. Croyez-vous que le coton _____

d. C'est choquant que _____

e. Je déteste _____

3. There are six errors in the following paragraph. Underline and correct them:

Quand on va à un mariage, il faut apportez un cadeau. Mes parents aiment que je mettre une cravate mais moi, je déteste porte une cravate. Je préfrèrerais porter mes vêtements ordinaires. D'ailleurs, je n'aime pas les mariages. Il faut toujours que j'attends deux heures pour manger et après, la vieille tante Berthe exige que je danse avec elle. C'est est dommage qu'elle a de si grands pieds!

Although the **passive voice** is used less frequently than in English, it's still important to master it. The active voice and the passive voice describe an action quite differently.

In the active voice, the subject "acts upon" an object (e.g., The cat eats the mouse — *Le chat mange la souris*). Conversely, in the passive voice, the subject is "acted upon" (The mouse is eaten by the cat — *La souris est mangée par le chat*).

HOW DO YOU FORM THE PASSIVE VOICE?

Let's begin by looking at the formula for an active sentence.

> **Subject + Verb + Direct Object**

Notice now the difference in a passive construction:

New Subject (direct object of active sentence)	**+**	**Form of** ***être***	**+**	**Past Participle** (agrees with new subject)	**+**	***Par***	**+**	**Agent** (old subject of active sentence)

1) CONVERTING FROM ACTIVE VOICE TO PASSIVE VOICE

To change a sentence from the active voice to the passive voice, the direct object of the active sentence becomes the new subject. In turn, the old subject of the active sentence becomes what is called the <u>agent</u> and is introduced by the word *"par."*

EXAMPLES: *Les jeunes gens sont arrêtés **par** la police.*
The young people are arrested by the police.

*Dans ce film les méchants sont tous tués **par** James Bond!*
In this film all the bad guys are killed by James Bond!

*Prince William et Kate Middleton ont été mariés **par** un pasteur.*
Prince William and Kate Middleton were married by a minister.

*De nouvelles planètes seront découvertes **par** les astronomes.*
New planets will be discovered by the astronomers.

LET'S CONVERT A FEW SENTENCES:

Active: *Tous les garçons aiment la nouvelle élève.*
Passive: ***La nouvelle élève est aimée par tous les garçons.***

Active: *Mon oncle a construit cette nouvelle maison.*
Passive: ***Cette nouvelle maison a été construite par mon oncle.***

Active: *Le petit chien a mangé trois paires de chaussures!*

Passive: ***Trois paires de chaussures ont été mangées par le petit chien!***

2) SOME ALTERNATIVES TO THE PASSIVE VOICE

a) **When there is no agent in the passive sentence, it is common to use the active voice of the reflexive form of the verb.**

⚜ **EXAMPLES:** *Le pain **s'achète** à la boulangerie.*
Bread is bought at the bakery.

*Les dictionnaires **se trouvent** en haut à droite dans la bibliothèque.*
Dictionaries are found on the upper right shelf in the library.

b) **Another way of avoiding the passive voice when there is no agent is to use *"on"* and the active voice:**

⚜ **EXAMPLES:** *Au Brésil, **on parle** portugais.*
Portugese is spoken in Brazil.

*Maintenant, **on vend** des lunettes dans les pharmacies.*
Now, glasses are sold in drugstores.

THINGS TO REMEMBER ABOUT THE PASSIVE VOICE:

◆ The past participle agrees with the new subject.

◆ These pronouns follow the preposition *"par"* if the agent is deemed important to the action *(moi, toi, lui, elle, nous, vous eux, elles)*.

◆ The verb *"être"* can be used in any tense; use the same tense as you would have for the active voice.

◆ It is not essential to include *"par"* and the agent.

EXERCICES

1. Change the following active sentences into the passive voice:

a. Mon grand frère a fait ce beau gâteau.

_____

_____

b. Les journalistes ont complimenté Mark Wahlberg pour son dernier film, *The Fighter.*

_____

_____

c. La police arrêtera bientôt les trois voleurs.

_____

_____

d. Personne ne comprend tes explications.

_____

_____

e. Quand j'étais petit, ma mère rangeait ma chambre.

_____

_____

2. Write the following sentences in the active voice:

a. Mon livre a été trouvé sous le matelas du chien.

_____

_____

b. Le swahili est parlé au Kenya.

_____

_____

c. Quelle horreur! Cette femme va être attaquée par Dracula!

_____

_____

d. Vous avez cru que ces billets étaient achetés au guichet de la gare.

_____

_____

e. Aux États-Unis, le hockey sur gazon est joué par les filles.

_____

_____

These two sets of questions use grammatical structures and vocabulary from this lesson. Working with a partner, alternate asking and answering each question. When you get to the bottom of each list, start over at the top, switching roles. As a variation, write out the answers in complete sentences.

A) Les Knicks se sont-ils fait battre **par** les Celtics hier soir?

Le gâteau a-t-il été mangé **par** ton frère ou ton père?

Cette **série** télévisée a-t-elle été réalisée **par** un réalisateur célèbre?

Cette **tâche** a-t-elle été accomplie?

Ce **portrait** a-t-il été peint **par** Sokey Edorh ou Picasso?

Cette **conférence** a-t-elle été donnée **par** un professeur célèbre?

Ce **système** a-t-il été conçu **par** un ingénieur?

B) **Est-il possible** que la **tortue puisse** courir aussi vite que le **lapin**?

Vaut-il mieux que nous **fassions** nos valises ce soir?

Est-il possible que vous **gagniez** à la loterie?

Se peut-il que la **cloche** de l'église **sonne** depuis six heures ce matin?

Faut-il que nous **prenions** la **route** pour Porto-Novo?

Est-il dommage que le vingtième **siècle soit** terminé?

Est-il nécessaire que vous **témoigniez** autant d'**affection**?

"La Cuisine Sénégalaise"

 Near the back of the book (p.310), you will find an article about the exquisite cuisine in Senegal. Listen to the audio as you read along. Afterwards, answer the comprehension questions (p.312) either aloud or in written form. &

A & B) UTILISATIONS DU SUBJONCTIF

1. **Write the appropriate form of the verb in the space provided. Not all sentences will call for the subjunctive:**

   a. Je préfère _____ les films sur un grand écran plutôt qu'à la télévision. (voir)

   b. Penses-tu que la sorcière _____ faire ce grand voyage sur ce vieux balai? (pouvoir)

   c. J'espère que vous aussi vous _____ les films de science-fiction. (aimer)

   d. Valentine est ravie de _____ au festival de musique africaine. (aller)

   e. Ce soir il faut absolument que nous _____ à Play Station 3. (jouer)

   f. Le directeur doute que cet élève _____ la vérité. (dire)

   g. Mon père voudrait que je _____ moins vite. (conduire)

   h. C'est évident que nous _____ assez bien français. (parler)

   i. Patricia est désolée que son petit ami _____ de si grandes oreilles. (avoir)

   j. Je crois que Célestine _____ avec Balthazar l'année prochaine. (se marier)

   k. Je suis enchanté de _____ mes vacances dans un endroit aussi charmant. (passer)

   l. Je crains que cette chanteuse _____ plus d'ambition que de talent. (avoir)

m. Dans la vie, il faut souvent _____ des choses désagréables. (faire)

n. Monsieur Lavelle pense que les racines de cet arbre _____ son mur. (détruire)

2. **There are eight errors in the following advertisement. Underline and correct them:**

Vous pensez vraiment que vous soyez la plus belle fille du monde?

Je regrette de doive vous dire que ce n'est pas vrai. Mais il est possible que vous le deveniez bientôt grâce à "Beauté Éclair." Il faut absolument que vous essayez notre crème miracle pour les cheveux. Cette crème empêche que vos cheveux tomberont quand vous allez à la discothèque. Votre petit ami sera ravi que vous être la reine du bal. Vous devrez achetez trois bouteilles et vous serez sûre que tout le monde vous choisissez pour devenir Miss France! Nous ne pensons pas que vous puissiez résister à notre offre.

3. **Your curfew was 11:00 P.M., but you came back at 2:30 A.M. Write what your parents might say as they speak to you:**

a. Nous sommes furieux que _____

_____

b. À partir de maintenant, il faut que _____

_____

c. Nous pensons que _____

_____

d. C'est incroyable que tu _____

_____

e. Au moins, est-ce que tu regrettes _____

_____

f. C'est dommage que _____

_____

g. C'est évident que _____

_____

h. Je ne veux plus que _____

_____

i. J'ai peur que _____

_____

j. Il faut que _____

_____

C) LA VOIX PASSIVE

1. Change the following sentences to the passive voice:

a. Les voisins ont entendu le son de ta trompette, et ils n'ont pas été contents!

_____

_____

b. On m'a bien expliqué la leçon.

_____

_____

c. Le chien mangera le morceau de gâteau qui est sur la table.

_____

_____

d. Le public applaudit les acteurs de cette pièce.

_____

_____

e. Autrefois, des chevaux tiraient les voitures.

_____

_____

f. On leur a dit que le garagiste ferait la réparation avant ce soir.

_____

_____

2. Change the following verbs into the passive voice:

a. ils ont mangé   → _____

b. tu frapperas   → _____

c. elle examine   → _____

d. vous aviez invité   → _____

e. elles construiraient   → _____

f. que nous choisissions → _____

g. je recommanderai   → _____

h. vous aurez vu   → _____

i. j'ai critiqué   → _____

j. il aurait réparé   → _____

3. Translate the following sentences:

a. I don't want you to laugh when I speak.

_____

_____

b. That portrait was done by Renoir.

_____

_____

c. Do you want to go on the roof?

_____

_____

d. French is spoken in many African countries. *(3 réponses possibles)*

_____

_____

e. It is a pity that the dog is eating my piece of cake.

_____

_____

f. I hope the tent will not fall down.

_____

_____

4. There are 13 errors in the following paragraph. Underline and correct them:

 Mon cher Paul,

Tu es mon petit frère et je t'aime beaucoup mais je ne veux plus que tu viens dans ma chambre quand je n'y sois pas. Il paraît que c'est toi qui as emprunté ma raquette de tennis. C'est évident que tu ne saches pas jouer au tennis parce que toutes les cordes sont cassées. J'exige que tu attends ma permission avant d'emprunter mes affaires. Il est temps que tu comprennes que je suis généralement gentil mais je veux pas perde tous mes CD. Il vaut mieux que tu vas chez tes amis quand tu veux écouter de la musique. Je pense que tu sois fâché quand tu liras cette lettre, mais je suis sûr que tu comprendras que je sois exaspéré. C'est possible que tu deviens plus responsable et alors, tu pourras empunter mes affaires. Je suis furieux aussi quand tu viennes dans ma chambre avec tes amis. Je préfère que vous allez jouer dans le jardin. Je ne pense pas que ma chambre est l'endroit idéal pour jouer. J'espère que tu me comprennes.

Bien affectueusement,

Georges

LE NIGER & LE TCHAD

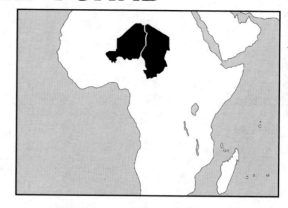

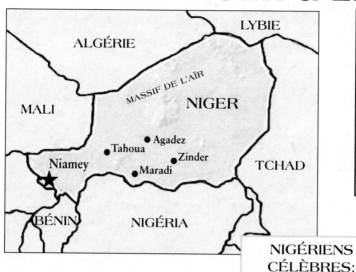

LE NIGER

Capitale:	Niamey
Population:	15.900.000
Gouvernement:	République
Chef d'état:	Président Djibo Salou
Monnaie:	Franc CFA (XOF)
Langues:	Français (langue officielle), hausa, djerma
Ressources:	Fer, or, pétrole, phosphates, textiles, uranium
Principales richesses touristiques:	La Cure Sale, Désert du Ténéré, Grand Marché de Niamey, Grande mosquée, Massif de l'Air, Musée National, Parc National W, ville d'Agadez
Cuisine:	Couscous, ragoût de mouton, riz

NIGÉRIENS CÉLÈBRES:

Moustapha Alassane
(CINÉASTE)

Clair Andrée
(ÉCRIVAIN)

Boubou Hama
(ÉCRIVAIN)

Haruna Ishola
(MUSICIEN)

Mamar Kassey
(CHANTEUR ET ACTIVISTE POUR LA PAIX)

LE TCHAD

Capitale:	N'Djamena
Population:	10.500.000
Gouvernement:	République
Chef d'état:	Président Idriss Deby Itno Premier Ministre Emmanuel Nadingar
Monnaie:	Franc CFA (XAF)
Langues:	Français, arabe (langues officielles) et d'autres langues africaines
Ressources:	Kaolin, pêche, pétrole, uranium
Musique/Danse:	Afro-pop, Dala, Griot (chanteurs), Soudanais, rap, reggae
Principales richesses touristiques:	Grand Marché de N'Djamena, Musée national, Oasis de Faya, vieille ville d'Abéché
Cuisine:	Boule de petit mil (céréale), boulettes aux œufs (bœuf haché), sauce moundourou (poisson), soupe de queue de bœuf

TCHADIENS CÉLÈBRES:

Ndolar Blaise
(JOUEUR DE FOOT)

Clément Masdongar
(CHANTEUR)

Baba Moustapha
(ÉCRIVAIN)

Kaltouma Nadjina
(ATHLÈTE, 400 M.)

Joseph Brahim Seid
(ÉCRIVAIN)

MC Solaar
(CHANTEUR DE RAP)

Kaar Kass Sonn
(CHANTEUR DE RAP)

VOCABULAIRE
LEÇON HUIT

LES NOMS

l' *avantage (m.)*   an advantage
les *bagages (m.)*   luggage
le *bois*   forest, wood
la *boîte aux lettres*   mailbox
le *casque*   helmet
la *colère*   anger
le *conte*   story, tale
le *contraire*   opposite
le *courrier*   e-mail
    électronique,
    le *e-mail,* le *mail*
le *défaut*   defect
l' *emploi du*   schedule
    temps (m.)
l' *énergie*   nuclear energy
    nucléaire (f.)
l' *enfance (f.)*   childhood
la *ferme*   farm
le *gouvernement*   government
la *honte*   embarrassment
l' *horaire (m.)*   schedule
                                (transportation)
la *langue*   language,
                                tongue
la *nature*   nature
le *niveau*   level

les *nouvelles (f.)*   news
l' *ordinateur (m.)*   computer
l' *orgueil (m.)*   pride
le *pouvoir*   power
la *publicité*   advertisement,
                                announcement
la *punition*   punishment
le *répondeur*   answering
                                machine
le *sable*   sand
le *sac*   bag, handbag,
                                purse
le *savoir*   knowledge
le *tas*   heap, pile
le *tissu*   fabric, cloth,
                                material
la *vague*   wave
le/la *vendeur/*   store clerk
      vendeuse
la *vengeance*   revenge,
                                vengeance
la *victime*   victim
la *vieillesse*   old age
la *violence*   violence
le *vol*   flight, theft
le *vote*   vote

LEÇON HUIT

KEY GRAMMAR
CONCEPTS

A) LE SUBJONCTIF APRÈS CERTAINES CONJONCTIONS → *The subjunctive after certain conjunctions*

B) LE SUBJONCTIF APRÈS UN ANTÉCÉDENT → *The subjunctive after an antecedent*

C) LE PASSÉ DU SUBJONCTIF → *The past subjunctive*

D) UTILISATIONS DE L'INFINITIF → *Uses of the infinitive*

A) LE SUBJONCTIF APRÈS CERTAINES CONJONCTIONS

Most **conjunctions** take the indicative, but there are some that take the **subjunctive**. The reason is that, in many cases, the action in the subordinate clause (following *"que"*) is not reality yet — it's hypothetical, contingent on something, or unrealized.

Here are the most commonly used conjunctions that take the subjunctive:

à moins que	→	unless
avant que	→	before
bien que	→	although, even though
de peur que	→	for fear that
en attendant que	→	waiting for, until
jusqu'à ce que	→	until
pour que	→	so that, in order that
pourvu que	→	provided that
sans que	→	without

EXAMPLES: *Il est venu en classe **bien qu'il soit** malade.*
He came to class even though he was sick.

*Je lisais **en attendant que** tu **finisses** tes devoirs.*
I was reading (while) waiting for you to finish your homework.

*Vous avez dû entrer **sans que** je vous **voie**.*
You must have come in without my seeing you.

Remember that these conjunctions always take the indicative:

après que	→	after
aussitôt que	→	as soon as
dès que	→	as soon as
parce que	→	because
pendant que	→	while
peut-être que	→	maybe, perhaps
quand, lorsque	→	when

EXAMPLES: *Je pourrai conduire **dès que** j'**aurai** mon permis.*
I will be able to drive as soon as I have my license.

*Elle est heureuse **parce qu**'elle **a gagné** le match.*
She is happy because she won the match.

*Tu faisais du sport **pendant que** je **dormais**.*
You were doing sports while I was sleeping.

***Peut-être** qu'il **viendra** me voir.*
Maybe he will come to see me.

EXERCICES

1. Write the appropriate form of the verb in the space provided. Most sentences, but not all, call for the subjunctive:

a. Je n'ai pas apporté assez de vêtements bien que je _____ beaucoup de bagages. (avoir)

b. Je vous enverrai les horaires des trains pour que vous _____ me chercher à la gare. (venir)

c. Après que la vague _____ mon château de sable sera détruit. (passer)

d. Je ne veux pas passer mes vacances en Amazonie de peur que la nature y

_____ trop hostile. (être)

e. Dès que tu _____ une tache, il faut laver ta robe.
(faire)

f. Si nous allons à Hollywood peut-être que nous _____
Angéline Jolie. (rencontrer)

g. Le voleur a réussi à prendre trois montres en or sans que le vendeur le

_____. (voir)

h. Nous ne pourrons pas nager dans la piscine avant que le niveau d'eau

_____ la ligne bleue. (atteindre)

2. **There are seven errors in the following paragraph. Underline each error and write the correct word above it:**

Pendant que nous soyons en vacances en Bretagne, il a fait

mauvais tout le temps. À la plage j'ai beaucoup lu en attendant que le

soleil est revenu; je ne m'ennuie jamais pourvu que j'ai un bon roman

policier. Mes amis, Julie et Gaspard priaient pour que nous pouvions aller

faire du bateau, et Séraphine regrettait de ne pas puisse bronzer. Dès

qu'il ait fait chaud, nous sommes montés sur le bateau,

malheureusement les vacances étaient presque finies. Pourvu que l'année

prochaine il fait meilleur!

1) "GHOST" ANTECEDENT

French also uses the **subjunctive** when the **antecedent** of the relative pronoun (subject of the main clause) is <u>not definite</u> or <u>may not even exist</u>. It is almost as if a "ghost" were the antecedent. In the dependent clause, therefore, the subjunctive is needed. However, when this antecedent exists for sure, you use the indicative.

 **EXAMPLES:** *Je cherche un secrétaire qui **sache** le chinois.*
I am looking for a secretary who can speak Chinese.
(This is a "ghost" secretary; we aren't sure one exists.)

BUT: *Mme Dupond a trouvé un secrétaire qui sait le chinois.*
Mrs. Dupond found a secretary who can speak Chinese.
(This is a very real secretary.)

*Il n'y a personne qui **soit** sportif dans cette classe.*
There is no one athletic in this class.
(An athletic person doesn't exist; it's a ghost.)

BUT: *Mais dans l'autre classe, il y a trois élèves qui sont sportifs.*
But in the other class, there are three three students who are athletic.
(They <u>are</u> real; they exist!)

2) SUPERLATIVES

The subjunctive is used after **superlative** expressions that convey a personal opinion or experience.

 **EXAMPLES:** Harry Potter and the Deathly Hallows? *C'est le meilleur film qui **j'aie** vu récement.*
Harry Potter and the Deathly Hallows? It is the best movie that I've seen recently.

*New York est la plus grande ville que je **connaisse**.*
New York is the largest city I know.

The Wire *est la série télévisée la plus violente que **j'aie** vue cette année.*
The Wire is the most violent TV series I've seen this year.

EXERCICES

1. Complete the following sentences using the subjunctive or the indicative:

a. Mon frère cherche un bon mécanicien qui _____ réparer son camion rapidement. (pouvoir)

b. J'ai écouté un CD de MC Solaar qui _____ vraiment excellent. (être)

c. Avez-vous trouvé un appartement qui _____ tous les avantages que vous cherchez? (avoir)

d. *"Versus"* est le meilleur CD que nous _____. (connaître)

e. Mon cousin a trouvé un vol direct qui le _____ à Ouagadougou, l'été prochain. (conduire)

f. Cette publicité est la plus stupide qui _____! (être)

2. Complete these sentences using your imagination and your knowledge of the subjunctive:

a. Juliette a acheté un chien qui _____.

b. *The Sound of Music* est le meilleur film que _____.

c. Dracula cherche une victime qui _____.

d. Est-ce que tu as trouvé un secrétaire qui _____?

e. Le français est la langue que _____.

f. L'orgueil est le plus grand défaut que _____.

HOW DO YOU FORM THE PAST SUBJUNCTIVE?

Forming the **past subjunctive** is quite simple:

◆ Start with the present subjunctive of *"avoir"* or *"être"*

◆ Then add the past participle of the verb you are conjugating

que j'aie parlé	*que nous ayons parlé*
que tu aies parlé	*que vous ayez parlé*
que il/elle ait parlé	*que ils/elles aient parlé*

Other examples:

s'asseoir	→	*qu'elles se soient assises, etc.*
danser	→	*que nous ayons dansé, etc.*
descendre	→	*que vous soyez descendus, etc.*
finir	→	*que j'aie fini, etc.*

The past subjunctive expresses an action that has taken place before that of the main clause.

EXAMPLES: *Je regrette que tu **aies été** malade hier.*
I am sorry that you were sick yesterday.

*Hier, **j'ai regretté** que tu **aies été** malade avant-hier.*
Yesterday, I was sorry that you were sick the day before.

ATTENTION! If the two actions are taking place at the same time, use the present subjunctive, even in a past sentence.

EXAMPLES: *Je regrette que tu **sois** malade maintenant.*
I am sorry that you are sick now.

***J'ai regretté** que tu **sois** malade hier.*
I was sorry that you were sick yesterday.

EXERCICES

1. Write the correct form of the past subjunctive using the verb and subject provided:

a. avoir (il) _____

b. sortir (nous) _____

c. se souvenir (tu) _____

d. lire (je) _____

e. vendre (vous) _____

f. tomber (elles) _____

2. Complete the following sentences using the present or past subjunctive:

a. Elle a eu un accident de moto très grave. C'est dommage qu'elle

_____ sans casque. (partir)

b. Je ne pense pas que la punition que le directeur donne à Pétronille

_____ juste. (être)

c. Il est regrettable que tu _____ ton répondeur. Tu aurais su que nous t'invitions ce soir. ([ne . . . pas] écouter)

d. Le voleur a ouvert la porte sans que je le _____.
(entendre)

e. Les dirigeants américains ont décidé de bombarder l'Irak bien que certains gouverments _____ leur opposition aux États-Unis.
(manifester)

f. Il vaut mieux que vous _____ une table en bois plutôt qu'une table en plastique. (acheter)

Throughout this book, we have come across many **uses of the infinitive**. This section will review those uses as well as present new ones.

1) The infinitive may function as a noun

In English, we often use a gerund (the "-ing" form of the verb) as a noun.

a) The infinitive as a subject

Examples: *Parler la bouche pleine est impoli.*
    Speaking with one's mouth full is impolite.

Fumer est mauvais pour la santé.
    Smoking is bad for one's health.

Voir c'est croire.
    Seeing is believing.

b) The infinitive as a direct object

Examples: *Elle aimerait se reposer maintenant.*
    She'd like to rest now.

J'aime courir au bord de la rivière.
    I like running by the river.

Il préfère s'asseoir près de la fenêtre.
    He prefers to sit down near the window.

Tu penses manger maintenant?
    Are you thinking about eating now?

c) The infinitive as an object of a preposition

The infinitive is used after all prepositions except *"en."* In English, we often use the "-ing" form of a verb after a preposition.

Examples: *Il a gagné sans faire d'effort.*
    He won without (making) any effort.

Réfléchis avant de te mettre en colère!
    Think before getting angry!

Nous venons d'arriver au Tchad.
    We have just arrived in Chad.

James Bond a commencé à organiser sa vengeance.
    James Bond began organizing his revenge.

Exception: *"En,"* the preposition, is followed by a present participle: *Ne parle pas en mangeant!* Don't speak while eating!
    "En," the pronoun, can be followed by an infinitive: *Je veux en manger.* I want to eat (some).

2) OTHER USES OF THE INFINITIVE

a) **The infinitive follows a conjugated verb when the subject of both verbs is the same.**

⚜ **EXAMPLES:** *Il voudrait **visiter** la ferme.*
He would like to visit the farm.

*J'étais désolée de **perdre** mon sac.*
I was sorry to lose my bag.

b) **You can use the infinitive after verbs of perception** *(écouter, entendre, regarder, sentir, voir . . .).*

In this case, what would have been the subject of the second verb becomes the object pronoun.

⚜ **EXAMPLES:** *Il **me** regarde **danser**.*
He is watching me dance.

*Je t'ai vu **prendre** les biscuits!*
I saw you take the cookies!

3) THE PAST INFINITIVE

a) **Used mainly after prepositions**

The past infinitive is mainly used after prepositions to indicate that one action took place before another.

⚜ **EXAMPLES:** *Je suis allé au cinéma après **avoir fait** mes devoirs.*
I went to the movies after having done my homework.

*Marie-Louise a téléphoné à Pierre avant d'**avoir écouté** son message sur le répondeur.*
Marie-Louise called Pierre before listening to his message on the answering machine.

b) **To form the past infinitive . . .**

◆ Start with the infinitive of the auxiliary of *"avoir"* or *"être"*
◆ Then add the past participle of the verb

choisir → *avoir choisi* (to have chosen)	*mourir* → *être mort* (to have died)
se dépêcher → *s'être dépêché* (to have hurried)	*parler* → *avoir parlé* (to have spoken)

1. Choose the correctly written sentence:

a. _____ Est-ce que tu aimerais faire une robe avec ce tissu vert?

_____ Est-ce que tu aimerais que tu fasses une robe avec ce tissu vert?

b. _____ Ils sont revenus après qu'ils ont regardé leur courrier électronique.

_____ Ils sont revenus après avoir regardé leur courrier électronique.

c. _____ Je ne veux pas que tu aies honte.

_____ Je ne veux pas que tu avoir honte.

d. _____ Il mange trop de gâteaux fait grossir.

_____ Manger trop de gâteaux fait grossir.

e. _____ Je il ai entendu chanter.

_____ Je l'ai entendu chanter.

f. _____ Il est défendu de marcher sur la pelouse.

_____ Il est défendu qu'il marche sur la pelouse.

2. Translate these sentences using the infinitive:

a. I'd like to dance with you tonight.

_____

b. Could you please call me before midnight?

_____

c. We ought to order the tomato salad.

_____

These two sets of questions use grammatical structures and vocabulary from this lesson. Working with a partner, alternate asking and answering each question. When you get to the bottom of each list, start over at the top, switching roles. As a variation, write out the answers in complete sentences.

A) Est-ce que tu regrettes que je t'**aie battu** au poker hier soir?

Est-il possible que tu **aies parlé** avec mes parents hier?

N'est-il pas dommage que tu n'**aies** pas **eu** le temps de venir avec nous au Tchad?

Ne valait-il pas mieux que vous **ayez acheté** une plus petite voiture?

Se pourrait-il que nous **ayons manqué** notre **vol** pour N'djamena?

Le **gouvernement** a-t-il le droit d'augmenter les impôts bien que plusieurs milliers de personnes **aient manifesté** leur mécontentement?

N'est-il pas déplorable qu'elle **ait été victime** de violence?

B) **Manger** du chocolat est-il nocif pour la santé?

Est-il légal de **manifester** contre le **gouvernement** au Niger?

Aimerais-tu écrire un livre un jour?

Comment peut-il **réussir sans faire** d'effort?

Voudrais-tu **travailler** pour une agence de **publicité**?

M'as-tu vu **surfer** sur la **vague** géante?

As-tu rappelé ton ami après **avoir écouté** son message sur le **répondeur**?

EXERCICES DE RÉVISION

A–C) UTILISATIONS DU SUBJONCTIF

1. Write the appropriate form of the verb in the space provided.
ATTENTION! Not all sentences will call for the subjunctive.

a. Je ne peux pas accepter ton invitation parce que mon emploi du temps

_____ déjà plein. (être)

b. Mon frère a fait le plus grand gâteau que je _____ jamais

_____. (voir)

c. Je suis désolé que tu _____ une enfance si malheureuse avant
ton arrivée ici. (avoir)

d. La violence ne diminuera pas à moins que le gouvernement _____
des mesures énergiques. (prendre)

e. Je suis furieuse que tu _____ toujours le contraire de ce que
je dis. (dire)

f. Il n'y a personne qui _____ la réponse à cette question.
(savoir)

g. Quand il me _____ dans ses bras, je vois la vie en rose. (prendre)

h. Le voleur a pris le sac de la victime avant que l'agent de police

_____ l'arrêter. (pouvoir)

i. Il faut que nous _____ tous les messages du répondeur

jusqu'à ce que nous _____ celui qui nous intéresse.
(écouter/trouver)

j. Aussitôt que je _____ l'horaire du train je te l'enverrai par
courriel. (recevoir)

2. There are seven errors in the following paragraph. Underline each error and write the correct word above it:

Gone With The Wind *est le meilleur film que j'avais jamais vu. Il est évident que Scarlett soit une femme difficile. Elle exige toujours que les autres font ce qu'elle veut. Il est certain aussi que, dans les situations difficiles, c'est elle qui prenne toutes les responsabilités et choisi les meilleures solutions. C'est admirable qu'elle ait pu soigner des blessés pendant la bataille d'Atlanta bien qu'elle a eu une enfance très gâtée. C'est dommage que son orgueil la rend souvent antipathique.*

3. Write the following verbs in the past subjunctive:

    a. être (tu) _____

    b. naître (vous) _____

    c. se dépêcher (elles) _____

    d. ne pas boire (je) _____

    e. voir (nous) _____

4. Complete the following sentences using the present or past subjunctive:

    a. Le petit garçon a une indigestion. Sa mère est furieuse qu'il

    _____ toute la glace au chocolat. (manger)

b. Il était temps que vous _____ la voiture au garage. (rentrer)

c. Elle t'a expliqué longuement ce problème pour que tu le _____ bien. (comprendre)

d. Elle t'a expliqué le problème longuement bien que tu le

_____ depuis longtemps. (comprendre)

e. Sa mère sera très surprise que Bernice _____ ce vieux tee-shirt demain pour aller à la fête. (mettre)

f. Mais la copine de Bernice n'est pas du tout étonnée qu'elle le

_____. (choisir)

D) UTILISATIONS DE L'INFINITIF

1. Choose the correctly written sentence:

a. _____ Les enfants sont heureux qu'ils jouent dans le tas de sable.

_____ Les enfants sont heureux de jouer dans le tas de sable.

b. _____ J'ai peur que les vagues soient trop grandes pour faire du surf.

_____ J'ai peur que les vagues soient trop grandes pour que nous faisons du surf.

c. _____ Buvant trop de bière avant de conduire est dangereux.

_____ Boire trop de bière avant de conduire est dangereux.

d. _____ Je vous vois danser.

_____ Je vous vois dansez.

e. _____ Tu étais ravi que tu aies gagné ton match.

_____ Tu étais ravi d'avoir gagné ton match.

2. Change the following verbs to the past infinitive:

a. écrire   → _____

b. vouloir   → _____

c. aller   → _____

d. pouvoir   → _____

e. se déshabiller → _____

3. Complete the following sentences using either the indicative, the subjunctive or the infinitive:

a. Dans le programme de télé ce soir, je ne trouve pas d'émission qui me

_____. (plaire)

b. Tu devrais regarder *Gossip Girl;* c'est une émission qui me _____ beaucoup. (plaire)

c. Il faut _____ la grammaire pour pouvoir parler correctement. (étudier)

d. Gaspard espère que Jennifer _____ avec lui. (sortir)

e. Il n'a pas plu depuis longtemps et je crains que nous ne _____

pas nager dans le lac, parce que le niveau d'eau _____ trop bas. (pouvoir/être)

f. Après _____ le droit de vote, les femmes ont participé davantage à la vie politique. (obtenir)

g. Est-ce que tu aimerais _____ avec moi à l'Oasis de Faya cet été? (venir)

h. _____ du sport est excellent pour la santé. (Faire)

i. Aussitôt que je _____ l'adresse du consulat, j'irai faire renouveler mon passeport. (avoir)

j. C'est lui qui _____ cette tache sur mon dessin? (faire)

k. Je ne crois pas que ces joueurs de foot _____ prendre un abonnement au magazine Mademoiselle. (vouloir)

4. Translate the following sentences:

a. I'd like to ask you a question.

_____

_____

b. He'd like you to go out with him.

_____

_____

c. It is a pity that he did not find his belongings after the theft.

_____

_____

d. You may not ride your bike before buying a helmet.

_____

_____

e. On the 14th of July, after singing the Marseillaise, they all went dancing in the neighborhood.

_____

_____

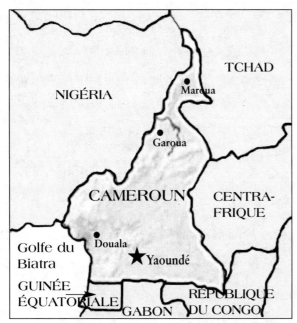

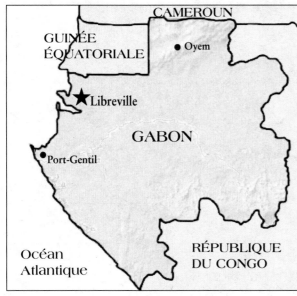

LA RÉPUBLIQUE DU CONGO

Capitale:	Brazzaville
Population:	4.100.000
Gouvernement:	République
Chef d'état:	Président Denis Sassou-Nguesso
Monnaie:	Franc CFA (XAF)
Langues:	Français (langue officielle), lingala, monokutuba, kikongo
Ressources:	Agriculture (canne à sucre, café, cacao), bois, pêche, pétrole
Musique/Danse:	Rap franco-congolais (Bisso Ne Bisso), "zouk"
Principales richesses touristiques:	Cases sur pilotis de l'île Mbamou, le Fespam (grand festival de musique), parcs nationaux (Odzala Lefini), ville de Mossaka
Cuisine:	Bananes, bovidé, chèvre, gibier, insectes (chenilles, sauterelles), pâte de manioc ou de maïs, poisson, poule, riz

CONGOLAIS CÉLÈBRES

Henri Lopes (ÉCRIVAIN)

Jean Malonga (ÉCRIVAIN)

Théophile Obenga (ÉCRIVAIN)

Odongo (PEINTRE)

LE CAMEROUN, LE GABON, LA RÉPUBLIQUE DÉMOCRATIQUE DU CONGO & LA RÉPUBLIQUE DU CONGO

LE CAMEROUN

Capitale:	Yaoundé
Population:	19.300.000
Gouvernement:	République
Chef d'état:	Président Paul Biya
Monnaie:	Franc CFA (XAF)
Langues:	Français, anglais (langues officielles), et d'autres langues africaines
Ressources:	Aluminium, café, coton, cultures vivrières et maraîchères, filatures, industrie du bois, pétrole, tissage
Musique:	Makossa
Principales richesses touristiques:	Forêts, Foumban (Palais Royal), Musée d'Art Nègre, Musée du Sultan, Parc National du Waza
Cuisine:	Fruits, fufu, garri, maïs, manioc, millet

LE GABON

Capitale:	Libreville
Population:	1.500.000
Gouvernement:	République
Chef d'état:	Président Ali Ben Bongo Ondimba Premier Ministre Paul Biyoghe
Monnaie:	Franc CFA (XAF)
Langues:	Français (langue officielle), fang, myene, nzebi, bapounou/eschira, bandjabi
Ressources:	Bois, cultures de canne à sucre, de bananes, de cacao, de café, d'hévéas, d'huile de palme et de plantain, de manioc, de riz, mines d'or, pétrole, produits chimiques
Musique/Danse:	Biguine, rap, rumba, "zouk"
Principales richesses touristiques:	Franceville et les plateaux Batékés, la Lopé (réserve), parcs nationaux, la plage d'Ekwata
Cuisine:	Crustacés, escargots, patates douces, poissons, riz

LA RÉPUBLIQUE DÉMOCRATIQUE DU CONGO (ZAÏRE)

Capitale:	Kinshasa
Population:	71.000.000
Gouvernement:	République
Chef d'état:	Président Joseph Kabila
Monnaie:	Franc congolais (CDF)
Langues:	Français (langue officielle), lingala, kikongo, kingwana, tshiluba
Ressources:	Argent, bauxite, bois, cobalt, cuivre, diamants, manganèse, pétrole, radium, uranium
Musique/Danse:	Rumba, soukous
Principales richesses touristiques:	Forêt équatoriale, Lac Kivu, Lac Tanganyika, Ruwenzori
Cuisine:	Bananes, insectes, pommes de terre

CAMEROUNAIS CÉLÈBRES

Francis Bebey
(POÈTE, MUSICIEN)

Mongo Beti
(ÉCRIVAIN)

Calixte Beyola
(ÉCRIVAIN)

Manu Dibango
(MUSICIEN)

Ferdinand
(ÉCRIVAIN)

Lions Indomptables du Cameroun
(ÉQUIPE DE FOOTBALL)

Wes Madiko
(CHANTEUR)

Marie Claire Matip
(ÉCRIVAIN)

Rabiatou Nioya
(THÉÂTRE)

GABONAIS CÉLÈBRES

Pierre Akendengué
(MUSICIEN)

Angèle Assélé
(CHANTEUSE)

Pierre-Marie Dong
(CINÉASTE)

Allogho-Oke
(SATIRISTE ET AUTEUR)

CONGOLAIS CÉLÈBRES

Patrice Lumumba
(HOMME POLITIQUE)

Mobutu Seseseko
(ANCIEN PRÉSIDENT)

Papa Wemba
(MUSICIEN)

VOCABULAIRE
LEÇON NEUF

LES VERBES

abandonner	to abandon	*effrayer*	to frighten, to scare
abîmer	to damage, to ruin	*(s') embrasser*	to kiss, to embrace
accuser	to accuse	*enlever*	to take off, to kidnap
acquérir	to acquire		
ajouter	to add	*épeler*	to spell
apparaître	to appear	*grandir*	to grow, to expand
(s') appuyer	to lean	*(s') habituer à*	to get used to
arracher	to tear out, to pull out	*louer*	to rent
assister à	to attend	*mentir*	to lie
attirer	to attract	*mettre*	to put, to place, to put on
avertir	to warn		
bavarder	to chat	*oser*	to dare, to have the courage to
briller	to shine		
causer	to cause	*pendre*	to hang
chauffer	to heat	*punir*	to punish
confondre	to confuse	*remercier*	to thank
conseiller	to advise	*renverser*	to spill
déranger	to bother, to disturb	*réparer*	to fix, to repair
développer	to develop	*(se) reposer*	to rest
disparaître	to disappear	*sauver*	to save
économiser	to save money	*serrer*	to tighten, to squeeze
effacer	to erase		

LEÇON NEUF

KEY GRAMMAR
CONCEPTS

A) LES ADJECTIFS → *Adjectives*

B) LES ADVERBES → *Adverbs*

C) LES NOMBRES CARDINAUX ET ORDINAUX → *Cardinal and ordinal numbers*

 A) LES ADJECTIFS

Adjectives are used to describe nouns and pronouns. In French, these adjectives always agree in number and gender with the noun they describe.

1) THE FEMININE OF ADJECTIVES

a) **To form the feminine of many adjectives, simply add an "*e*" to the masculine form.**

un grand garçon →	a tall boy
une grande fille →	a tall girl
un ciel bleu →	a blue sky
une fleur bleue →	a blue flower
un jardin carré →	a square garden
une table carrée →	a square table

b) **Masculine adjectives that end in "*-e*" do not change in the feminine form.**

un camion rouge →	a red truck
une robe rouge →	a red dress
un conseil utile →	a useful piece of advice
une explication utile →	a useful explanation

Helpful Tip: Do not confuse masculine adjectives ending in "*-é*," which follow the basic rule, with those ending in "*-e*."

un renard rusé →	a sly fox
une sorcière rusée →	a sly witch

c) **Masculine adjectives ending in "-er" change to "-ère" in the feminine.**

un pays étranger → a foreign country
une voiture étrangère → a foreign car

le premier jour → the first day
la première page → the first page

d) **Masculine adjectives ending in "-f" change to "-ve" in the feminine.**

un chapeau neuf → a new hat
une jupe neuve → a new skirt

un résultat négatif → a negative result
une réponse négative → a negative answer

e) **Masculine adjectives ending in "-eur" or "-eux" change to "-euse" in the feminine.**

un conseil trompeur → a deceiving advice
une question trompeuse → a deceiving question

un endroit dangereux → a dangerous place
une autoroute dangereuse → a dangerous highway

f) **Masculine adjectives ending with a consonant usually double the consonant before adding an "e" in the feminine.**

un bon dîner → a good dinner
une bonne amie → a good friend

un animal cruel → a cruel animal
une remarque cruelle → a cruel remark

g) **These masculine adjectives have an irregular feminine form that must be memorized.**

beau → **belle** (beautiful)
blanc → **blanche** (white)
doux → **douce** (soft, sweet)
faux → **fausse** (false, wrong)
fou → **folle** (mad, crazy)
frais → **fraîche** (fresh, cool)
long → **longue** (long)
nouveau → **nouvelle** (new)
roux → **rousse** (redhead)
sec → **sèche** (dry)
vieux → **vieille** (old)

ATTENTION! Three adjectives *(beau, nouveau, vieux)* have an extra masculine form that is used before a vowel or a silent *"h."*

> un **bel** animal → a beautiful animal
> un **nouvel** ordinateur → a new computer
> un **vieil** homme → an old man

2) THE PLURAL OF ADJECTIVES

a) To form the plural of most adjectives, add an *"s."*

> un enfant blond → a blond child
> des enfants blond**s** → blond children

> une petite fille française → a French girl
> des petites filles française**s** → French girls

b) Adjectives that end in *"-s"* or *"-x"* do not change in the masculine plural form.

> un gros cochon → a fat pig
> des gros cochons → fat pigs

> un homme malheureux → an unhappy man
> des hommes malheureux → unhappy men

ATTENTION! However, the plural feminine form of the adjective does take an *"s"*:

> une glace délicieuse → a delicious ice cream
> des glaces délicieuse**s** → delicious ice creams

c) Most masculine adjectives that end in *"-al"* change to *"-aux"* in the plural.

> un problème social → a social problem
> des problèmes soci**aux** → social problems

d) Masculine adjectives that end in *"-eau"* change to *"-eaux"* in the plural.

> un beau château → a beautiful castle
> de **beaux** chât**eaux** → beautiful castles

But for feminine adjectives, just add an *"s"* to form the plural:

> une fête nationale → a national holiday
> des fêtes nationale**s** → national holidays

> une belle robe → a beautiful dress
> de belles robe**s** → beautiful dresses

> une grosse pêche → a big peach
> de grosses pêche**s** → big peaches

Notes:

1) When adjectives are placed before the noun, *"des"* traditionally becomes *"de"* in the plural. However, this rule is often ignored, especially in conversation.

> ⚜ **EXAMPLES:** *un grand hôtel*
> a big hotel
> *de grands hôtels*
> big hotels

2) The adjective *"tout"* changes to *"tous"* in the masculine plural, while *"toute"* (feminine, singular) becomes *"toutes"* in the feminine plural.

> ⚜ **EXAMPLES:** | | |
> |---|---|---|
> | ***tout** l'appartement* | → | the whole apartment |
> | ***tous** les appartements* | → | all the apartments |
> | ***toute** la classe* | → | the whole class |
> | ***toutes** les classes* | → | all the classes |

3) PLACEMENT OF ADJECTIVES

Most "long" adjectives (more than two syllables) are placed after the noun.

> | | | |
> |---|---|---|
> | *un film **ennuyeux*** | → | a boring film |
> | *des journaux **italiens*** | → | Italian newspapers |
> | *des giraffes **élégantes*** | → | elegant giraffes |
> | *une vidéo **intéressante*** | → | an interesting video |

It is more difficult to place "short" adjectives, but here are two rules of thumb:
- Adjectives of color always go after the noun.
- Adjectives of **b**eauty, **a**ge, **g**oodness and **s**ize (BAGS) go before the noun.

> | | | |
> |---|---|---|
> | *un casque **rouge*** | → | a red helmet |
> | *de **bonnes** nouvelles* | → | some good news |
> | *un **gentil** petit chien* | → | a nice little dog |

EXERCICES

1. Change the following adjectives to their feminine form:

a. poli → _____

b. cher → _____

c. curieux → _____

d. fou → _____

e. fatigué → _____

f. européen → _____

g. attentif → _____

h. gros → _____

i. nul → _____

j. faible → _____

2. There are eight errors in the following paragraph. Underline and correct them:

Hier après-midi, je suis allée faire des achats avec ma meilleur amie Mireille au nouveau centre commercial. Mireille s'est acheté une longe jupe vert, mais moi je préfère les robes courtes. Donc, je me suis acheté une ravissant petite robe avec de groses fleurs jaunes. Pour bavarder, nous sommes allées dans une bel pâtisserie modernee où nous avons pris une boisson frais.

3. Write the correct form of the adjective in parentheses:

a. Les (jeune) _____ garçons ont loué de (beau)

_____ bicyclettes pour les (grand) _____

vacances au Parc National du Waza.

b. Les (méchant) _____ parents de Hansel et Gretel ont

abandonné leurs (gentil) _____ enfants dans une forêt

(dangereux) _____.

c. Le gouvernement a développé des programmes (spécial) _____

pour résoudre les (grave) _____ problèmes (national)

_____.

d. (Tout) _____ le monde peut poser des questions (oral)

_____ pendant les (long) _____ et

(laborieux) _____ conférences de ce professeur.

4. **Change the following phrases from the singular to the plural form:**

    a. un gros fromage   → _____

    b. une belle chemise   → _____

    c. un bel hôtel   → _____

    d. un ami loyal   → _____

    e. une vache hollandaise → _____

    f. le nouveau pull   → _____

    g. une grosse pomme verte → _____

5. **Rewrite the following sentences, placing the adjectives in their proper positions and making sure they agree with the nouns they describe.**

    a. Vers 1924, on a accusé Landru d'avoir tué des femmes (jeune, joli).

    _____

    _____

    _____

    b. Ces femmes (malheureux) disparaissaient après des voyages (petit) qui avaient des conséquences (fatal).

    _____

    _____

    _____

c. La police avait été avertie par des voisins (soupçonneux) qui avaient vu beaucoup de fumée (noir, dense) sortir de la cheminée (vieux).

_____

_____

_____

d. Il attirait ces victimes (naïf) et leur mentait avec des déclarations (amoureux) et des demandes en mariage (secret).

_____

_____

_____

e. Il espérait acquérir la fortune (entier) de ces femmes (faible) avec des promesses (mensonger).

_____

_____

_____

f. Il est probable que ce fiancé (cruel) tuait ses épouses (futur) dans sa maison (isolé) et qu'il brûlait les cadavres (tout).

_____

_____

_____

g. Il n'a pas été pendu parce que la punition (traditionnel, français) était la guillotine. Beaucoup de spectateurs (curieux) ont assisté à sa mort (sanglant).

_____

_____

_____

h. J'espère que cette punition (horrible) fera peur aux assassins (futur) qui veulent enlever des femmes (riche, vulnérable).

_____

_____

_____

6. Translate the following sentences:

a. He found a nice, blue tie in a little shop.

_____

_____

b. We must save that old tree.

_____

_____

c. Last year, I quickly got used to my new French family.

_____

_____

d. Marie was bored because the lecture was long and endless.

_____

_____

B) LES ADVERBES

Adverbs are used to modify verbs, adjectives or other adverbs. These words tell how, when, or with what intensity something was done. They are all invariable.

WHERE DO YOU PLACE ADVERBS?

◆ Adverbs generally follow the verbs they modify.

> ⚜ **EXAMPLE:**   *Maman parle **gentiment** à ma petite sœur.*
> Mom speaks kindly to my little sister.

◆ In compound tenses they generally follow the past participle.

> ⚜ **EXAMPLE:**   *Le voleur est sorti **rapidement** de la banque.*
> The thief left the bank quickly.

◆ A few common adverbs, however, are placed between the auxiliary and the past participle *(assez, beaucoup, bien, encore, mal, peu, souvent, toujours, trop, vite, vraiment)*.

> ⚜ **EXAMPLE:**   *Nous avons **beaucoup** aimé It's a Wonderful Life.*
> We liked *It's a Wonderful Life* a lot.

1) ADVERBS THAT END IN "-MENT"

a) When an adjective ends with a vowel, simply add "-ment" to form an adverb.

> *absolu → absolument*
> *vrai → vraiment*

b) When the adjective ends with a consonant, add "-ment" to the feminine form of the adjective.

> *heureux → heureuse → heureusement*
> *premier → première → premièrement*

c) When adjectives end in "-ant" or "-ent," replace the ending with "-amment" or "-emment."

> *méchant → méchamment*
> *prudent → prudemment*

Note: *"Emme"* is pronounced like *"femme"* (an "a" sound).

ATTENTION! Make sure to memorize these important exceptions:

> bon → bien
> gentil → gentiment
> mauvais → mal
> meilleur → mieux

2) ADVERBS THAT DO NOT COME FROM ADJECTIVES

There are many adverbs that are not formed from adjectives.

aujourd'hui → today	demain → tomorrow	loin → far
aussi → also, too	encore → still	puis→then
bientôt → soon	hier → yesterday	tant → so much
d'abord → first	ici → here	tôt → early
dedans → inside	jamais → never	toujours → always
dehors → outside	là → there	trop → too much

3) PREPOSITIONAL PHRASES USED INSTEAD OF ADVERBS AT THE END OF A SENTENCE

At times, a prepositional phrase is an elegant substitute for an adverb at the end of a sentence.

> d'un air + adjectif   d'une façon + adjectif

 EXAMPLES: *Elle m'a répondu **d'un air arrogant**.*
She answered me arrogantly.

*Jules et son frère ont fait cela **d'une façon stupide**.*
Jules and his brother did that stupidly.

EXERCICES

1. Change the following adjectives to adverbs:

a. curieux → _____   **d.** entier → _____

b. étrange → _____   **e.** bon → _____

c. évident → _____   **f.** vrai → _____

2. Instead of adverbs, use *"d'un air"* or *"d'une façon"* with the following adjectives:

a. triste _____   **c.** charmant _____

b. timide _____   **d.** vif _____

3. Translate the following sentences:

a. The plants grow rapidly in the rain forest.

_____

b. Santa Claus quickly added another present under the tree.

_____

_____

c. The cook heated the onion soup slowly and carefully.

_____

_____

4. There are six errors in the following paragraph. Underline and correct them:

Le fantôme est apparu brutallement à la dame. Evidentement,

elle a eu affreusement peur. Le fantôme a voulu l'embrasser gentillement

et c'est alors que la dame a bon vu que c'était son défunt mari qui

revenait tendrement lui rendre visite. Malheureuxment pour le fantôme,

la dame avait immédiatment retrouvé un nouveau mari jeune et beau!

1) LES NOMBRES CARDINAUX

0	*zéro*	10	*dix*	20	*vingt*
1	*un(e)*	11	*onze*	21	*vingt et un(e)*
2	*deux*	12	*douze*	22	*vingt-deux*
3	*trois*	13	*treize*	23	*vingt-trois*
4	*quatre*	14	*quatorze*	24	*vingt-quatre*
5	*cinq*	15	*quinze*	25	*vingt-cinq*
6	*six*	16	*seize*	26	*vingt-six*
7	*sept*	17	*dix-sept*	27	*vingt-sept*
8	*huit*	18	*dix-huit*	28	*vingt-huit*
9	*neuf*	19	*dix-neuf*	29	*vingt-neuf*

It then continues in the same pattern:

30	*trente*	31	*trente et un(e)*	32	*trente-deux*
40	*quarante*	41	*quarante et un(e)*	42	*quarante-deux*
50	*cinquante*	51	*cinquante et un(e)*	52	*cinquante-deux*
60	*soixante*	61	*soixante et un(e)*	62	*soixante-deux*
70	*soixante-dix*	71	*soixante et onze*	72	*soixante-douze*
80	*quatre-vingts*	81	*quatre-vingt un(e)*	82	*quatre-vingt-deux*
90	*quatre-vingt-dix*	91	*quatre-vingt-onze*	92	*quatre-vingt-douze*
100	*cent*	101	*cent un(e)*	102	*cent deux*
200	*deux cents*	201	*deux cent un(e)*	202	*deux cent deux*
300	*trois cents*	301	*trois cent un(e)*	302	*trois cent deux*
400	*quatre cents*	401	*quatre cent un(e)*	402	*quatre cent deux*

500	*cinq cents*	1000	*mille*
600	*six cents*	10 000	*dix mille*
700	*sept cents*	100 000	*cent mille*
800	*huit cents*	1 000 000	*un million*
900	*neuf cents*	1 000 000 000	*un milliard*

Helpful Tip: *Vingt* and *cent* take an "s" in the plural:

> *quatre-vingts*   *trois cents*   *six cents*

ATTENTION! These numbers do <u>not</u> take an "s" when followed by another number:

> *quatre-vingt-un*   *trois cent soixante*   *six cent dix*

2) LES NOMBRES ORDINAUX

Except for *premier,* you can form the ordinal numbers by adding *"-ième"* to the cardinal number.

1ER	*premier, première*	11ÈME	*onzième*	30ÈME	*trentième*
2ÈME	*deuxième*	12ÈME	*douzième*	40ÈME	*quarantième*
3ÈME	*troisième*	13ÈME	*treizième*	50ÈME	*cinquantième*
4ÈME	*quatrième*	14ÈME	*quatorzième*	60ÈME	*soixantième*
5ÈME	*cinquième*	15ÈME	*quinzième*	70ÈME	*soixante-dixième*
6ÈME	*sixième*	16ÈME	*seizième*	80ÈME	*quatre-vingtième*
7ÈME	*septième*	17ÈME	*dix-septième*	90ÈME	*quatre-vingt-dixième*
8ÈME	*huitième*	18ÈME	*dix-huitième*	100ÈME	*centième*
9ÈME	*neuvième*	19ÈME	*dix-neuvième*	1.000ÈME	*millième*
10ÈME	*dixième*	20ÈME	*vingtième*	1.000.000ÈME	*millionième*

Helpful Tip: *Premier* is the only ordinal number to change in the feminine form. It becomes *première.* Also, how do you think they say 21ST? —*Vingt et unième!*

3) N'OUBLIEZ PAS!

a) **Cardinal numbers are used for dates.**

> *le quatorze juillet* → the fourteenth of July
> *le vingt-neuf août* → the twenty-ninth of August

ATTENTION! The first day of the month requires the ordinal number: *Aujourd'hui, c'est le premier février.*

b) **Use the ordinal number to identify a chapter, lesson, problem, street, row, etc.**

> *le premier exercice* → the first exercise
> *la troisième partie* → the third part
> *le septième paragraphe* → the seventh part
> *la huitième strophe* → the eighth stanza

c) **In a title, cardinal numbers are generally used.**

> *Louis XIV (quatorze)*
> *Henri IV (quatre)*

ATTENTION! You need to use *"premier (première)"* for the word "first."

> *François IER (premier)*

d) Cardinal and ordinal numbers in the same sentence.
   If both a cardinal and an ordinal number are used in the same sentence, a French speaker will normally put the <u>cardinal number first</u> and the <u>ordinal number second</u>. In English, we tend to do just the opposite.

    EXAMPLES: *Les **cinq premiers** mots de la Marseillaise sont "Allons, enfants de la patrie . . ."*
   The first five words of the Marseillaise are [translated as] "Let's go, children of the fatherland . . ."

   *Les **deux premières** chansons de* Taylor Swift *ont été des tubes.*
   Taylor Swift's first two songs were hits.

EXERCICE

Translate the following phrases:

a. 21 scissors _____

b. 32 hangers _____

c. 101 tickets _____

d. 2,000 drops of water _____

e. the fifth exit _____

f. the second press conference _____

g. the first ten students _____

h. the twentieth miracle _____

i. the first mystery _____

j. the third toenail _____

k. 2,571 suitcases _____

l. 1,000,000 legends   _____

m. Fifth Avenue   _____

n. 1998   _____

o. fourteen days   _____

p. the sixtieth student   _____

q. the third part   _____

r. February 10, 1931   _____

s. June 5, 1923   _____

t. a thousand brooms   _____

u. 10,546 stars   _____

These two sets of questions use grammatical structures and vocabulary from this lesson. Working with a partner, alternate asking and answering each question. When you get to the bottom of each list, start over at the top, switching roles. As a variation, write out the answers in complete sentences.

 A) Pleut-il **abondamment** au Congo?

Avez-vous **beaucoup** pleuré à l'enterrement de votre grand-mère?

Usain Bolt court-il **vite**?

Dois-tu **absolument** fumer une cigarette?

Pourquoi me réponds-tu aussi **méchamment**?

Ta mère te demande-t-elle de conduire **prudemment**?

M'aimes-tu **vraiment**?

B) Mangez-vous souvent du poisson **frais**?

Où allez-vous planter ce **bel** arbre?

Combien avez-vous payé votre **nouvel** ordinateur?

Connaissez-vous des hommes **malheureux**?

Célébrez-vous toujours les fêtes **nationales**?

As-tu reçu de **bonnes** nouvelles récemment?

Promenez-vous souvent votre **gentil petit** chien?

A) LES ADJECTIFS

1. Write the appropriate form of the definite/indefinite article and adjective:

a. personne (un/nerveux) _____

b. magasins (un/énorme) _____

c. entrevue (un/long) _____

d. goût (un/vulgaire) _____

e. conseils (le/inutile) _____

f. table (vieux) _____

g. assemblée (un/attentif) _____

h. tortues (un/géant) _____

i. plateau (un/rouge) _____

j. fille (un/jeune/étranger) _____

2. Translate the following phrases:

a. my old red dressing gown _____

b. beautiful true stories _____

c. an old bald man _____

d. the expensive new Italian car _____

e. the beautiful white snow _____

f. Are all the English
cows mad?   _____

3. Write the correct form of the article and adjective in the appropriate place:

a. _____ conférence _____ (un/long)

b. _____ feuilles _____ (un/sec)

c. _____ hommes _____ (un/petit/vert)

d. _____ autoroute _____ (un/dangereux)

e. _____ vache _____ (un/bon/gros)

f. _____ femme _____ (un/petit/
                                                    arrogant)

g. _____ chemise _____ (le/beau/blanc)

h. _____ pharmaciens _____ (un/charmant/
                                                       espagnol)

i. _____ histoires _____ (un/ennuyeux/
                                                     long)

j. _____ chapeau _____ (le/grand/violet)

4. Change the following phrases from the singular to the plural form:

a. une jolie fleur   → _____

b. le gros monsieur désagréable → _____

c. un petit pois   → _____

d. un beau garçon irlandais → _____

e. le problème social   → _____

f. un bel arbre   → _____

5. There are 15 errors in the following paragraph. Underline and correct them.
<u>ATTENTION!</u> **Make sure the adjectives are in the right place.**

Julie doit acheter un cadeau d'anniversaire pour son oncle

Bernard. C'est un grosse homme antipathique qui dit toujours des choses

désagréable à tout la famille. Mais Julie qui est gentil, est allé dans

un magasin grand au rayon des cravates et des chaussettes. Un vendeuse

avec une grande noire barbe a proposé de l'aider à faire son choix. La

premier cravate jaune qu'il a montrée était trop laid. Ensuite, il a suggéré

des chaussettes blancs avec de petites bleues fleurs ridicules. Julie était

irritée parce qu'elle ne voulait pas acheter des chaussettes hideux. Pour

finir elle a acheté une beau cravate grise avec de petites lignes verts.

L'oncle Bernard était ravi.

B) LES ADVERBES

1. Change the following adjectives to adverbs:

a. dangereux → _____   **d.** excessif → _____

b. léger   → _____   **e.** patient → _____

c. fort   → _____   **f.** seul   → _____

g. courant → _____ **i.** gentil → _____

h. vrai → _____ **j.** bon → _____

2. Translate the following sentences:

a. First, he went outside, then he dug a hole secretly and, finally, he buried the body silently.

_____

_____

b. I had never thought that he could eat so much chocolate.

_____

_____

c. Yesterday she was happy because they had delivered her new piano.

_____

_____

d. He thanked me a thousand times.

_____

_____

C) LES NOMBRES CARDINAUX ET ORDINAUX

1. Write out the answers to these problems:

a. 175 + 24 = _____

b. 42 + 33 = _____

c. 122 – 11 = _____

d. 527 − 12 = _____

e. 67 + 15 = _____

2. Translate the following phrases:

a. a million dollars _____

b. the first of December _____

c. the third example _____

d. the first four suitcases _____

e. July 4, 1776 _____

f. 100,321 scholarships _____

3. Write out the following numbers:

Example: 1022 __mille vingt-deux_____

a. 1492 _____

b. 16 _____

c. 299 _____

d. 40.738 _____

e. 901 _____

f. 351 _____

MADAGASCAR

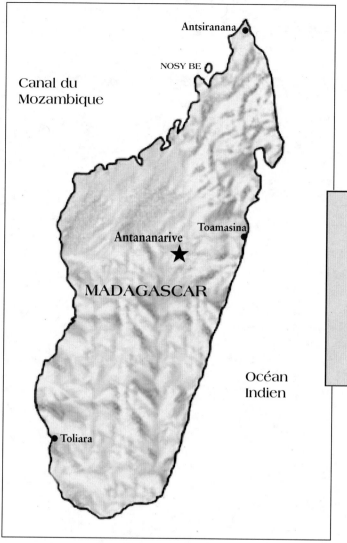

Canal du Mozambique

Antsiranana

NOSY BE

Antananarive

Toamasina

MADAGASCAR

Océan Indien

Toliara

MALGACHES CÉLÈBRES:

Refis Gizavo
(MUSICIEN)

Joajoby
(MUSICIEN)

Rajery
(MUSICIEN)

Michèle Rakotoson
(ÉCRIVAIN MALGACHE)

Ranavalona Ière
(REINE 19ÈME SIÈCLE)

Ranivoson
(PEINTRE)

MADAGASCAR

Capitale:	Antananarive
Population:	21.300.000
Gouvernement:	République
Chef d'état:	Président Andry Nirina Rajoelina Premier Ministre Albert Camille Vital
Monnaie:	Madagascar ariary (MGA)
Langues:	Français, malgache (langues officielles)
Ressources:	Café, cacao, clous de girofle, minerais, sisal, vanille
Musique:	Influences africaines et indonésiennes, rythmes Vaky-Soava, salegy, valiha (instrument à cordes)
Principales richesses touristiques:	Canotage sur le Mangoky, chutes d'eau, exploration sous-marine, geysers, lémurs, Marché de Zuma (un des plus grands du monde), orchidées tropicales, paradis environnemental (géographiquement isolé), randonnées, Réserve de Tsingy
Cuisine:	Curry de poulet et de poisson, légumes, thé au riz, ravitoto (soupe de porc), riz, vanille

VOCABULAIRE
LEÇON DIX

LES VERBES

aboyer	to bark	*juger*	to judge
allumer	to light, to turn on (electricity)	*jurer*	to swear
		livrer	to deliver, to hand over
(s') amuser	to enjoy, to have a good time	*nettoyer*	to clean
attendre	to wait for	*pleurer*	to cry, to weep
avoir mal	to ache, to hurt	*plier*	to fold
blesser	to wound	*ranger*	to tidy, to put away
cacher	to hide (something)	*remarquer*	to notice
choisir	to choose, to select	*rendre*	to give back
durer	to last	*réussir*	to succeed, to pass (an exam)
éclater	to burst		
empêcher	to prevent	*sécher*	to dry
(s') enfuir	to run away	*signer*	to sign
essayer	to try, to try on	*tirer sur*	to shoot
éteindre	to extinguish, to turn off	*tourner*	to turn, to revolve, to rotate
exiger	to require, to demand	*traverser*	to go across, to cross
(se) fâcher	to become angry	*tricher*	to cheat
faire confiance	to trust	*tromper*	to deceive
geler	to freeze	*(se) tromper*	to be mistaken, to make a mistake
gouverner	to govern		
imprimer	to print	*tuer*	to kill
jeter	to throw away		

LEÇON DIX

KEY GRAMMAR CONCEPTS

A) LES PRONOMS RELATIFS → *Relative pronouns*

B) LES ADJECTIFS ET LES PRONOMS DÉMONSTRATIFS → *Demonstrative adjectives and pronouns*

C) LES ADJECTIFS ET LES PRONOMS POSSESSIFS → *Possessive adjectives and pronouns*

 A) LES PRONOMS RELATIFS

A **relative pronoun** connects two parts of a sentence. The relative pronoun connects the relative clause (usually the second part of a sentence) to the noun or pronoun for which it stands (the antecedent).

The following is a list of French relative pronouns:

Relative Pronouns
qui
que
dont
lequel, laquelle, lesquels, lesquelles

Helpful Tip: While a relative pronoun is often omitted in English, it is required in French. (e.g., "The pizza (that) I ate was delicious." → *"La pizza que j'ai mangée était délicieuse."*)

1) QUI

"Qui" acts as a subject pronoun. It refers to people and things, and introduces the relative clause. It is always followed by a conjugated verb.

In English, it is translated as "who," "which," or "that."

 EXAMPLES: *Le chien **qui** aboie tout le temps me fait peur.*
   The dog that barks all the time scares me.

   *L'homme **qui** m'attend est le plus beau.*
   The man who is waiting for me is the most handsome.

ATTENTION! *"Qui"* <u>never</u> becomes *"qu'."*

2) QUE, QU'

"*Que*" acts as a direct object pronoun and refers to people and things. It is always followed by a noun or pronoun. In English, it can be translated as "whom," "which," or "that."

 EXAMPLES: *L'enfant cherche les œufs de Pâques **que** tu as cachés dans le jardin.*
The child is looking for the Easter eggs that you hid in the garden.

*Je connais l'homme **qu'**on a jugé.*
I know the man who was judged.

*Je connais l'homme **que** le policier a arrêté.*
I know the man whom the policeman arrested.

3) DONT

"*Dont*" acts as an object pronoun of "*de*" and refers to people and things. "*Dont*" is used to express possession or it is used with a verb which is constructed with "*de.*"

In English, it could be translated as "whose," "of whom," or "of which."

 EXAMPLES: *Elle connaît quelqu'un **dont** le frère est joueur de football professionnel.*
She knows someone whose brother is a professional football player.

*Le garçon **dont** je parle est le fils de M. Dupond.*
The boy of whom I speak is Mr. Dupond's son.

*Je suis sûre que tu réussiras à l'examen **dont** tu as peur.*
I am sure you will pass the exam of which you are afraid.

Note: Prepositions constructed with *de* such as *à côté de, en face de, au milieu de, etc.,* are not replaced by *dont* in the relative clause.

4) LEQUEL, LAQUELLE, LESQUELS, LESQUELLES

These relative pronouns are used after prepositions such as *avec, pour, sans, sur, sous, devant, etc.* Though these four words can refer both to people and things, it is more common to use "*qui*" with people.

 EXAMPLES: *Je ne trouve pas l'aspirateur avec **lequel** je veux nettoyer ma chambre.*
I'm not finding the vacuum cleaner with which I want to clean my room.

*Sais-tu la raison pour **laquelle** il pleure tout le temps?*
Do you know the reason why he cries all the time?

*Je connais bien la fille avec **qui** (or "avec **laquelle**") tu joues au tennis.*
I know the girl well with whom you are playing tennis.

*L'avocat avec **qui** elle travaille est intelligent.*
The lawyer with whom she is working is bright.

Lequel, laquelle, lesquels, and *lesquelles* will contract with *"à"* and *"de"* (the way articles do), forming *auquel, auxquels, auxquelles, duquel, desquels,* and *desquelles.*

EXAMPLES: *Le jardin en face **duquel** il habite est charmant.*
The garden in front of which he lives is charming.

*Les problèmes **auxquels** tu penses sont vraiment graves.*
The problems you are thinking of are really serious.

But: *Damien est tombé amoureux de la fille à côté de **laquelle** il est en classe.*
Damien fell in love with the girl next to whom he is in class.

5) Où

"Où" can also be used as a relative pronoun when the antecedent is a place. *"Où"* is often translated as "where," or "in which."

EXAMPLES: *Le placard **où** j'ai rangé mes affaires est trop petit.*
The closet in which I put away my things is too small.

*La ville **où** tu habites n'est pas sur la carte.*
The town where you live is not on the map.

6) RELATIVE PRONOUNS WITH NO NOUN AS AN ANTECEDENT

When there is no noun as an antecedent and no indication from the context what you are talking about, simply put *"ce"* directly before the relative pronouns *"qui," "que,"* or *"dont."*

In these sentences, *"ce"* signals an <u>indefinite</u> antecedent.

EXAMPLES: *Est-ce que vous voyez **ce qui** se passe là-bas?*
Do you see what is going on over there?

*Antoine a entendu **ce que** tu as dit.*
Antoine heard what you said.

*Nous achèterons tout **ce dont** nous avons besoin au centre commercial.*
We will buy everything we need at the shopping center.

1. **Write an appropriate relative pronoun in the space provided.**
   <u>ATTENTION!</u> **Include** *"ce"* **if necessary.**

   a. *Le Monde* est un journal _____ est imprimé en France.

   b. Le lac _____ j'aime patiner est complètement gelé.

   c. Le gouvernement a accepté les documents _____ les
   députés ont signés.

   d. Range tout _____ tu as acheté sur cette étagère.

   e. Le bois près _____ nous habitons est plein d'orchidées
   et d'oiseaux.

   f. Le petit garçon _____ livre le journal est le fils de nos
   voisins.

   g. Julie a trouvé tout _____ elle avait envie au Monoprix.

   h. Est-ce que Valentine est la fille avec _____ tu t'es
   fâchée?

   i. Les Malgaches _____ tu as écrit te répondront bientôt.

   j. Connais-tu ce chien _____ le maître est si méchant?

   k. Les chaussettes _____ tu as choisies sont affreuses.

   l. As-tu remarqué cet homme étrange _____ traverse
   la rue?

   m. Elle va nous raconter tout _____ est arrivé dimanche au
   Marché de Zuma.

2. There are ten errors in the following paragraph. Underline and correct them:

Cendrillon *que* avait une méchante belle-mère était obligée de nettoyer la maison toute la journée. Le matin elle allumait le feu dont elle devait éteindre le soir. Un jour, on a apporté une invitation du château à côté de *qui* elle habitait. Le prince donnait un bal *duquel* il invitait toutes les belles jeunes filles du royaume. Les deux horribles sœurs *lesquels* détestaient Cendrillon ont tout fait pour l'empêcher d'y aller, *qui* était très triste. Heureusement, Cendrillon *duquels* la marraine était fée a reçu une belle robe et une voiture. Le prince avec *dont* elle a beaucoup dansé est tombé amoureux d'elle. À minuit, elle devait rentrer à la maison *qui* elle habitait. Mais dans sa course, elle a perdu une des chaussures qu'elle portait, *ce que* a permis au prince de la retrouver plus tard.

B) LES ADJECTIFS ET LES PRONOMS DÉMONSTRATIFS

1) LES ADJECTIFS DÉMONSTRATIFS

Demonstrative adjectives ("this," "that," "these," and "those") help to identify and distinguish one noun from other nouns of the same type.

These adjectives <u>precede</u> the nouns that they modify.

Here are the demonstrative adjectives in French:

> *ce* → masculine, singular (it means both "this" and "that")
> *cet* → if the masculine noun begins with a vowel or a silent *"h"* ("this"/"that")
> *cette* → feminine, singular ("this"/"that")
> *ces* → feminine and masculine plural (it means both "these" and "those")

EXAMPLES:
ce parapluie	this (that) umbrella
cet oiseau	this (that) bird
cette église	this (that) church
ces ciseaux	these (those) scissors
ces femmes	these (those) women

Helpful Tip: To distinguish two items or groups of the same category, you can add *"-ci"* (this or that) or *"-là"* (these or those).

EXAMPLES: *Est-ce qu'il faut tourner dans **cette** rue-**ci** ou dans **cette** rue-**là**?*
Should we turn on this street or that street?

*Je préfère **ces** chaussures-**ci** et toi tu préfères **ces** chaussures-**là**.*
I prefer these shoes, and you prefer those shoes.

2) LES PRONOMS DÉMONSTRATIFS

The **demonstrative pronouns** are used to replace a noun modified by a demonstrative adjective. They agree with the noun they replace and are never used alone.

	SINGULAR	PLURAL
MASCULINE	*celui*	*ceux*
FEMININE	*celle*	*celles*

◆ Demonstrative pronouns never appear alone. They are followed by:

a) **"-ci" or "-là"**

❧ EXAMPLES: *J'ai beaucoup d'amis dans ma classe.* **Celui-ci** *s'appelle Paul et* **celui-là** *s'appelle Stéphane.*
I have many friends in my class. This one is called Paul and that one is called Stéphane.

Ces fleurs-ci sont plus fraîches que **celles-là**.
These flowers are fresher than those.

b) **a relative pronoun**

❧ EXAMPLES: *De tous ces ordinateurs, je préfère* **celui que** *tu as acheté hier.*
Of all these computers, I prefer the one you bought yesterday.

N'emporte pas ces livres inutiles; prends **ceux dont** *nous avons besoin pour travailler.*
Don't take these useless books; take those which we need to study.

c) **a preposition**

❧ EXAMPLES: *Aimes-tu le sac de Pauline? –Non, mais j'aime* **celui de** *Colette.*
Do you like Pauline's bag? –No, but I like Colette's.

Regarde les cadeaux de Noël que j'ai achetés. **Celui pour** *Cédric a coûté très cher.*
Look at the Christmas presents that I bought. The one for Cédric was very expensive.

3) LES PRONOMS DÉMONSTRATIFS IMPERSONNELS

Here are the **neuter demonstrative pronouns**: *"cela, "ça," "ceci,"* and *"ce."*

a) **Use *"cela," "ça,"* and *"ceci"* to replace an object, a sentence or an idea.**

❧ EXAMPLES: *Tu m'as raconté l'histoire du film et* **cela** *m'a beaucoup intéressé.*
You told me the plot of the movie, and that interested me a lot.
(*"Cela"* replaces "You told me the plot of the movie.")

Si tu portes **cela**, *moi je porterai* **ceci**.
If you carry that, I will carry this.
(Both *"cela"* and *"ceci"* refer to objects you are pointing to.)

"Ça" is simply a contraction of *"cela"* and is commonly used.

❧ EXAMPLE: *Regarde* **ça**! *C'est une catastrophe!*
Look at this! It's a disaster!

b) You can use the impersonal demonstrative pronoun *"ce" (c')* as the subject of the verb *"être."*

⚜ **Examples:** *Qui est ce garçon? –C'est mon cousin.*
Who is this boy? –It is my cousin.

Qui a dit cela? –C'est toi!
Who said that? –It's you!

Il pleut, c'est dommage.
It is raining, it's a pity.

ATTENTION! If *"c'est"* is followed by an adjective, the adjective will always be masculine.

⚜ **Example:** *Tu as vu cette robe? – Oui, c'est joli.*
Did you see this dress? –Yes, it's pretty.

 EXERCICES ▶

1. Complete these sentences with an appropriate form of a demonstrative adjective or pronoun:

a. _____ fille ne veut pas revenir en classe.

b. _____ montagnes là-bas sont couvertes de neige.

c. J'ai mal à _____ dent-ci, mais je n'ai pas mal à _____-là.

d. Bill Clinton et Ronald Reagan sont deux présidents américains. _____

est de Californie, _____ est de l'Arkansas.

e. Elle a allumé des bougies dans sa chambre; je trouve que _____
est dangereux.

f. Mes boucles d'oreilles et _____ de Virginie sont pareilles.

g. D'abord nous irons en voiture à Wendy's et ensuite nous irons à pied à

Coldstone Creamery. Que penses-tu de _____?

h. Crois-tu qu'on doive conduire les blessés à _____ hôpital?

i. Nous nous sommes bien amusés à la fête de Victor, mais nous nous sommes

horriblement ennuyés à _____ d'Ariane.

j. Il y a des éléphants en Afrique, mais moi _____ que je

préfère, _____ est Babar et Céleste.

k. Est-ce que tu as vu le deuxième film de *Star Wars*? –Oui, mais je préfère

_____ que j'ai vu quand j'étais petit.

l. _____ me fait mal aux pieds de porter des chaussures élégantes!

2. There are seven errors in the following dialogue. Underline and correct them:

Conversation dans une laverie entre Adrien Letournier et

Marie-Christine Lavial:

A. *Mademoiselle, j'ai déjà mis mes vêtements dans celle*

machine, prenez cette-là.

M.C. *Mais cette machine ne marche pas, Monsieur. Ne jetez pas*

ceux vêtements par terre! Ça est sale!

A. *Si elle ne marche pas, prenez celui qui est là-bas au fond!*

M.C. *Mais Monsieur, ces détergent est à moi!*

A. *Cet n'est pas vrai! Celui-là est à vous.*

M.C. *C'est incroyable comme les gens peuvent être désagréables!*

C) LES ADJECTIFS ET LES PRONOMS POSSESSIFS

1) LES ADJECTIFS POSSESSIFS

Possessive adjectives let you know to whom something belongs. They agree with the noun they describe.

ATTENTION! Possessive adjectives do <u>not</u> agree with the possessor. They agree with what is possessed.

Possessor	Possessive Adjectives		
	For Singular Nouns		For Plural Nouns
	masculine	feminine	masculine <u>and</u> feminine
je	*mon* → my	*ma* → my	*mes* → my
tu	*ton* → your	*ta* → your	*tes* → your
il/elle	*son* → his/her	*sa* → his/her	*ses* → his/her
nous	*notre* → our	*notre* → our	*nos* → our
vous	*votre* → your	*votre* → your	*vos* → your
ils/elles	*leur* → their	*leur* → their	*leurs* → their

When a feminine word begins with a vowel or a silent *"h,"* the possessive adjectives *mon, ton, son* will replace *ma, ta, sa.*

 EXAMPLES: ***Mon** ami Paul et **mon** amie Amélie viennent à **ma** fête.*
My friend Paul and my friend Amélie are coming to my party.

*Les Dupont rangent **leurs** vélos dans **leur** garage.*
The Duponts store their bicycles in their garage.

*Mais Monsieur, **nos** enfants ne trichent jamais!*
But Sir, our children never cheat!

2) LES PRONOMS POSSESSIFS

Possessive pronouns replace a noun modified by a possessive adjective. The pronoun agrees with the noun it replaces.

ATTENTION! Possessive pronouns are always coupled with a definite article.

Possessor	Possessive Pronouns			
	For Singular Nouns		For Plural Nouns	
	masculine	feminine	masculine	feminine
je	*le mien*	*la mienne*	*les miens*	*les miennes*
tu	*le tien*	*la tienne*	*les tiens*	*les tiennes*
il/elle	*le sien*	*la sienne*	*les siens*	*les siennes*
nous	*le nôtre*	*la nôtre*	*les nôtres*	*les nôtres*
vous	*le vôtre*	*la vôtre*	*les vôtres*	*les vôtres*
ils/elles	*le leur*	*la leur*	*les leurs*	*les leurs*

EXAMPLES: *J'ai perdu mon livre; prête-moi le tien!*
I have lost my book; lend me yours!

Moi, j'emporte mes affaires, mais eux, ils laissent les leurs ici.
I take my things away, but they leave theirs here.

Si vous prenez ma chemise, je prends la vôtre.
If you take my shirt, I'll take yours.

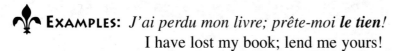 **EXERCICES**

1. Translate the following sentences:

a. My drawing is more beautiful than yours.

_____

_____

b. He did not give me his e-mail address, but he has mine.

_____

_____

c. Now, Anne Hathaway comes to my hairdresser because she does not like hers anymore.

_____

_____

d. Their dog and ours play in our garden.

_____

_____

2. Fill in each blank with the correct form of the possessive adjective or pronoun:

a. Nous recevons beaucoup de cadeaux pour _____ anniversaire.

b. Où avez-vous garé _____ voiture, nous avons garé _____ derrière l'université.

c. Elle va chercher _____ courrier dans _____ boîte aux lettres.

d. Albertine a mis _____ livres et _____ calculatrice dans _____ sac, comme c'est _____ habitude.

e. Pendant toute _____ enfance, Jacques passait _____ vacances dans la maison de _____ grand-mère à Monte-Carlo.

f. Les oiseaux font _____ nid dans les arbres et protègent _____ petits de _____ ennemis.

g. Je ne vois pas pourquoi nous vous inviterions à _____ mariage, vous ne nous avez pas invités _____.

h. Cette journaliste a écrit _____ article avec _____ talent habituel.

i. Cet enfant m'exaspère avec _____ jeux vidéo et je l'ai envoyé dans _____ chambre.

j. _____ chambre est tellement en désordre que j'ai perdu _____ ciseaux, _____ livre de chimie, et _____ devoir de français. Tu seras furieux parce que j'ai aussi perdu _____ devoir de français.

PRATIQUE DE L'ORAL
QUESTIONS PAR DEUX

These two sets of questions use grammatical structures and vocabulary from this lesson. Working with a partner, alternate asking and answering each question. When you get to the bottom of each list, start over at the top, switching roles. As a variation, write out the answers in complete sentences.

A) As-tu vu **mes** lunettes?

Comment **ta** grand-mère s'appelle-t-elle?

J'ai perdu **ma** crème solaire. Peux-tu me prêter la **tienne**?

Vas-tu venir à **ma** fête?

Tes voisins ont-ils planté des tulipes sur **leur** pelouse?

Qu'as-tu fais avec **mon** livre?

Si je te prête **mon** chandail, est-ce que je peux emprunter le **tien**?

B) As-tu fait une sieste **cet** après midi?

Joues-tu au football **ce** soir?

Manges-tu beaucoup de frites **ces** temps-ci?

Pourquoi me regardes-tu avec **cet** air?

Est-ce que **c'est** toi qui **as jeté** mes vêtements dans la piscine?

Préfères-tu mes boucles d'oreilles ou **celles de** France?

As-tu déjà fait **ça**?

246 BREAKING THE FRENCH BARRIER (ADVANCED)

A) LES PRONOMS RELATIFS

1. **Write an appropriate relative pronoun in the space provided. Include "ce" if necessary.**

   a. J'ai accepté la bourse _____ l'école m'a offerte.

   b. Connais-tu cette jeune fille _____ habite au dernier étage?

   c. Je ne comprends pas _____ tu me dis.

   d. Nous habitons maintenant en Corse dans l'île _____ Napoléon est né.

   e. J'aimerais voir ce film _____ on a beaucoup parlé.

   f. C'est la fille à côté de _____ nous sommes assis.

   g. Il n'a pas apporté _____ nous avions besoin pour le pique-nique.

   h. Regarde le beau peignoir _____ j'ai acheté au Printemps.

   i. Nous avons reçu des cadeaux _____ nous sommes contents.

   j. Nous préférons aller sur une plage _____ il n'y a pas trop de monde.

2. **Combine the two sentences into one with a relative pronoun:**

   Example: Je voudrais relire ce livre. Je l'ai lu il y a deux ans.

   Je voudrais relire ce livre que j'ai lu il y a deux ans.

   a. J'aime les fruits rouges. On fait des confitures avec les fruits rouges.

   _____

   _____

b. Tu as fait un curry de poulet. Ce curry de poulet n'est pas bon.

Tu as fait un curry de poulet qui n'est pas bon.

c. Connaissez-vous cette pauvre femme? Les enfants de cette femme sont tous délinquants.

Connaissez-vous cette pauvre femme dont les enfants sont tous

délinquants?

d. Le livre n'est pas à la bibliothèque. Je parle du livre.

Le livre dont je parle n'est pas à la bibliothèque.

e. Antananarive est une grande ville. Il y a beaucoup de marchés à Antananarive.

Antananarive est une grande ville où il y a beaucoup de marchés.

f. Notre-Dame est une grande cathédrale. Près de la cathédrale, il y a un hôpital.

Notre-Dame est une grande cathédrale près de laquelle il y a un

hôpital.

g. Elle est sortie avec une robe. La robe était beaucoup trop courte.

Elle est sortie avec une robe qui était beaucoup trop courte.

B) LES ADJECTIFS ET LES PRONOMS DÉMONSTRATIFS

Translate the following sentences:

a. If you work on this computer, I will use that one.

_____

_____

b. Have you done these horrible exercises? –No, I have only done the ones that he gave us yesterday.

_____

_____

c. This insect is not part of this category. In this biology lesson, we have not studied those.

_____

_____

d. He hesitates between this and that.

_____

_____

e. Julie is not in love with Patrick—it's a pity! They would make such a nice couple!

_____

_____

C) LES ADJECTIFS ET LES PRONOMS POSSESSIFS

1. Fill in each blank with the appropriate possessive adjective:

a. _____ livres (je)   f. _____ cousine (nous)

b. _____ maison (elles)   g. _____ bicyclettes (ils)

c. _____ amies (tu)   h. _____ cousine (je)

d. _____ orchidées (vous)   i. _____ dictionnaire (tu)

e. _____ associée (il)   j. _____ valises (elle)

2. Replace the underlined words with the appropriate possessive pronoun:

Example: Ma voiture et <u>ta voiture</u>.

Ma voiture et la tienne. _____

a. Je parle à mon ami et à <u>son ami</u>.

_____

b. Ils essaient leurs chaussures et nous essayons <u>nos chaussures</u>.

_____

c. Nous faisons confiance à nos amis, et eux <u>à leurs amis</u>.

_____

d. Il m'a rendu mes CD et je lui rendrai <u>ses CD</u>.

_____

3. There are nine errors in the following letter. Underline and correct them:

 Une lettre à ma copine...

Chère Rosalie,

J'ai réfléchi à que tu m'as dit et je pense que je dois absolument faire du sport. La natation est un sport dont est bon pour se muscler en douceur. Il y a beaucoup de piscines publiques à Paris que ne sont pas chères. La piscine ce que allait Anne l'année dernière est très agréable. Ce que ne me plaît pas c'est que le chlore me fait mal aux yeux. Alors j'ai pensé au karaté. C'est une activité laquelle on a bien besoin maintenant pour se défendre. Et si je faisais du yoga? Cet exercice que est très ancien est aussi une philosophie. Je connais quelqu'un de laquelle la grand-mère est prof de yoga. Mais si je fais du yoga, j'aimerais avoir une amie avec dont je pourrais y aller. Veux-tu en faire avec moi?

Bises,

Anabelle

4. Change this account from the 1ST person to the 3RD person (i.e., from *"je"* to *"elle"*) making all the necessary corrections:

Un voyage raté

Mon voyage à Madagascar a été catastrophique. Mon avion est arrivé en retard et ma voiture de location avait été prise par quelqu'un d'autre. J'ai téléphoné à mon cousin pour qu'il vienne me chercher avec la sienne. Pendant que je téléphonais, on m'a volé mes bagages. Il y avait des valises dans le hall mais ce n'était pas les miennes. Je suis donc allée à la police pour faire ma déclaration et le policier m'a montré un sac qui était bien le mien, mais il n'y avait rien dedans! J'avais perdu toutes mes chaussures, ma chemise en coton rose et mon maillot de bain si sexy! Comment est-ce que je vais pouvoir aller à la plage?

_____

_____

_____

_____

_____

_____

_____

_____

_____

_____

HAÏTI

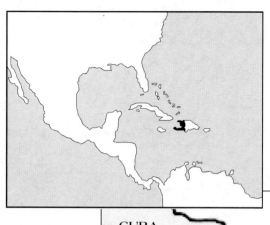

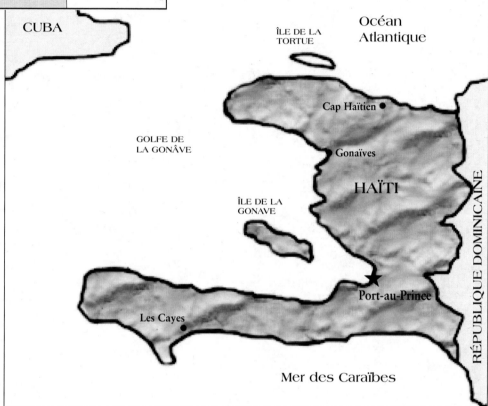

CUBA

ÎLE DE LA TORTUE

Océan Atlantique

Cap Haïtien ●

GOLFE DE LA GONÂVE

Gonaïves

HAÏTI

ÎLE DE LA GONAVE

RÉPUBLIQUE DOMINICAINE

★ Port-au-Prince

Les Cayes ●

Mer des Caraïbes

HAÏTI

Capitale:	Port-au-Prince
Population:	9.600.000
Gouvernement:	République
Chef d'état:	Président René Préval
Monnaie:	La gourde (HTG)
Langues:	Français, créole (langues officielles)
Ressources:	Bauxite, cacao, café, cuivre, sisal, sucre, textiles
Musique/Danse:	Bamboche, meringue (danse nationale), salsa, reggae, "zouk"
Principales richesses touristiques:	Cap Haïtien, La Citadelle, côte nord, marché au fer, Musée d'Art Haïtien, plages
Cuisine:	Bananes au rhum, créole, langouste flambée, patates douces, piment oiseau, riz et pois, rhum, tassot de dinde

HAÏTIENS CÉLÈBRES:

Le Père Jean-Bertrand Aristide
(ANCIEN PRÉSIDENT)

Marie Chauvet
(ÉCRIVAIN)

Edwidge Danticat
(ÉCRIVAIN)

René Depestre
(ÉCRIVAIN)

Hector Hippolyte
(PEINTRE)

Wyclef Jean
(CHANTEUR)

Toussaint Louverture
(LIBÉRATEUR)

VOCABULAIRE
LEÇON ONZE

LES VERBES

appartenir à	to belong to	*paraître*	to seem, to appear
arrêter	to stop	*patiner*	to skate
arriver	to happen, to arrive	*(se) peigner*	to comb
atteindre	to reach	*peindre*	to paint
augmenter	to increase	*(se) plaindre*	to complain
(se) battre	to fight	*prévenir*	to warn
couvrir	to cover	*promettre*	to promise
deviner	to guess	*quitter*	to leave
discuter	to discuss	*raconter*	to tell (a story)
entourer	to surround	*recevoir*	to receive
gagner	to earn, to win	*réfléchir*	to reflect, to think
garder	to keep	*régner*	to reign
gêner	to embarrass, to bother	*remplir*	to fill
		ressembler à	to look like
laisser	to leave	*rester*	to stay, to remain
mélanger	to mix	*résoudre*	to resolve, to solve a problem
mériter	to deserve		
mesurer	to measure	*soigner*	to care for
mordre	to bite	*sonner*	to ring
mouiller	to wet	*suivre*	to follow
nommer	to name	*verser*	to pour

LEÇON ONZE

KEY GRAMMAR
CONCEPTS

A) LE PLURIEL DES NOMS → *Plural nouns*

B) LES ADJECTIFS, LES PRONOMS ET LES ADVERBES INDÉFINIS → *Indefinite adjectives, pronouns and adverbs*

C) LES PARTICIPES PRÉSENTS ET PASSÉS → *Present and past participles*

D) LE PASSÉ SIMPLE → *Past definite*

E) LE DISCOURS INDIRECT → *Indirect speech*

 A) LE PLURIEL DES NOMS

These guidelines explain the formation of plural nouns:

1 **To form the plural of most nouns, add an "*s*":**

> *la ferme* → *les fermes*
> *le sac* → *les sacs*
> *le vendeur* → *les vendeurs*

2 **Nouns ending in "-*s*," "-*x*" and "-*z*" do not change in the plural:**

> *le bois* → *les bois*
> *le prix* → *les prix*
> *le nez* → *les nez*

3 **Most nouns ending in "-*al*" change to "-*aux*" in the plural:**

> *le cheval* → *les chevaux*
> *le journal* → *les journaux*

Note: The word "festival" is an exception: *festival* → *festivals*

4 **Nouns ending in "-*eau*" and "-*eu*" add an "*x*" in the plural:**

> *le bureau* → *les bureaux*
> *le jeu* → *les jeux*
> *l'oiseau* → *les oiseaux*

BEWARE OF THE FOLLOWING:

a) These nouns are irregular in the plural:

> *l'œil* → *les **yeux***
> *le travail* → *les **travaux***

b) These nouns are used <u>only</u> in the plural:

> *les ciseaux* → scissors
> *les gens* → people
> *les lunettes* → glasses
> *les mathématiques* → mathematics
> *les vacances* → vacation

c) There are also some nouns that are used only in the singular.

> *la morale* → morals
> *la physique* → physics
> *la politique* → politics

EXERCICES

1. Change the following phrases from the singular to the plural form:

a. un bel animal → _____

b. le manteau rouge → _____

c. le gros tas → _____

d. un vieil hôpital → _____

e. la dernière fois → _____

f. un avantage social → _____

2. Translate the following sentences:

a. He receives many international newspapers.

_____

b. He combs his hair everyday.

_____

c. Birds have two wings.

_____

d. Nobody has two noses.

_____

e. They study physics during the vacation.

_____

B) LES ADJECTIFS, LES PRONOMS ET LES ADVERBES INDÉFINIS

1) LES ADJECTIFS ET LES PRONOMS INDÉFINIS

Here is a helpful list of common adjectives and indefinite pronouns:

Adjectifs et Pronoms
l' (les) autre(s) → the other one, the others
certain(e)(s) → some, certain
chacun(e) → each one, everyone
chaque → each
n'importe quel (quelle, quels, quelles) → any
n'importe qui → anybody
n'importe quoi → anything
la plupart → most
la plupart de (des) → most of
plusieurs → several
quelque(s) → some, a few
quelque chose → something
quelqu'un, quelques-unes, quelques → someone, some, **or** a few
tout, toute, tous, toutes (adjectifs) → all, every
tout, toute, tous, toutes (pronoms) → all, everything, anything

Helpful Tip: When *"tous"* is an adjective, you don't pronounce the final *"s,"* but when it is a pronoun, you do pronounce the *"s."*

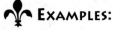 **EXAMPLES:** *Pour la fête, **chacun** apporte un cadeau.*
For the party, everyone is bringing a present.

*L'entraîneur lit **chaque** numéro de* Sports Illustrated *avec enthousiasme.*
The coach reads each issue of *Sports Illustrated* with enthusiasm.

***La plupart** de mes amies achètent leurs vêtements à J.Crew.*
Most of my friends buy their clothes at J.Crew.

*Réfléchis avant de dire **n'importe quoi**.*
Think before saying just anything.

2) LES ADVERBES INDÉFINIS

n'importe où	→	anywhere
n'importe quand	→	anytime
quelque part	→	somewhere

🔷 **EXAMPLES:** *Ne laisse pas tes affaires **n'importe où**.*
Don't leave your things just anywhere.

*Il m'a quittée pour aller **quelque part**, mais je ne sais pas où.*
He left me to go somewhere, but I don't know where.

Helpful Tip: The expressions with *"n'importe"* (adjectives, pronouns, or adverbs) are literally negative, but they are translated in English as "any" in the sense of "any old" or "just any."

🔷 **EXAMPLES:** *Ne mets pas **n'importe quelle** robe pour sortir!*
Don't wear any old dress when you go out!

*Je n'écris pas **n'importe quoi**; je réfléchis d'abord.*
I don't write just anything; I think first.

3) EXPRESSIONS AVEC "TOUT"

pas du tout	→	not at all
tout à fait	→	completely
tout le monde	→	everybody, everyone
tout le temps	→	all the time
tous (toutes) les deux, trois, quatre	→	both, all three, the four of them

🔷 **EXAMPLES:** *Maurice ressemble **tout à fait** à Wyclef Jean.*
Maurice looks exactly like Wyclef Jean.

***Tout le monde** parle du nouveau Harry Potter.*
Everyone is talking about the new *Harry Potter*.

*Il y sont allés **tous les trois**.*
The three of them went there.

*Ils sont **tous** venus.*
They all came.

1. Use these words and expressions in the paragraph below.
ATTENTION! You may use each word only once.

certains	*plusieurs*	*quelqu'un*
n'importe quoi	*quelque part*	*tous*
la plupart	*quelques*	*tout le monde*

Dans ma classe, nous sommes _____ intelligents,

mais _____ ont des difficultés pour faire le travail de

classe. _____ n'aiment pas faire les devoirs et écrivent

_____ aux examens. _____ a même mis

des verbes français à l'examen d'espagnol. Cependant, _____

des élèves ne trichent pas et font seulement _____ fautes.

_____ ira à l'université _____ l'année

prochaine.

2. Translate the following sentences:

a. He guessed most of the answers.

_____

_____

b. Why do you complain all the time?

_____

_____

c. Come for dinner anytime!

_____

_____

d. These children have skated several times, but they are completely incapable (hopeless).

_____

_____

e. Don't stop just anywhere on the highway!

_____

_____

 C) LES PARTICIPES PRÉSENTS ET PASSÉS

1) LES PARTICIPES PRÉSENTS

Present participles may be used as adjectives or as verbs. In French, they are not used as often as in English.

HOW DO YOU FORM THE PRESENT PARTICIPLE?

To form the present participle:

◆ Start with the _"nous"_ form of the present indicative.
◆ Take off the _"-ons."_
◆ Replace it with _"-ant."_

> _devoir: nous devons_ → _devant_
> _finir: nous finissons_ → _finissant_
> _manger: nous mangeons_ → _mangeant_

ATTENTION! _"Être," "avoir"_ and _"savoir"_ have irregular present participles.

> _avoir_ → _ayant_
> _être_ → _étant_
> _savoir_ → _sachant_

HOW IS THE PRESENT PARTICIPLE USED?

a) Present participles may be used as adjectives

Like all adjectives, present participles used as adjectives agree with the nouns they modify.

✠ EXAMPLES: *Lisez les pages **suivantes** pour demain!*
Read the following pages for tomorrow!

Nintendo's Mario Kart *est un jeu **amusant**, mais la musique est **exaspérante**!*
Nintendo's *Mario Kart* is a fun game, but the music is exasperating!

b) Present participles may be used as verbs

When used as a verb, the present participle is preceded by *"-en." "En"* can be translated as "while," "by," "upon," or "in."

✠ EXAMPLES: *Il s'est cassé une dent **en mordant** son frère!*
He broke a tooth (while) biting his brother!

*Little Bo Peep pleurait **en cherchant** ses moutons.*
Little Bo Peep was crying while looking for her sheep.

*C'est **en discutant** avec des Français que vous progresserez en français.*
It is (by) talking with French people that you will improve your French.

2) LES PARTICIPES PASSÉS

You are already very familiar with one use of past participles: They are the second part of the compound in the *passé composé* and pluperfect, for example.

Past participles are also commonly used as adjectives. These past participles always agree with the nouns they modify.

✠ EXAMPLES: *La bibliothèque est **ouverte**.*
The library is opened.

*Le petit chien **mouillé** aboie parce qu'il a froid.*
The wet little dog is barking because he is cold.

*Les langues **parlées** me semblent plus utiles que les langues mortes.*
Spoken languages seem more useful to me than dead languages.

EXERCICES

1. Change the following verbs to the present participle:

a. promettre → _____   **d.** comprendre → _____

b. réussir → _____   **e.** boire → _____

c. être → _____   **f.** recevoir → _____

2. There are six errors in the following paragraph. Underline and correct them:

> *Pour devenant acteur de cinéma, il faut apprendre à parler en sourissant. Il ne faut pas charmer les jolies actrices en les couvrir de baisers. Ce n'est pas en flattant le metteur en scène qu'on devient célèbre, mais en jouer bien. Si tu bavardes avec des acteurs amusaient, tu apprendras la comédie. Et un jour, en recevoyant un Oscar tu te souviendras de mes bons conseils.*

3. Write the proper form of the past participle in the following sentences:

a. Allons patiner sur le lac _____. (geler)

b. Les balles _____ par Tom Brady sont difficiles à intercepter. (lancer)

c. La vieille dame est trop _____ par son corset pour nettoyer le plancher. (gêner)

d. La princesse _____ au méchant prince ne veut pas se marier avec lui. (promettre)

e. Vous pouvez lire tous les articles _____ dans *Rolling Stone* sur Internet. (paraître)

f. Ces tableaux _____ par Picasso se vendent très chers. (peindre)

g. Toutes les lettres d'amour _____ à Elvis sont au musée. (écrire)

h. Mes acteurs _____ sont Colin Firth et Javier Bardem. (préférer)

i. _____ de l'arrivée de son fils adoré, Madame la Marquise a préparé des bananes au rhum. (prévenir)

j. John Wayne, _____ en plein cœur d'une flèche tirée par des Indiens, fait semblant de mourir pendant l'attaque du train. (atteindre)

D) LE PASSÉ SIMPLE

The *passé simple* (**historical past**) is similar to the *passé composé,* but is used rarely in modern French. It occurs mostly in literature and history books.

1) THE CONJUGATION OF THE "PASSÉ SIMPLE"

To form the *passé simple,* drop the infinitive endings (**-ER, -IR, -RE**) and add the following endings:

◆ For all **-ER** verbs: *-ai, -as, -a, -âmes, -âtes, -èrent*
◆ For all regular **-IR** and **-RE** verbs: *-is, -is, -it, -îmes, -îtes, -irent*

PARLER	FINIR	ENTENDRE
je parl**ai**	je fin**is**	j'entend**is**
tu parl**as**	tu fin**is**	tu entend**is**
il parl**a**	elle fin**it**	il entend**it**
nous parl**âmes**	nous fin**îmes**	nous entend**îmes**
vous parl**âtes**	vous fin**îtes**	vous entend**îtes**
elles parl**èrent**	ils fin**irent**	elles entend**irent**

ATTENTION! You will find the same spelling changes in the *passé simple* as in other tenses.

> "*c*" becomes "*ç*" before "*a*" and "*u*"
> "*g*" becomes "*ge*" before "*a*" and "*u*"

⚜ **EXAMPLES:** *je commençai*
vous mangeâtes
elles reçurent

ARE THERE IRREGULAR FORMS IN THE PASSÉ SIMPLE?

Many verbs have irregular forms in the *passé simple*.

Here a few of the most common:

AVOIR	ÊTRE	FAIRE
j'eus	je fus	je fis
tu eus	tu fus	tu fis
elle eut	il fut	il fit
nous eûmes	nous fûmes	nous fîmes
vous eûtes	vous fûtes	vous fîtes
ils eurent	elles furent	ils firent
LIRE	**SAVOIR**	**VENIR**
je lus	je sus	je vins
tu lus	tu sus	tu vins
il lut	elle sut	il vint
nous lûmes	nous sûmes	nous vînmes
vous lûtes	vous sûtes	vous vîntes
elles lurent	ils surent	elles vinrent

2) USE OF THE "PASSÉ SIMPLE"

The *passé simple* is used as an historical past tense.

⚜ **EXAMPLE:** *Georges Haussmann qui **fut** préfet de la Seine de 1853 à 1870, **voulut** faire de Paris une ville modèle. Il **dirigea** les grands travaux qui **transformèrent** Paris. Il **attira** de grands architectes et urbanistes qui **construisirent** l'Opéra et les Champs Elysées.*

You will also find that many literary texts use the *passé simple*.

⚜ **EXAMPLE:** *"Javert **loua** une chambre. Le soir même il s'y **installa**. Il vint écouter à la porte du locataire mystérieux, espérant entendre le son de sa voix, mais Jean Valjean **aperçut** sa chandelle à travers la serrure et **déjoua** l'espion en gardant le silence."* (**Les Misérables**, Victor Hugo)

1. Write all the verbs in parentheses in the *passé simple*:

Jeanne d'Arc (être) _____ une héroïne française. Elle

était très croyante, et un jour, elle (entendre) _____ des

voix qui la (encourager) _____ à délivrer la France de la

domination des Anglais. Les soldats (faire) _____ des

difficultés pour l'accepter comme leur chef, mais Jeanne (voir)

_____ le roi de France et (réussir) _____

à le persuader de sa mission. Elle (obliger) _____ les

Anglais à lever le siège d'Orléans, mais elle (échouer) _____

devant Paris et (tomber) _____ aux mains des Anglais. Ils

la (déclarer) _____ "sorcière." Elle (se défendre)

_____ avec habileté et courage, mais déclarée hérétique,

elle (être) _____ brûlée le 14 mai 1431.

2. Give the infinitive of these verbs:

Example: nous entendîmes ___**entendre**_____

a. il fit _____ **f.** je fus _____

b. tu vins _____ **g.** ils devinrent _____

c. nous déclarâmes _____ **h.** nous voulûmes _____

d. vous grossîtes _____ **i.** elles écrivirent _____

e. elle eut _____ **j.** il courut _____

When quoting the words of another person, you can either use **direct speech** with quotation marks:

> *Quand Joséphine est en colère, elle dit toujours: "Tu es méchante!"*
> When Joséphine is angry, she always says: "You are mean!"

or, use **indirect speech**:

> *Quand Joséphine est en colère, elle dit toujours que je suis méchante.*
> When Joséphine is angry, she always says that I am mean.

Helpful Tip:	In this context, *"que"* introduces an <u>indirect</u> quotation.

When you want to incorporate a quote — direct or indirect — into a sentence, keep these things in mind:

1 principal verb in the present or future tense

When the principal verb is in the present or the future tense, the other verb maintains its original tense in both direct and indirect speech.

EXAMPLES: *Mon père **dit**: "Tu **dois** sortir le chien."*
  My father says: "You must take the dog out."

  *Mon père **dit** que je **dois** sortir le chien.*
  My father says that I must take the dog out.

  *Le professeur **demandera** aux élèves: "Où **allez**-vous en vacances?"*
  The teacher will ask the students: "Where are you going on vacation?"

  *Le professeur **demandera** aux élèves où ils **vont** en vacances.*
  The teacher will ask the students where they go on vacation.

  *Julie me **raconte**: "Mon frère **est tombé** amoureux de toi."*
  Julie tells me: "My brother has fallen in love with you."

  *Julie me **raconte** que son frère **est tombé** amoureux de moi.*
  Julie tells me that her brother has fallen in love with me.

2 **principal verb in the past tense**

In indirect speech, when the principal verb is in the past, the verb in the original quotation will change as follows:

principal verb in **+** the past	If the original quotation was in the present . . . . . . /	then	the quotation will be in the imperfect tense.
	If the original quotation is in the future	then	the quotation will be in the present conditional tense.
	If the original quotation was in the past (either *passé composé* or imperfect) . . .	then	the quotation will be in the pluperfect tense.

EXAMPLES: *Pierre m'a déclaré: "Cette conférence **est** ennuyeuse!"*
Pierre declared to me: "This lecture is boring!"

*Pierre m'a déclaré que cette conférence **était** ennuyeuse.*
Pierre declared to me that this lecture was boring.

*L'entraîneur a prévenu les coureurs: "La course **sera** difficile!"*
The coach warned the runners: "The race will be difficult!"

*L'entraîneur a prévenu les coureurs que la course **serait** difficile.*
The coach warned the runners that the race would be difficult.

*Sébastien s'est plaint: "Ton chat **a mordu** mon chien!"*
Sébastien complained: "Your cat has bitten my dog!"

*Sébastien s'est plaint que mon chat **avait mordu** son chien.*
Sébastien complained that my cat had bitten his dog.

*Fatima m'a dit ce matin: "Hier, le professeur de maths **était** de mauvaise humeur."*
Fatima told me this morning: "Yesterday the math teacher was in a bad mood."

*Fatima m'a dit ce matin que hier, le professeur de maths **avait été** de mauvaise humeur.*
Fatima told me this morning that yesterday, the math teacher had been in a bad mood.

1. Put the verbs in parentheses in the correct tense:

a. Mon oncle m'a écrit qu'il _____ Port-au-Prince demain soir à six heures. (quitter)

b. Nous promettons au professeur d'art que nous _____ comme Picasso à la fin de l'année! (peindre)

c. Le gérant a dit: "Vous _____ entourer votre piscine d'une barrière." (devoir)

d. Les enfants ont appris que Louis XIV _____ pendant 54 ans. (régner)

e. La dame a dit à la petite fille: "Il ne _____ pas mouiller tes vêtements." (falloir)

f. La petite fille a répondu qu'ils _____ déjà mouillés. (être)

g. La cliente s'est plainte: "Vous _____ du thé sur ma nouvelle robe!" (verser)

h. Tu m'as dit ce matin que nous _____ le Cap Haïtien avant la nuit. (atteindre)

2. Change these sentences to indirect speech:

a. Nicolas a deviné: "C'est toi qui m'a envoyé cette carte pour la Saint-Valentin!"

_____

_____

b. Le journaliste a dit: "Alberto Contador gagnera sûrement le Tour de France."

_____

_____

c. Paul déclare: "Tu es la plus belle fille du monde."

_____

_____

d. Paul jure: "Je t'aimerai toujours."

_____

_____

e. Mais elle répond: "Je ne te crois pas!"

_____

_____

These two sets of questions use grammatical structures and vocabulary from this lesson. Working with a partner, alternate asking and answering each question. When you get to the bottom of each list, start over at the top, switching roles. As a variation, write out the answers in complete sentences.

 A) As-tu vu de beaux **animaux** l'été dernier?

As-tu terminé tes **devoirs** pour demain?

Quelle est la **morale** de *La cigale et la fourmi*?

Lis-tu les **journaux** internationaux?

As-tu reçu des **jeux** vidéo pour ton anniversaire?

Fermes-tu les **yeux** quand tu réfléchis?

Es-tu allé(e) en Haïti pendant les **vacances**?

B) As-tu **résolu tous** tes problèmes de famille?

Les médecins sont-ils obligés de soigner **n'importe qui**?

Est-ce que **la plupart** de tes amis savent **patiner**?

Pourquoi **tout le monde** se plaint du gouvernement?

Leonard Da Vinci était-il capable de peindre n'importe quoi?

As-tu vu **chaque** épisode des *Simpson*?

Pourquoi vas-tu aux toilettes **toutes les** deux secondes?

"LE RAP FRANÇAIS"

TRACK 10 DISC 3

Near the back of the book (p.313), you will find an article about rap music. Listen to the audio as you read along. Afterwards, answer the comprehension questions (p.315) either aloud or in written form. **TRACK 11 DISC 3** & **TRACK 12 DISC 3**

EXERCICES DE RÉVISION

A) LE PLURIEL DES NOMS

1. There are ten errors in the following paragraph. Underline and correct them:

> *Mon oncle est vendeur de jouet dans un grand magasins. Grâce à lui, les prixs sont très avantageux pour moi. Il vend des animals en bois qui ont des formes marrantes. Il y a des cheveaux avec des œils violettes. Des lapins avec des lunette rondes et des nezs pointus. Il vend aussi des jeus vidéo amusants. J'aime bien lui rendre visite.*

2. Rewrite the following phrases in plural form:

    a. la serviette mouillée   _____

    b. le bureau couvert de papiers _____

    c. leur travail intéressant   _____

    d. le pays exotique   _____

    e. le fils ennuyeux   _____

    f. tout le bateau   _____

    g. ta punition méritée   _____

B) LES INDÉFINIS

Translate the following sentences:

a. Most people like Duke Ellington.

_____

_____

b. This is not hard; any child can do it.

_____

_____

c. Each person can bring one guest to the party.

_____

_____

d. I will go anywhere with you, my love.

_____

_____

e. Several people told me that Jack Lalanne died last year.

_____

_____

C) Les participes présents et passés

1. Combine the two sentences with a present participle indicating that the two actions are done at the same time.

Example: Malheureusement mon père chante. Il prend sa douche.

<u>**Malheureusement, mon père chante en prenant sa douche.**</u>

a. L'explorateur était fatigué. Il a atteint le pôle nord.

_____

b. Les garçons se sont fait mal. Ils se sont battus à l'école.

_____

c. Il s'est brûlé. Il versait du thé.

_____

d. On peut faire ce dessert. On mélange du chocolat avec du sucre.

_____

e. Il fera fortune. Il gagnera à la loterie.

_____

f. Vous me faites plaisir. Vous restez quelques jours de plus.

_____

2. Circle the correct present or past participle:

a. Les verres (remplis, remplissants) de whiskey ne sont pas pour les enfants.

b. Les élèves (mérités, méritants) recevront des prix à la fin de l'année.

c. Page 8, il y a un problème (suivi, suivant) par des explications.

d. Elle a beaucoup de chance; son mari est très (charmé, charmant).

e. Ce bébé, (nommé, nommant) Gustave comme son grand-père, est vraiment adorable.

f. Les bagages (laissés, laissants) à la gare sont détruits par la police.

g. Ils n'ont pas aimé cette histoire (gênée, gênante).

h. Le chien a sauté par-dessus la barrière (entouré, entourant) le jardin.

i. Qui a volé les billets (posés, posants) sur la cheminée?

j. Christiane Amanpour est très jolie et (attirée, attirante).

D) Le passé simple

1. Identify and underline the verbs in the *passé simple*:

a. Napoléon qui était petit mais intelligent gagna la bataille d'Austerlitz, mais plus tard perdit celle de Waterloo.

b. Lorsque le vampire parut, il terrifa tous les habitants qui habitaient au château.

c. Si le lac gèle, mon cousin patinera avec ses amis et j'espère qu'ils réfléchiront avant de prendre des risques.

d. La princesse peignait sa chevelure blonde qui tombait jusque sur ses pieds quand le prince entra et fut ébloui par sa beauté.

e. Ne remplis pas ton verre de vin toutes les cinq minutes, tu vas être ivre!

f. Ils eurent peur d'entrer dans le restaurant qui leur paraissait trop chic.

g. Jeanne d'Arc a vécu en Lorraine avant d'aller à Reims où le roi a été couronné.

h. Cette remarque indiscrète de l'ambassadeur gêna beaucoup le premier ministre qui était un homme très modeste.

i. Le peintre Rubens fit des portraits de femmes qui n'étaient pas très minces.

j. Lorsque les soldats entendirent le canon de l'ennemi, ils partirent à l'attaque.

2. Give the infinitive of these verbs:

Example: nous entendîmes   **entendre** _____

a. nous fûmes _____   **f.** tu pris _____

b. vous dîtes _____   **g.** ils surent _____

c. ils firent _____   **h.** je lus _____

d. elle nagea _____   **i.** elle vint _____

e. vous perdîtes _____   **j.** ils crièrent _____

E) LE DISCOURS INDIRECT

1. There are six errors in the following text. Underline and correct them:

Hier après-midi, je voulais garer ma voiture près des Champs-

Élysées quand un agent de police est arrivé et il m'a dit:

   –"Vous ne pourriez pas stationner ici!"

J'ai répondu que je suis pressé et que je dois stationner là pour aller au

cinéma. Il n'a pas aimé ma réponse et a dit:

   –"Vous recevrais une contravention si vous restiez là."

Je lui ai expliqué que ma copine m'attendra et qu'elle partirait si je

n'arrivais pas à l'heure. L'agent a été touché par mon histoire

sentimentale et m'a dit:

   –"Pour une fois, restez ici!"

2. Change these sentences to indirect speech:

a. Ma mère m'a dit: "Tu dois prendre soin de ton petit frère pendant que ton père et moi allons au cinéma."

_____

_____

b. L'arbitre crie: "Les spectateurs ne peuvent pas entrer sur le terrain de foot."

_____

_____

c. Le directeur de Citröen a dit: "Je signerai le contrat la semaine prochaine."

_____

_____

d. Le professeur a dit: "Vous avez tous triché!"

_____

_____

e. Le petit garçon répond: "Le poulet traversera la route pour aller de l'autre côté."

_____

_____

f. Sylvain m'a dit: "Je te rendrai toutes tes vidéos avant la fin du trimestre."

_____

_____

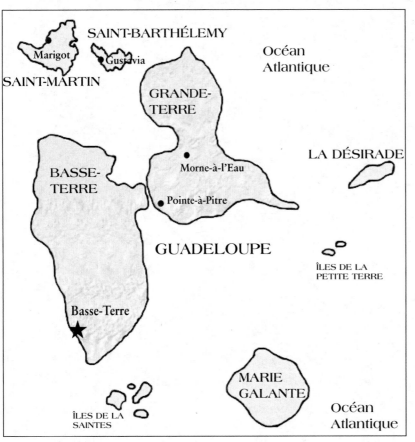

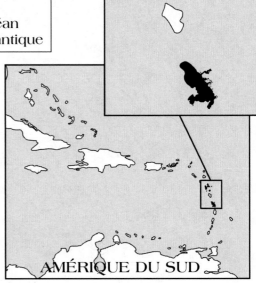

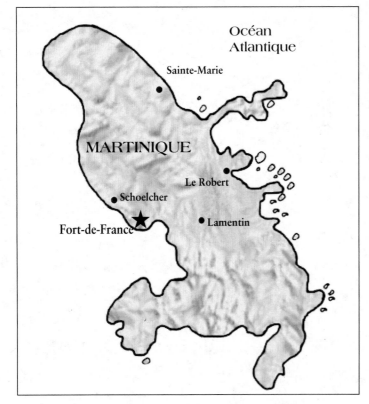

LA MARTINIQUE & LA GUADELOUPE

LA MARTINIQUE

Capitale:	Fort-de-France
Population:	410.000
Gouvernement:	Département d'outre-mer
Chef d'état:	Gouverné par le président français (Nicolas Sarkozy)
Monnaie:	Euro
Langues:	Français, créole (langues officielles)
Ressources:	Ananas, bananes, palmes, rhum, sucre, tourisme
Musique/Danse:	Limbo, steel band, "zouk"
Principales richesses touristiques:	La Montagne Pelée (volcan), plages, Les Trois Îlets, lieu de naissance de l'impératice Joséphine, première femme de Napoléon Bonaparte)
Cuisine:	Conques, curry, épices exotiques de tradition française, Franco-Caribéenne, fruits de mer, indienne et africaine, langoustes, "planteur" (jus de fruits et rhum), poissons

MARTINIQUAIS CÉLÈBRES:

Joséphine Bonaparte
(FEMME DE NAPOLÉON BONAPARTE)

Aimé Césaire
(POÈTE)

Patrick Chamoiseau
(ÉCRIVAIN)

Le Père Labat
(QUI A PERFECTIONNÉ LA RECETTE DU RHUM)

Ronny Turiaf
(JOUEUR DE BASKETBALL)

LA GUADELOUPE

Capitale:	Basse-Terre
Population:	460.000
Gouvernement:	Département d'outre-mer (République française)
Chef d'état:	Gouverné par le président français (Nicolas Sarkozy)
Monnaie:	Euro
Langues:	Français, créole (langues officielles)
Ressources:	Bananes, cacao, café, rhum, sucre, tourisme, vanille
Musique/Danse:	Biguine (danse créole), disco, Ken'nida (groupe musical), percussions, "zouk"
Principales richesses touristiques:	Fête des Cuisinières, forêts, plages, Parc National de Guadeloupe, Ste. Marie de Capesterre (Christophe Colomb y a débarqué)
Cuisine:	Cabri, columbo, conques, Française-créole, langoustes, oursins, punch au rhum, tortues

GUADELOUPÉENS CÉLÈBRES:

Dany Bébel
(SOCIOLOGUE, LINGUISTE, ÉCRIVAIN)

Maryse Condé
(ÉCRIVAIN)

Victor Hugues
(RÉVOLUTIONNAIRE ET OPPORTUNISTE)

Alexis Léger Perse
(SAINT-JOHN PERSE)
(POÈTE ET RÉCIPIENDAIRE DU PRIX NOBEL DE LITTÉRATURE)

Mickael Pietrus
(ATHLÈTE)

Simone Schwarz-Bart
(ÉCRIVAIN)

VOCABULAIRE LEÇON DOUZE

LES EXPRESSIONS IDIOMATIQUES

aller voir	to visit someone	*faire la cuisine*	to cook
apprendre par cœur	to learn by heart	*faire la queue*	to wait in line
(s') attendre à	to expect	*faire le tour de*	to go around
avoir des ennuis	to have problems	*faire semblant de*	to pretend to
avoir horreur de	to hate, to loathe	*faire un tour*	to take a walk/ drive
avoir rendez-vous	to have an appointment	*faire un voyage*	to take a trip
(se) débrouiller	to manage	*laisser tomber*	to drop, to give up
(se) demander	to wonder	*(se) mettre à*	to start doing something
(se) disputer	to quarrel with		
(s') entendre avec	to get along	*mettre le couvert*	to set the table
entendre dire	to hear (a rumor)	*(se) passer*	to happen
être à l'heure	to be on time	*poser une question*	to ask a question
être en colère	to be angry	*prendre des notes*	to take notes
être en retard	to be late	*prendre soin de*	to take care of
être ennuyé	to be worried	*prendre une décision*	to make a decision
être ennuyeux	to be boring		
être pressé	to be in a hurry	*servir à*	to be used for/to
faire attention	to pay attention	*(se) servir de*	to use
faire des progrès	to improve	*suivre un cours*	to take a course
faire exprès	to do something on purpose	*tomber amoureux de*	to fall in love with
		valoir la peine	to be worth the trouble

LEÇON DOUZE

KEY GRAMMAR
CONCEPTS

A) EXPRESSIONS DE TEMPS → *Expressions of time*

B) VERBES À EMPLOIS DIVERS → *Verbs with special uses*

C) "IL EST" VS. À "C'EST" → *"Il est" vs. "c'est"*

A) EXPRESSIONS DE TEMPS

This section will present some useful constructions to express time.

1) DEPUIS

a) ***Depuis combien de temps?*** (How long?) (Literally: "Since how much time?")

> *Depuis* + amount of time

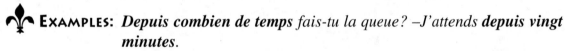 **EXAMPLES:** ***Depuis combien de temps*** *fais-tu la queue?* –*J'attends* ***depuis vingt minutes****.*
How long have you been waiting in line? –I have been waiting for twenty minutes.

J'étudie le français ***depuis deux ans****.*
I have been studying French for two years.

b) ***Depuis quand?*** (Since when?)

> *Depuis* + specific point in time

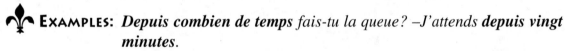 **EXAMPLE:** ***Depuis quand*** *fais-tu la queue?* –*J'attends* ***depuis midi****.*
Since when have you been waiting in line? –I have been waiting since noon.

Helpful Tip: In all of the examples above, a French speaker uses the present tense when the action began in the past and is continuing in the present. (In English, speakers will use a construction with "have been <u>doing</u> something.")

However, when the action begins in the past and is still going on at the time of a second past action, French uses the <u>imperfect</u> with the *passé composé* (English uses the pluperfect with the preterite).

 EXAMPLES: *Elle **étudiait** le français depuis deux ans quand elle **a décidé** de faire du Coréen.*
She had been studying French for two years when she decided to take Korean.

*J'**étais** à la piscine quand tu **as téléphoné**.*
I was at the pool when you called.

2) IL Y A . . . QUE

The use of *"il y a"* + amount of time + *que* expresses duration in the same manner as *"depuis"* + amount of time.

 EXAMPLES: *Il y a deux heures que je fais la queue.*
I've been in line for two hours.

Je fais la queue depuis deux heures.
I've been in line for two hours.

*Il y avait dix minutes **que** les enfants se disputaient quand leur mère les a séparés.*
The children had been quarreling for ten minutes when their mother separated them.

ATTENTION! Remember to include *"que"* to introduce the second part of the sentence!

3) PENDANT

"Pendant" is used to introduce an action completed in a "floating block" of time. We know how long the action lasted, but not necessarily when it took place.

When you use *"pendant,"* use the same tense in French as you would in English to convey this notion of duration of time.

 EXAMPLES: *Pendant combien de temps as-tu travaillé pour l'examen?*
How long did you study for the exam?

*J'ai travaillé **pendant** cinq heures.*
I studied for five hours.

*Ma fille fera un voyage **pendant** trois semaines.*
My daughter will take a trip for three weeks.

 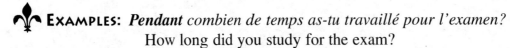

1. Fill in the blanks with the correct expression:

a. Il s'ennuyait _____ deux heures à la conférence quand il s'est endormi.

b. Prenez des notes _____ le cours d'histoire.

c. _____ trois jours que tu fais semblant d'être malade, mais maintenant je ne te crois plus.

d. _____ le mois de septembre, le petit garçon attend le Père Noël.

e. _____ combien de temps est-ce que tu parles créole?

f. _____ combien de temps est-ce que tu as voyagé dans les Antilles?

g. Je ne trouve pas la tortue et pourtant _____ dix minutes que je fais le tour du jardin.

h. _____ toute l'après-midi, mon frère a fait exprès de faire du bruit parce que je travaillais.

2. Write the correct form of the verb:

a. Est-ce que ça _____ la peine de pleurer pendant une heure pour ça? (valoir)

b. Thierry Henry _____ au foot depuis cinq minutes quand il a marqué un but. (jouer)

c. Mon père _____ en colère depuis ce matin parce qu'il ne sait pas se servir de son nouvel ordinateur. (être)

d. Il faut s'entendre avec les gens quand on _____ travailler avec eux pendant un an. (devoir)

e. Il y a longtemps que je me _____ à quoi servait un tire-bouchon quand tu me l'as expliqué. (demander)

f. Roméo mourait d'amour depuis des mois quand Juliette _____ ses propositions. (accepter)

g. Il _____ des ennuis d'argent depuis trois mois quand il a enfin trouvé un bon emploi. (avoir)

h. Tu _____ des progrès en francais quand tu iras à la Martinique pendant les vacances. (faire)

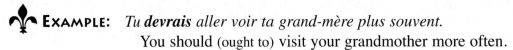

B) VERBES À EMPLOIS DIVERS

1) DEVOIR

a) *"Devoir"* means "must," or "to have to." It will usually be followed by an infinitive.

 EXAMPLES: *On doit travailler pour réussir.*
One must (has to) work to succeed.

Tu devras apprendre par cœur tous les poèmes de Victor Hugo.
You will have to (must) memorize all of Victor Hugo's poems.

b) In the conditional tense, *"devoir"* means "should," or "ought to."

EXAMPLE: *Tu devrais aller voir ta grand-mère plus souvent.*
You should (ought to) visit your grandmother more often.

c) *"Devoir"* also suggests probability.

EXAMPLES: *Il court; il doit être pressé.*
He is running; he must be in a hurry.

Leur maison est beaucoup plus jolie; ils ont dû la repeindre.
Their house looks much prettier; they must have repainted it.

d) *"Devoir"* has another completely unrelated meaning. It can also mean "to owe."

    ⚜ EXAMPLE: *M. Cazeilles a trop joué au casino de Monte Carlo et maintenant il **doit** beaucoup d'argent.*
                 Mr. Cazeilles has gambled too much in the Monte Carlo casino, and now he owes a lot of money.

2) POUVOIR

a) *"Pouvoir"* means "to be able to" or "can."

    ⚜ EXAMPLE: *Céline **ne peut pas** atteindre le pot de confiture parce qu'elle est trop petite.*
                 Céline cannot reach the jar of preserves because she is too small.

b) *"Pouvoir"* can also mean "may."

    ⚜ EXAMPLE: *Est-ce que je **peux** vous parler?*
                 May I speak to you?

c) *"Pouvoir"* vs. *"savoir"*

Make sure to differentiate between *"pouvoir"* (to have the physical ability) and *"savoir"* (to have the knowledge or skill).

    ⚜ EXAMPLES: *Il **ne peut pas** nager aujourd'hui parce qu'il s'est cassé les deux jambes.*
                 He cannot swim today because he broke both of his legs (he is physically unable).

                 *Ce bébé **ne sait pas** encore nager.*
                 This baby cannot swim yet (he has not learned how to).

3) SAVOIR/CONNAÎTRE

Both *"savoir"* and *"connaître"* mean "to know."

◆ *"Savoir"* implies having knowledge of a fact or piece of information, something you can say or recite with words or numbers or something you know how to do.

◆ *"Connaître"* is used in the sense of being familiar or acquainted with a person or place.

    ⚜ EXAMPLES: *Savez-vous la date de la révolution française?*
                 Do you know the date of the French Revolution?

                 Connaissez-vous Port-au-Prince?
                 Do you know Port-au-Prince?

*Julie **sait** où il habite.*
Julie knows where he lives.

*Est-ce que tu **sais** conduire un tracteur?*
Do you know how to drive a tractor?

*Je ne **connais** pas sa maison, mais je **sais** où il habite.*
I don't know his house, but I know where he lives.

4) FAIRE

a) **"Faire" means "to do" or "to make."**

 **EXAMPLE:** *Qu'est-ce que tu **as fait** hier? –J'ai fait une sculpture superbe!*
What did you do yesterday? –I made a fabulous sculpture!

b) **In the construction "*faire* + infinitive," the subject makes someone else do something.**

EXAMPLES: *Je fais **manger** le bébé.*
I feed the baby (the baby does the eating).

*Elle **se fait couper** les cheveux par un bon coiffeur.*
She has her hair cut by a good hairdresser.

*Gustave **fait faire** ses devoirs à sa grande sœur.*
Gustave has (makes) his big sister do his homework.

 EXERCICES ▶

1. Translate the following sentences:

a. Where is he? He must be sick.

_____

_____

b. Could I have an appointment with the manager, please?

_____

_____

c. You should tidy your room!

_____

_____

d. They know a good restaurant near Fort-de-France.

_____

_____

e. My friend owes me twenty euros.

_____

_____

f. This girl really knows how to dance the rumba.

_____

_____

g. I had this dress made for my wedding.

_____

_____

h. Marie's parents had her hang up the phone.

_____

_____

2. Choose *connaître, savoir* or *pouvoir* in the appropriate form:

a. Tu ne devrais pas aller en France sans _____ quelqu'un là-bas.

b. Je crois que Benoît _____ assez de français pour se débrouiller pendant son séjour à Marseille.

c. Il est regrettable que vous ne _____ pas prendre une décision immédiatement.

d. _____ -vous les cousins de Virginie?

e. Tous les Américains _____ la date de la révolution.

f. Antoine ne _____ pas pourquoi Suzanne l'a laissé tomber.

g. Je ne _____ pas ce qui s'est passé hier soir chez Alain.

h. Dominique, est-ce que je _____ vous poser encore une question indiscrète?

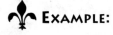

C) "IL EST" VS. À "C'EST"

1) IL EST

"Il est" is used before adjectives (or nouns used as adjectives indicating professions, nationalities or religions).

⚜ **EXAMPLE:** *Connaissez-vous M. Youssef? **Il est** médecin, **il est** tunisien et **il est** musulman. –Je le connais bien; **il est** très sympa!*
> Do you know Mr. Youssef? He is a doctor, he is Tunisian and he is a Muslim. –I know him well; he is very nice!

In the above example *"il"* replaces a specific noun. If the noun were feminine, it could be *"elle."* If the noun were plural, *"ils"* or *"elles"* would be followed by *"sont."*

⚜ **EXAMPLE:** *Hier j'ai dîné avec Mélanie Suchard. **Elle est** suisse. **Elle est** chanteuse de jazz. **Elle est** très célèbre.*
> Yesterday I had dinner with Mélanie Suchard. She is Swiss. She is a jazz singer. She is very famous.

2) C'EST

"C'est" has two common uses:

◆ Before a proper noun or a pronoun
◆ Before a noun preceded by an article, a possessive or demonstrative adjective.

⚜ **EXAMPLES:** *Qui c'est? –C'est moi! –Qui toi? –C'est Louise! –Quelle Louise?*
–C'est ta cousine adorée!

    Who is it? –It is I! –Who, you? –It's Louise! –Which Louise?
    –It is your beloved cousin!

M. Youssef? C'est un médecin célèbre, c'est un Tunisien qui
habite à Carthage et c'est un musulman. –Je le connais bien;
c'est un homme très sympa! C'est lui qui a reçu le prix de médecine
il y a trois ans.

    Mr. Youssef? He is a famous doctor, he is a Tunisian living in
    Carthage, and he is a Muslim. –I know him well; he is a very
    nice man! It is he who received the medical prize three years ago.

If the noun is plural, *"est"* becomes *"sont."*

⚜ **EXAMPLE:** *Est-ce que tu connais Paul et Virginie? Ce **sont** mes cousins. Ce **sont***
eux qui ont voyagé aux Antilles avec moi.

    Do you know Paul and Virginie? They are my cousins. It is they who
    traveled to the West Indies with me.

"C'est" replaces an idea or a sentence previously expressed as follows:

Est-ce que vous voulez lire Shakespeare?

*–Non, **c'est** difficile.* (adjective alone)

*–Non, **c'est** difficile à lire.* (adjective + infinitive)

*–Non, **c'est** difficile de lire ses tragédies.* (adjective + infinitive + direct object)

⚜ **EXAMPLES:** *C'est agréable d'aller à la plage!*
    Going to the beach is pleasant!

*Pierre et Sylvie divorcent. **C'est dommage de divorcer** si vite.*
    Pierre and Sylvie are divorcing. It's a pity to divorce so fast.

*Nous suivons des cours de danse folklorique. **C'est amusant***
***de danser la polka**!*
    We take folk dancing classes. It is fun to dance the polka!

Fill in the blanks with *il est, elle est, ils sont, elles sont, c'est,* **or** *ce sont*:

a. Mme. Gouda a téléphoné hier soir. _____ hollandaise; _____ une amie de ma mère; _____ très bavarde. Elle va venir passer le weekend; _____ ennuyeux parce que je voulais inviter mes copains.

b. Je n'étudie ni le latin ni le grec; _____ des langues mortes; _____ difficiles et _____ impossible de les parler avec les indigènes!

c. Je viens de voir le dernier film de Catherine Deneuve; _____ une excellente actrice et _____ très jolie. Je ne l'ai jamais rencontrée, _____ dommage!

d. Vous voulez venir nager avec moi dans la rivière? Tu es idiot? _____ très dangereux! _____ fou de regarder les crocodiles de si près!

These two sets of questions use grammatical structures and vocabulary from this lesson. Working with a partner, alternate asking and answering each question. When you get to the bottom of each list, start over at the top, switching roles. As a variation, write out the answers in complete sentences.

 A) *Ton ami Alexandre*—**Est-il** canadien ou français?

Est-il intelligent?

Apprendre le mandarin—**Est-ce** difficile?

Les pommes et les poires—Est-ce que **ce sont** des légumes?

Sauter en parachute—Est-ce que **c'est** dangereux?

Est-il bizarre de manger de la glace aux concombres?

Est-ce que **c'est toi** qui a mangé le sac de biscottes?

B) Est-ce que tu **fais des progrès** en français?

Peux-tu avaler dix hamburgers à la suite?

Sais-tu faire des œufs brouillés?

Connais-tu bien Angelina Jolie?

Devrions-nous promener nos chiens plus souvent?

Pourquoi **fais**-tu **exprès** de m'énerver?

Doit-on seulement parler anglais dans cette classe?

EXERCICES DE RÉVISION

A) EXPRESSIONS DE TEMPS

1. Fill in the blanks with *il y a, depuis* or *pendant*:

a. _____ combien de temps est-ce que tu vas dans cette école?

b. _____ très longtemps que je ne crois plus au Père Noël.

c. Le téléphone sonnait _____ quelques minutes quand je l'ai enfin entendu.

d. Où étais-tu? –J'attends sous la pluie _____ une demi-heure.

e. J'ai regardé Meryl Streep dans *Julie et Julia* _____ toute la soirée.

f. _____ quand est-ce que tu as les cheveux courts?

2. Write the correct form of the verb:

a. Ma petite sœur _____ à un camp de tennis en Provence pendant trois semaines. (aller)

b. Il y avait déjà bien longtemps que je _____ Gaston quand je l'ai rencontré par hasard dans un bar. (ne voir plus)

c. Hier les athlètes _____ pendant un bon moment avant de recommencer l'entraînement. (se reposer)

d. Ils louaient une maison depuis quelques mois quand ils _____ d'acheter un appartement. (décider)

e. Le dîner sera certainement délicieux, il y a trois heures que mon père

_____ dans la cuisine! (travailler)

B) VERBES À EMPLOIS DIVERS

1. There are seven errors in the following letter. Underline and correct them:

 Mon cher Christophe,

J'ai entendu dire que tu allais passer tes vacances dans les Alpes, là où j'étais l'année dernière. Je vais te donner quelques conseils. Est-ce que tu sais la région? Tu devais acheter de bonnes chaussures pour savoir faire de l'escalade. Je sais un excellent magasin où tu connaîtras trouver tout l'équipement nécessaire. Tu ne saurais pas aller trop vite au commencement des randonnées. Tu seras vite fatigué et tu ne pourras pas arriver au sommet. Il faut conserver ton énergie et connaître quand tu dois t'arrêter. Bon courage et bonnes vacances!

Philippe

2. Translate the following sentences:

a. I don't owe you anything!

_____

b. Do you know how to paint like Matisse?

_____

c. I hate having my hair cut by a hairdresser.

_____

_____

d. You ought to give all these books back to the library.

_____

_____

e. I cannot set the table because I have an appointment with the manager.

_____

_____

C) "IL EST" OPPOSÉ À "C'EST"

Fill in the blanks with _il est, elle est,_ or _c'est_:

Qui est-ce? _____ un journaliste et _____ américain.

_____ un journaliste qui a toujours beaucoup d'ennuis; _____

vert, mais il n'est pas malade, _____ sa couleur naturelle;

_____ lui dont Miss Piggy est amoureuse. Il ne l'aime pas et il

voudrait être seul, mais _____ très difficile de se débarrasser de cette

star. En effet _____ agressive et elle pense qu'il l'adore.

_____ le reporter pour les histoires de princesses. Malheureusement,

les histoires ne finissent jamais comme elles devraient et _____ bien

triste pour notre héros!

UN CONTRÔLE FINAL:
BRISER LA BARRIÈRE!

This final section contains forty sentences that test material which you have learned throughout the book. Answers with explanations follow this final exercise:

1. L'année prochaine, je _____ avec Suzanne. (nager)

2. Si tu avais fait tout ton travail, tu _____ te coucher tôt. (pouvoir)

3. Quand nous étions petits, nous _____ toujours des Captain Crunch. (manger)

4. Tous les jours, je _____ le train pour aller à mon travail. (prendre)

5. Je ne me marierai pas avant de _____ cette année scolaire. (finir)

6. Je ne crois pas que tu _____ des notes hier pendant la classe. (prendre)

7. Michel m'a dit qu'il ne _____ pas à la fête demain soir. (aller)

8. Nous bavardions quand l'alarme d'incendie _____. (sonner)

9. Pendant que je _____ la cuisine, les enfants sont arrivés. (faire)

10. Ça ne vaut pas la peine de te faire tant de soucis. Est-ce que tu n'es pas

    fatigué de tant _____? (pleurer)

11. Hier, Françoise et Henri _____ le livre d'anglais en français. (traduire)

12. Je suis si contente que mon fils et ta fille _____ amoureux! (tomber)

13. Nous ne _____ pas _____ nos bagages quand le taxi est arrivé! (finir)

14. Nous ne doutons pas que tu _____ un cousin à la Martinique! (avoir)

15. Ils espèrent que les enfants _____ les voir dimanche prochain. (venir)

16. S'il vous plaît, Messieurs, _____-vous immédiatement! (s'asseoir)

17. S'il _____ maintenant, nous ne pourrions pas nager dans la piscine. (pleuvoir)

18. Si nous avions eu de la chance, notre parti _____. (gagner)

19. Il faut _____ beaucoup de questions en classe. (poser)

20. Dans mon dortoir, il n'y a pas un seul élève qui _____ jouer du piano. (savoir)

21. Quand tu _____ à Paris, tu m'écriras une carte postale. (être)

22. Il n'est pas poli de parler en _____. (manger)

23. Après _____ le film *Harry Potter* une deuxième fois, nous irons nous coucher. (voir)

24. Tu te doucheras avant que je _____ mon bain puisque nous n'avons qu'une salle de bains! (prendre)

25. Si elles _____ de l'argent, elles iraient à New York pour voir Justin Bieber. (avoir)

26. Je cherche une personne qui me _____. (comprendre)

27. Mes chers enfants, _____ sages pendant que je ne serai pas là. (être)

28. Quand il arrivera à Point-à-Pitre, il _____ pendant dix-huit heures. (voyager)

29. J'aurais préféré que tu _____ ce travail avec moi. (faire)

30. Les enfants sont heureux de vous _____. (voir)

In nine of the following sentences, you will find one error. Identify and correct each error. There is one correct sentence.

31. Nous avons regardé la télévision depuis quatre heures.

> **Hint:** Is this a completed action in a "floating block" of time? Do we know when it took place?

32. Tu connais Céleste? Elle est la femme de Babar!

> **Hint:** Can *"elle est"* be followed by an article?

33. Pour devenant musicien, il faut beaucoup jouer.

> **Hint:** Can *"pour"* be followed by the present participle?

34. C'est triste: nous aimerions voyager, mais personne ne va jamais nulle part.

> **Hint:** Can French line up negatives in this way?

35. Nous avons vu de bels animaux au zoo.

> **Hint:** When do you use the form of *"bel, nouvel, vieil"*?

36. Je ne comprends pas ce qui tu me dis!

> **Hint:** Which relative pronoun is correct here? Is it a subject in the relative clause?

37. C'est vrai fabuleux de passer des vacances au soleil!

> **Hint:** How do you form adverbs?

38. Elle va acheter cette petite rouge robe jolie pour la fête.

> **Hint:** Think of the placement of adjectives.

39. Ce sont les gens à qui j'ai parlés hier soir.

> **Hint:** In what situation does the past participle agree?

40. Tu veux bien me donner des fleurs? —Non, je ne veux pas te les donner.

> **Hint:** Is the direct object in the question preceded by *"les"*?

Answers to the previous exercises.

1. L'année prochaine je **nagerai** avec Suzanne.

> **Why?** *"L'année prochaine"* indicates that the action will take place in the future.

2. Si tu avais fait tout ton travail, tu **aurais pu** te coucher tôt.

> **Why?** In *"si"* clauses, when you have the pluperfect on one side, you have the conditional past on the other.

3. Quand nous étions petits, nous **mangions** toujours des Captain Crunch.

> **Why?** Habitual actions in the past are in the imperfect.

4. Tous les jours, je **prends** le train pour aller à mon travail.

> **Why?** Habitual actions in the present are in the present tense.

5. Je ne me marierai pas avant de **finir** cette année scolaire.

> **Why?** All verbs following a preposition – except *"en"* – will be in the infinitive form.

6. Je ne crois pas que tu **aies pris** des notes hier pendant la classe.

> **Why?** *"Croire"* in the negative takes the subjunctive–in this case the past subjunctive because the action of taking notes precedes the believing.

7. Michel m'a dit qu'il **n'irait** pas à la fête demain soir.

> **Why?** This conditional is used to describe an action subsequent to another past action or to a time in the past *(Leçon 5)*.

8. Nous bavardions quand l'alarme d'incendie **a sonné**.

> **Why?** This action interrupts an ongoing action. Both are in the past.

9. Pendant que je **faisais** la cuisine, les enfants sont arrivés.

> **Why?** The "cooking" action is an ongoing action, and the other completed action "interrupts" it.

10. Ça ne vaut pas la peine de te faire tant de soucis. Est-ce que tu n'es pas fatigué de tant **pleurer**?

> **Why?** The preposition *"de"* is followed by an infinitive.

11. Hier, Françoise et Henri **ont traduit** le livre d'anglais en français.

> **Why?** This is a specific event in the past. It takes the *passé composé*, no matter how long it lasted.

12. Je suis si contente que mon fils et ta fille **soient tombés** amoureux!

> **Why?** Adjectives of feeling take the subjunctive, the past subjunctive in this case because the action precedes the comment made about it.

13. Nous **n'avions** pas **fini** nos bagages quand le taxi est arrivé!

> **Why?** The pluperfect indicates that the *"finir"* action began and ended before the taxi arrived.

14. Nous ne doutons pas que tu **aies** un cousin à la Martinique!

> **Why?** The verb *"douter"* takes the subjunctive even in the negative.

15. Ils espèrent que les enfants **viendront** les voir dimanche prochain.

> **Why?** *"Espérer"* does not take the subjunctive. Here the future is necessary because of *"dimanche prochain."*

16. S'il vous plaît, Messieurs, **asseyez**-vous immédiatement!

> **Why?** This is a command; you use the imperative.

17. S'il **pleuvait** maintenant, nous ne pourrions pas nager dans la piscine.

> **Why?** In *"si"* clauses, the present conditional is paired with the imperfect.

18. Si nous avions eu de la chance, notre parti **aurait gagné**.

> **Why?** In *"si"* clauses, the pluperfect is paired with the past conditional on the other.

19. Il faut **poser** beaucoup de questions en classe.

> **Why?** With impersonal expressions, the infinitive is used when the subject is not specific

20. Dans mon dortoir, il n'y a pas un seul élève qui **sache** jouer du piano.

> **Why?** This is a "ghost" antecedent. There could not be such a person.

21. Quand tu **iras** à Paris, tu m'écriras une carte postale.

> **Why?** After *"quand,"* future actions are in the future (unlike English).

22. Il n'est pas poli de parler en **mangeant**.

> **Why?** When *"en"* is followed by a verb, it requires the present participle.

23. Après **avoir vu** le film *Harry Potter* une deuxième fois, nous irons nous coucher.

> **Why?** When *"Après"* is followed by a verb, it requires the past infinitive .

24. Tu te doucheras avant que je **prenne** mon bain puisque nous n'avons qu'une salle de bains.

> **Why?** *"Avant que"* demands the subjunctive.

25. Si elles **avaient** de l'argent, elles iraient à New York pour voir Justin Bieber.

> **Why?** In *"si"* clauses, the present conditional is paired with the imperfect.

26. Je cherche une personne qui me **comprenne**.

> **Why?** "Ghost antecedent" — this person may or may not exist. Use the subjunctive!

27. Mes chers enfants, **soyez** sages pendant que je ne serai pas là.

> **Why?** This is a command; use the imperative.

28. Quand il arrivera à Pointe-à-Pitre il **aura voyagé** pendant dix-huit heures.

> **Why?** Both actions are future, but one clearly precedes the other.

29. J'aurais préféré que tu **fasses** ce travail avec moi.

Why?	*"Préférer"* needs the subjunctive.

30. Les enfants sont heureux de vous **voir**.

Why?	The preposition *"de"* here requires the infinitive.

31. Nous avons regardé la télévision **pendant** quatre heures.

32. Tu connais Céleste? **C'est** la femme de Babar!

33. Pour **devenir** musicien, il faut beaucoup jouer.

34. C'est triste: nous aimerions voyager, mais personne ne va jamais nulle part
(This sentence is correct!)

35. Nous avons vu de **beaux** animaux au zoo.

36. Je ne comprends pas ce **que** tu me dis!

37. C'est **vraiment** fabuleux de passer des vacances au soleil!

38. Elle va acheter une **jolie petite** robe **rouge** pour la fête.

39. Ce sont les gens à qui j'ai **parlé** hier soir.

40. Tu veux bien me donner des fleurs? –Non, je ne veux pas t'**en** donner.

FÉLICITATIONS!
YOU'VE BROKEN THE FRENCH BARRIER!

Le hockey à Montréal

e vous apprends rien (apprendre): I teach you
thing (to teach)

ous disant (dire): by saying (to you)

occupe (occuper): (it) takes (to take)

eur: heart

bécois: people from Quebec

enfants (un, une enfant): children

jouent (jouer): (they) play (to play)

uelles (une ruelle): alleyways

ant (porter): wearing (to wear)

tunique: tunic

naillot: shirt, jersey

a ancrée: well established

trouve (trouver): we can find (trouver)

table: real

comparent (comparer): (they) compare
compare)

ne: even

rassemble (rassembler): that gather
gather)

que année (une année): each year

centaines (une centaine): hundreds

milliers (un millier): thousands

porters (masc): fans

ur de: around

eux rivés (un œil): eyes riveted on

équipes (une équipe): teams

latrices (fondatrice): founding

époque: time

oueur: player

était (être): (he) was (to be)

é: pride

identifiaient (identifier): they identified
mselves (to identify)

ement: strongly

nonde: world

iné: dominated

onstituait (constituer): (it) was (to be)

revanche: revenge

émeutes (une émeute): riots

ont aussi marqué (marquer): (they) also have
luenced (to influence)

noms (un nom): names

gardiens de but: goalkeepers

n'en nommer que certains: to name only
me of them

ur rend encore hommage (rendre): they are
paid tribute (to pay tribute).

urd'hui: today

nt souvent inventé (inventer): they have
en invented (to invent)

veaux (nouveau): new

Je ne vous apprends rien **en vous disant** que le hockey **occupe** une place considérable dans **le cœur** des **Québécois**. L'image habituelle **des enfants** qui **jouent** au hockey dans **les ruelles**, **portant** leur **tunique** ou leur **maillot** des «Canadiens» de Montréal est **bien ancrée** dans l'imaginaire collectif. **On y trouve** un **véritable** phénomène social,

que certains **comparent même** à la ferveur d'un culte, et **qui rassemble chaque année** des **centaines** de **milliers** de supporters **autour de** leur téléviseur, **les yeux rivés** sur les matchs des séries éliminatoires.

Le club des «Canadiens» de Montréal est l'une **des équipes fondatrices** de la Ligue Nationale de Hockey. A l'**époque** de Maurice («Rocket») Richard, **joueur** légendaire, le hockey **était** un symbole de **fierté** pour les Québécois. **Ils s'identifiaient fortement** au succès de l'équipe, dans **un monde dominé** économiquement et politiquement par les Anglophones. Le hockey **constituait** une sorte de **revanche** du peuple québécois. En 1955, la suspension temporaire de Maurice Richard provoque de violentes **émeutes** à Montréal.

Mais d'autres joueurs **ont aussi marqué** l'histoire de ce club. **Les noms des gardiens de but** Jacques Plante, Patrick Roy, ou de Guy Lafleur, Jean Beliveau et Bernard Geoffrion **pour n'en nommer que certains** que tout le monde connaît. **On leur rend encore hommage aujourd'hui** car **ils ont souvent inventé** de **nouveaux** styles et développé ce sport.

Le hockey est **un sujet** si «émotif» qu'il a souvent **tristement** fait **les gros titres** des journaux à cause des émeutes, **des vitrines fracassées, des voitures incendiées par** certains **fêtards** sur **la rue** Ste-Catherine après **les** victoires du club des Canadiens.

Ce club de hockey **tire sa réputation** de son impressionnant nombre de victoires. En 100 **ans** d'existence, **il a remporté** 24 coupes Stanley. C'est l'équipe professionnelle **la plus victorieuse après** les Yankees de New York.

Pourtant, les Montréalais sont aussi **très durs envers** les joueurs ou les entraineurs. **S'ils ne savent pas** répondre aux **énormes attentes** des supporters, **ils sont échangés** ou **congédiés rapidement. Ces dernières années**, les résultats **ont été plutôt décevants** pour l'équipe mais tous **les supporters croisent les doigts** pour que les récentes modifications **au sein de** l'équipe **ramènent** la coupe à Montréal.

un sujet: topic
tristement: sadly
les gros titres (un titre): headlines, front pages
des vitrines fracassées (une vitrine): broken windows
des voitures (une voiture): cars
incendiées par: burnt by
des fêtards (un fêtard): party-men
la rue: street

(il) tire sa réputation de: (he) owns his reputa from (to own)
ans (un an): years
il a remporté (remporter): he has won (to wir
la plus victorieuse: the most victorious
après: after

pourtant: however
très durs (dur): very hard
envers: towards
s'ils ne savent pas (savoir): if they don't know (to know)
répondre à: to answer to
énormes attentes (une attente): huge expectat
ils sont échangés (échanger): they are exchang
congédiés (congédier): fired (to fire)
rapidement: quickly
ces dernières années (une année): in the past few years
(ils) ont été plutôt décevants (être): (they) ha been rather disappointing (to be)
(ils) croisent les doigts: (they) keep their finge crossed
au sein de: inside
ramènent (ramener): to bring back

French Sports Vocabulary - Vocabulaire de sports

archery: le tir à l'arc
biking: le cyclisme
boxing: la boxe
cross-country skiing: le ski de randonnée/fond
diving: la plongée
downhill skiing: le ski de descente/piste
fishing: la pêche
jogging: le jogging
rollerskating: le patin à roulettes, le skating

sailing: la voile
skating: le patinage
skiing: le ski
soccer: le foot(ball)
swimming: la natation
tennis: le tennis
water skiing: le ski nautique
wrestling: la lutte

Hockey Vocabulary | Le Hockey

goalie: gardien de but
opponent: adversaire
rink: patinoire
goal: but, cage
goal: crease territoire de but
hockey stick: crosse de hockey
puck: palet

helmet: casque protecteur
face mask: protecteur facial
glove: gant
skate: patin
to play hockey: jouer au hockey
to check: mettre en échec
to clear the puck: dégager le palet
to score a goal marquer un but
to shoot lancer, tirer

1. Quelle image est-ce que l'auteur utilise pour démontrer l'importance du hockey chez les Québécois?

_____

_____

2. ¿A quoi est-ce que certains comparent la passion québécoise pour le hockey?

_____

3. Qui est Maurice Richard?

_____

4. Que représentait le hockey à l'époque de « Rocket » Richard? Pourquoi?

_____

_____

5. Pourquoi est-ce qu'il y a eu des émeutes à Montréal en 1955?

_____

_____

6. Pourquoi est-ce qu'on rend encore hommage aux grands joueurs du club des Canadiens?

_____

_____

7. Donnez trois raisons négatives pour lesquelles le hockey fait les gros titres des journaux après les victoires du club des Canadiens?

_____

_____

_____

8. En 100 ans d'existence, combien de coupes Stanley est-ce que le club a remporté?

_____

9. Qui est la seule équipe professionnelle plus victorieuse que le club des Canadiens?

_____

_____

10. Pourquoi les entraîneurs et les joueurs sont-ils souvent échangés ou congédiés?

_____

_____

La cuisine sénégalaise

on compare (comparer): we compare (to compare)
autres: other
culinaires (culinaire): culinary
sans doute: certainly
(elle) a subit (subir): (it) has be subjected to (to be sujected to)
étrangères: foreign
une ville: city
ouverte (ouvert): open
sur l'extérieur: to the outside

les recettes (une recette): recipes
(elles) ont tendance à: (they) tend to
céder: to give up, give way
des mets (un mets): dishes, foods
sans renoncer: without giving up
par ailleurs: in addition
(ils) proposent (proposer): (they) offer (to offer)
on trouve (trouver): we find (to find)
souvent: often
pays: countries
y compris: including
valorisant: promoting
disponibles (disponible): available
le marché: market

un peu curieux: a little bit curious
(il) découvrira (decouvrir): (he) will discover (to discover)
une panoplie: range
goûts
des saveurs (une saveur): flavors
un mélange: blend
il trouvera (trouver): he will find (to find)
les femmes (une femme): women
(elles) auront plaisir à (avoir plaisir à): (they) will enjoy (to enjoy)
préparer: to prepare
montrer: to show

bien sûr: of course
fortes (fort): strong
étonner: to surprise
le palais: palate
cela fait partie d: it is part of
le jeu: game
la découverte: discovery
la nouveauté: novelty
(elle) fait place à: (it) makes way for
un attrait: attraction
sans être: without being
tropétrangère (étranger): too foreign
reproduire: to reproduce
le retour: come back
les livres (un livre): books
(ils) aideront (aider): (they) will help (to help)
fières (fier): proud
un savoir-faire: know-how
(elles) seront prêtes: (they) will be ready
vos plats favoris: your favorite dishes

vous n'aurez pas l'occasion: you will not have the chance
quotidienne (quotidien): daily
moins riche: less rich
moins variée (varié): less varied
la gargote: diner, cheap restaurant
pauvreté: povery
cela ne leur permet pas (permettre): it does not allow them (to allow)

Si l'**on compare** la cuisine sénégalaise aux **autres** traditions **culinaires** du continent africain, c'est **sans doute** celle qui **a subit** le plus l'influence de cuisines **étrangères** et traditionnelles, en particulier à Dakar. La capitale du Sénégal est **une ville** multiethnique, multiculturelle et **ouverte sur l'extérieur**.

A Dakar, **les recettes** du terroir **ont tendance à céder** la place à **des m** européens, moyen-orientaux et asiatiques. **Sans renoncer** toutefois aux mo de préparation et de consommation traditionnels, ces plats sont adaptés habitudes culinaires locales. **Par ailleurs,** si les restaurants **proposent** des p sénégalais traditionnels, on trouve aussi **souvent** au menu des plats de différe **pays, y compris** du continent africain (Bénin, Cameroun), **valorisant** ains diversité des produits **disponibles** sur **le marché.**

Le voyageur **un peu curieux découvrira** à Dakar toute **une panoplie** de go de **saveurs** et d'odeurs issus de ce **mélange** de produits locaux et importés. D les provinces sénégalaises, **il trouvera** des plats plus traditionnels, spécifiq à certains terroirs ou ethnies, que **les femmes auront plaisir** à **préparer** p **montrer** à l'étranger leurs talents culinaires et la richesse des produits de l région...

Bien sûr, certains produits aux saveurs **fortes**, à la texture inhabituelle, pourr **étonner le palais** des «toubabs», mais cela **fait partie du jeu** de **la découve** La surprise de la **nouveauté fait** ensuite **place à un attrait** pour une cuis souvent accessible, originale **sans être trop étrangère**, que vous aurez plais **reproduire** de **retour** dans votre pays. **Les livres** de recettes vous y **aideron** les Sénégalaises, **fières** de leurs **savoir-faire**, **seront prêtes** à vous apprend cuisiner **vos plats favoris.**

Vous n'aurez sans doute pas **l'occasion** de découvrir l'alimentation **quotidie** de la grande majorité des Sénégalais, **moins riche** et **moins variée**, que celle restaurant ou de **la gargote**. L'état de pauvreté des familles urbaines et rur **ne leur permet pas** toujours de préparer **deux repas par jour** ni de divers leur alimentation.

Elles se contentent ainsi souvent **d'un bol de riz** ou de **mil**, **agrémenté** **parfois** de quelques **légumes**, **d'un peu de poisson**, **d'un morceau** de **viande à partager entre** les **nombreux** membres de la famille. **Sachez donc** qu'un plat bien **garni** est un privilège, **un cadeau offert** par votre hôtesse en signe d'hospitalité, qu'**il faut savoir apprécier même si** parfois **nos** **habitudes alimentaires** sont très différentes.

LA SAUCE ARACHIDE

La sauce **arachide** est une recette commune à **plusieurs** pays africains dont le Sénégal. Savoureuse, **elle se** **consomme** très régulièrement.

Ingrédients
(pour environ 4 personnes)

- 100g de **pâte** d'arachide
- 2 tomates **fraîches**
- 1 **cuillère** à soupe de pâte de tomates
- 1 kg de **viande** ou **poisson**
- 1-2 **piments**
- 1 **oignon**
- **sel**
- 1 **cube de bouillon de volaille**

Préparation

- **Préchauffer un chaudron** contenant un peu d'**huile** et y placer la viande **découpée en morceaux.**
- **Mettre** l'oignon et les tomates découpés en gros morceaux.
- **Ajouter** le piment, un peu de sel, ainsi que la pâte de tomate.
- Ajouter un peu d'**eau**, **couvrir** et **laisser bouillir** 15 minutes.
- **Diluer** la pâte d'arachide avec un peu d'eau et ajouter dans la préparation.
- **Lorsque** l'huile **commence à se former** à la surface, ajouter le cube de bouillon de volaille.
- Laisser **mijoter** encore quelques minutes.

Servir avec du riz ou des **ignames** pour **un régal assuré ! Écraser** le piment pour **donner** un peu plus de **piquant** au **mélange selon votre goût!**

Bon appétit !

deux repas (un repas): two meals
par jour: per day

elles se contentent de (se contenter de): they content themselves with (to content oneself with)
un bol de riz: a bowl of rice
le mil: millet
agrémenté: accompanied
parfois: sometimes
les légumes (un légume): vegetables
un peu de: a little
le poisson: fish
un morceau: piece
la viande: meat
à partager: to share
entre: between
nombreux: numerous
(vous) sachez (savoir): know (to know)
garni: filled, full
un cadeau: gift
offert (offrir): offered (to offer)
il faut savoir (falloir): it is necessary to know (to be necessary)
apprécier: to appreciate
même si: even if
nos habitudes (une habitude): our habits
alimentaires (alimentaire): dietary

une arachide: peanut
plusieurs: several
(elle) se consomme (consommer): (it) is consumed (to consume)
très savoureuse (savoureux): very tasty
environ: about

la pâte: paste
fraîches (frais): fresh
une cuillère: spoon
viande: meat
poisson: fish
des piments (un piment): hot peppers
un oignon: onion
le sel: salt
cube de bouillon de volaille: chicken bouillon cube

préchauffé: preheate
un chaudron: cooking pot
huile (fem.): oil
découpé: cut
en morceaux: in pieces
mettre: put
ajouter: add
l'eau (fem.): water
couvrir: to cover
laisser bouillir: to let boil
diluer: to dilute
lorsque: when
(cela) commence à (commencer): (it) starts to (to start)
se former: to form
mijoter: simmer
des ignames (un igname): yams
un régal: delight, treat
assuré: guaranteed
écraser: mash
donner: to give
piquant: hot, spicy
un mélange: blend
votre goût (le goût): your taste

1. En quoi la cuisine sénégalaise est-elle différente par rapport aux autres traditions culinaires africaines?

_____

_____

2. Quelle est la capitale du Sénégal?

_____

3. Quelles sont les trois influences étrangères sur la cuisine sénégalaise?

_____

_____

4. Selon l'article, est-ce que les Sénégalaises prépareraient des plats traditionnels pour des touristes pour leur montrer leurs talents culinaires?

_____

_____

5. Que signifie le mot « toubab »?

_____

6. Comment est l'alimentation quotidienne de la grande majorité des Sénégalais?

_____

_____

7. Décrivez un repas quotidien pour la majorité des Sénégalais.

_____

_____

8. Où se consomme la sauce arachide?

_____

9. Donnez quatre ingrédients de la sauce arachide.

_____

_____

10. Avec quoi est-ce qu'on doit servir la sauce arachide pour « un régal assuré » selon l'article?

_____

Le rap français
par Matt Westman

...ître): born
...nées 70: the seventies
...t devenu (devenir): (it) has become
...ecome)
...ue: known
...ite: produced
...nde entier: whole world
...volué (évoluer): (it) has evolved
...volve)
...pu trouver (pouvoir): (it) could find (can)
...e: as well as
... but also
...oyen d'expression: means of expression
...: even
...s (un jeune): youth
...uartiers défavorisés: underprivileged
...ighborhoods
...ntres urbains: urban centers

...s célèbre: the most famous
...s: since
...strer: to record
...: release
...se trouve (se trouver): (it) is
...e)
...usions (une allusion): his allusions
...x de mots (un jeu de mot): his wordplays

...anson: song
...uvre: works
...ivain: writer
...n: name
...adeleines: shell-shaped cookies
...file (filer): (it) flies by
...y by)
...tesse: at the speed
...lté: ability
...ser: to surpass
...llent à la peau (coller à la peau): which are
...k with (to be stuck with)
...lisant: by using
...gue: language

Né aux Etats-Unis dans le Bronx dans **les années 70**, le rap **est devenu** une forme musicale **connue** et **produite** dans **le monde entier**. Le genre américain **a évolué** et son alter-ego français **a pu trouver** une identité unique dans le contexte français. En France, **comme** aux Etats-Unis, le rap est **aussi un moyen d'expression** et **même** un type de musique de résistance pour certains **jeunes** issus **des quartiers défavorisés des centres urbains**.

Aux Etats-Unis, le rappeur **le plus célèbre** du monde francophone s'appelle MC Solaar. **Depuis** son premier succès en 1990 avec le single, « Bouge de là, » Solaar, d'origine sénégalaise, continue d'**enregistrer** des disques à succès : son septième et dernier disque en date, Chapitre 7, est **sorti** en 2007. La richesse unique des textes de Solaar **se trouve** dans la force de **ses allusions** et de **ses jeux de mots**.

Dans sa **chanson** « Obsolète, » Solaar fait référence à une des grandes **œuvres** de la littéraire française du XXème siècle, A la recherche du temps perdu de Marcel Proust en jouant avec les noms de l'**écrivain** et **le nom** du pilote automobile français du Formule 1, Alain Prost : « L'allégorie **des madeleines file, à la vitesse** de Prost. » Cet exemple illustre bien **la faculté** du rap à **dépasser** les stéréotypes de violence et de vulgarité **qui collent à la peau en utilisant** la richesse de **la langue** et de la culture françaises.

Dans les années 90, quand la dichotomie East/West **se développe** dans le rap américain, deux centres du rap français **naissent** avec le succès de deux groupes : IAM de Marseille et Suprême NTM de Paris. Avec MC Solaar, les deux groupes **restent toujours** les plus grands noms de l'histoire du rap.

Même si ces artistes **sortent** toujours des albums, le rap d'**aujourd'hui est dominé** par de **nouveaux** artistes qui constituent une nouvelle génération de rappeurs. La majorité d'entre eux sont français d'origine **étrangère**. Ces origines i**mmigrées irriguent** cette **communauté** et expliquent la richesse du rap français **contemporain**. On peut voir les influences culturelles dans la musique, les styles **vestimentaires** et le langage.

Plus récemment, quelques artistes français **ont renouvelé** un style **proche** du rap **venant des** Etats-Unis, le slam, **un mélange** de textes poétiques **récités avec ou sans** musique, y **intégrant** des éléments de traditions littéraires françaises. **C'est le cas, entre autres**, de Grand Corps Malade et d'Abd Al Malik **qui connaissent un succès grandissant grâce à** la qualité de leurs textes et de leur diction.

Ainsi, et **malgré** les stéréotypes bien connus, le rap tout comme le slam sont **des atouts** considérables pour l'**enseignement** secondaire du français **tant ils peuvent se rapprocher** des univers musicaux **des élèves tout en montrant** une nouvelle facette, **souvent plus actuelle**, de la langue et de la culture françaises.

1. Qu'est-ce que le rap?

_____

2. Qui est MC Solaar?

_____

3. A quelle oeuvre littéraire MC Solaar fait-il référence dans sa chanson « Obsolète »?

_____

4. Que représente la parole par rapport aux stéréotypes du rap?

_____

_____

5. Quels sont les deux groupes de rap français les plus connus des années 90 en France?

_____

6. D'où vient la nouvelle génération de rappeurs français?

_____

_____

7. Où peut-on voir les influences culturelles dans le rap français d'aujourd'hui?

_____

_____

8. Qu'est-ce que le slam?

_____

9. Comment s'appellent les deux artistes du slam français mentionnés dans le texte?

_____

10. Pourquoi est-ce que le rap peut servir à l'enseignement de la langue française?

_____

_____

CONJUGAISONS DE PARLER, CHOISIR ET VENDRE

CONJUGATIONS OF PARL**ER**, CHOIS**IR** AND VEND**RE**

PRÉSENT (present) (I speak, etc.)

	parler	choisir	vendre
je (I)	je parle	je choisis	je vends
tu (you)	tu parles	tu choisis	tu vends
il, elle (he, she)	il parle	il choisit	il vend
nous (we)	nous parlons	nous choisissons	nous vendons
vous (you)	vous parlez	vous choisissez	vous vendez
ils, elles (they)	ils parlent	ils choisissent	ils vendent

IMPARFAIT (imperfect) (I used to speak, I was speaking, etc.)

je parlais	je choisissais	je vendais
tu parlais	tu choisissais	tu vendais
il parlait	il choisissait	il vendait
nous parlions	nous choisissions	nous vendions
vous parliez	vous choisissiez	vous vendiez
ils parlaient	ils choisissaient	ils vendaient

FUTUR (future) (I will speak, etc.)

je parlerai	je choisirai	je vendrai
tu parleras	tu choisiras	tu vendras
il parlera	il choisira	il vendra
nous parlerons	nous choisirons	nous vendrons
vous parlerez	vous choisirez	vous vendrez
ils parleront	ils choisiront	ils vendront

CONDITIONNEL (conditional) (I would speak, etc.)

je parlerais	je choisirais	je vendrais
tu parlerais	tu choisirais	tu vendrais
il parlerait	il choisirait	il vendrait
nous parlerions	nous choisirions	nous vendrions
vous parleriez	vous choisiriez	vous vendriez
ils parleraient	ils choisiraient	ils vendraient

SUBJONCTIF (present subjunctive)

que je parle	que je choisisse	que je vende
que tu parles	que tu choisisses	que tu vendes
qu'il parle	qu'il choisisse	qu'il vende
que nous parlions	que nous choisissions	que nous vendions
que vous parliez	que vous choisissiez	que vous vendiez
qu'ils parlent	qu'ils choisissent	qu'ils vendent

IMPÉRATIF (imperative) (Speak!)

tu (you)	Parle!	Choisis!	Vends!
nous (we)	Parlons!	Choisissons!	Vendons!
vous (you)	Parlez!	Choisissez!	Vendez!

PARTICIPE PRÉSENT (present participle) (speaking)

parlant	choisissant	vendant

PARTICIPE PASSÉ (past participle) (spoken)

parlé	choisi	vendu

PASSÉ COMPOSÉ (past tense) (I spoke [I have spoken])

j'ai parlé	j'ai choisi	j'ai vendu
tu as parlé	tu as choisi	tu as vendu
il a parlé	il a choisi	il a vendu
nous avons parlé	nous avons choisi	nous avons vendu
vous avez parlé	vous avez choisi	vous avez vendu
ils ont parlé	ils ont choisi	ils ont vendu

PLUS-QUE-PARFAIT (pluperfect or past perfect) (I had spoken, etc.)

j'avais parlé	j'avais choisi	j'avais vendu
tu avais parlé	tu avais choisi	tu avais vendu
il avait parlé	il avait choisi	il avait vendu
nous avions parlé	nous avions choisi	nous avions vendu
vous aviez parlé	vous aviez choisi	vous aviez vendu
ils avaient parlé	ils avaient choisi	ils avaient vendu

FUTUR ANTÉRIEUR (future perfect) (I will have spoken, etc.)

j'aurai parlé	j'aurai choisi	j'aurai vendu
tu auras parlé	tu auras choisi	tu auras vendu
il aura parlé	il aura choisi	il aura vendu
nous aurons parlé	nous aurons choisi	nous aurons vendu
vous aurez parlé	vous aurez choisi	vous aurez vendu
ils auront parlé	ils auront choisi	ils auront vendu

CONDITIONNEL PASSÉ (past conditional) (I would have spoken, etc.)

j'aurais parlé	j'aurais choisi	j'aurais vendu
tu aurais parlé	tu aurais choisi	tu aurais vendu
il aurait parlé	il aurait choisi	il aurait vendu
nous aurions parlé	nous aurions choisi	nous aurions vendu
vous auriez parlé	vous auriez choisi	vous auriez vendu
ils auraient parlé	ils auraient choisi	ils auraient vendu

SUBJONCTIF PASSÉ (past subjunctive)

que j'aie parlé	que j'aie choisi	que j'ai vendu
que tu aies parlé	que tu aies choisi	que tu aies vendu
qu'il ait parlé	qu'il ait choisi	qu'il ait vendu
que nous ayons parlé	que nous ayons choisi	que nous ayons vendu
que vous ayez parlé	que vous ayez choisi	que vous ayez vendu
qu'ils aient parlé	qu'ils aient choisi	qu'ils aient vendu

CONJUGAISONS DE VERBES IRRÉGULIERS

TABLE DE VERBES IRRÉGULIERS

INFINITIF ET PARTICIPE PASSÉ/PRÉSENT	INDICATIF				CONDITIONNEL	SUBJONCTIF
	Présent	Imparfait	Passé composé	Futur	Présent	Présent
ALLER (to go) allé allant	je vais tu vas on/il/elle va nous allons vous allez ils/elles vont	allais allais allait allions alliez allaient	suis allé(e) es allé(e) est allé(e) sommes allé(e)s êtes allé(e)s sont allé(e)s	irai iras ira irons irez iront	irais irais irait irions iriez iraient	aille ailles aille allions alliez aillent
ASSEOIR (S') (to sit) assis asseyant	je m'assieds tu t'assieds il/elle s'assied nous asseyons vous asseyez ils/elles s'asseyent	asseyais asseyais asseyait asseyions asseyiez asseyaient	suis assis(e) es assis(e) est assis(e) sommes assis(e)s êtes assis(e)(s) sont assis(e)s	assiérai assiéras assiéra assiérons assiérez assiéront	assiérais assiérais assiérait assiérions assiériez assiéraient	asseye asseyes asseye asseyions asseyiez asseyent
AVOIR (to have) eu ayant	j'ai tu as il/elle a nous avons vous avez ils/elles ont	avais avais avait avions aviez avaient	ai eu as eu a eu avons eu avez eu ont eu	aurai auras aura aurons aurez auront	aurais aurais aurait aurions auriez auraient	aie aies ait ayons ayez aient
BOIRE (to drink) bu buvant	je bois tu bois il/elle boit nous buvons vous buvez ils/elles boivent	buvais buvais buvait buvions buviez buvaient	ai bu as bu a bu avons bu avez bu ont bu	boirai boiras boira boirons boirez boiront	boirais boirais boirait boirions boiriez boiraient	boive boives boive buvions buviez boivent
COMPRENDRE (to understand) compris comprenant	je comprends tu comprends il/elle comprend nous comprenons vous comprenez ils/elles comprennent	comprenais comprenais comprenait comprenions compreniez comprenaient	ai compris as compris a compris avons compris avez compris ont compris	comprendrai comprendras comprendra comprendrons comprendrez comprendront	comprendrais comprendrais comprendrait comprendrions comprendriez comprendraient	comprenne comprennes comprenne comprenions compreniez comprennent
CONDUIRE (to drive) conduit conduisant	je conduis tu conduis il/elle conduit nous conduisons vous conduisez ils/elles conduisent	conduisais conduisais conduisait conduisions conduisiez conduisaient	ai conduit as conduit a conduit avons conduit avez conduit ont conduit	conduirai conduiras conduira conduirons conduirez conduiront	conduirais conduirais conduirait conduirions conduiriez conduiraient	conduise conduises conduise conduisions conduisiez conduisent
CONNAÎTRE (to know) connu connaissant	je connais tu connais il/elle connaît nous connaissons vous connaissez ils/elles connaissent	connaissais connaissais connaissait connaissions connaissiez connaissaient	ai connu as connu a connu avons connu avez connu ont connu	connaîtrai connaîtras connaîtra connaîtrons connaîtrez connaîtront	connaîtrais connaîtrais connaîtrait connaîtrions connaîtriez connaîtraient	connaisse connaisses connaisse connaissions connaissiez connaissent

INFINITIF ET PARTICIPE PASSÉ/PRÉSENT	INDICATIF				CONDITIONNEL	SUBJONCTIF
	Présent	**Imparfait**	**Passé composé**	**Futur**	**Présent**	**Présent**
COURIR (to run) couru courant	je cours tu cours il/elle court nous courons vous courez ils/elles courent	courais courais courait courions couriez couraient	ai couru as couru a couru avons couru avez couru ont couru	courrai courras courra courrons courrez courront	courrais courrais courrait courrions courriez courraient	coure coures coure courions couriez courent
CRAINDRE (to fear, to be afraid of) craint craignant	je crains tu crains il/elle craint nous craignons vous craignez ils/elles craignent	craignais craignais craignait craignions craigniez craignaient	ai craint as craint a craint avons craint avez craint ont craint	craindrai craindras craindra craindrons craindrez craindront	craindrais craindrais craindrait craindrions craindriez craindraient	craigne craignes craigne craignions craigniez craignent
CROIRE (to believe) cru croyant	je crois tu crois il/elle croit nous croyons vous croyez ils/elles croient	croyais croyais croyait croyions croyiez croyaient	ai cru as cru a cru avons cru avez cru ont cru	croirai croiras croira croirons croirez croiront	croirais croirais croirait croirions croiriez croiraient	croie croies croie croyions croyiez croient
DEVOIR (to have to, to be obliged to) dû devant	je dois tu dois il/elle doit nous devons vous devez ils/elles doivent	devais devais devait devions deviez devaient	ai dû as dû a dû avons dû avez dû ont dû	devrai devras devra devrons devrez devront	devrais devrais devrait devrions devriez devraient	doive doives doive devions deviez doivent
DIRE (to say) dit disant	je dis tu dis il/elle dit nous disons vous dites ils/elles disent	disais disais disait disions disiez disaient	ai dit as dit a dit avons dit avez dit ont dit	dirai diras dira dirons direz diront	dirais dirais dirait dirions diriez diraient	dise dises dise disions disiez disent
DORMIR (to sleep) dormi dormant	je dors tu dors il/elle dort nous dormons vous dormez ils/elles dorment	dormais dormais dormait dormions dormiez dormaient	ai dormi as dormi a dormi avons dormi avez dormi ont dormi	dormirai dormiras dormira dormirons dormirez dormiront	dormirais dormirais dormirait dormirions dormiriez dormiraient	dorme dormes dorme dormions dormiez dorment
ÉCRIRE (to write) écrit écrivant	j'écris tu écris il/elle écrit nous écrivons vous écrivez ils/elles écrivent	écrivais écrivais écrivait écrivions écriviez écrivaient	ai écrit as écrit a écrit avons écrit avez écrit ont écrit	écrirai écriras écrira écrirons écrirez écriront	écrirais écrirais écrirait écririons écririez écriraient	écrive écrives écrive écrivions écriviez écrivent

INFINITIF ET PARTICIPE PASSÉ/PRÉSENT	INDICATIF				CONDITIONNEL	SUBJONCTIF
	Présent	Imparfait	Passé composé	Futur	Présent	Présent
ÊTRE (to be) été étant	je suis tu es il/elle est nous sommes vous êtes ils/elles sont	étais étais était étions étiez étaient	ai été as été a été avons été avez été ont été	serai seras sera serons serez seront	serais serais serait serions seriez seraient	sois sois soit soyons soyez soient
FAIRE (to do, to make) fait faisant	je fais tu fais il/elle fait nous faisons vous faites ils/elles font	faisais faisais faisait faisions faisiez faisaient	ai fait as fait a fait avons fait avez fait ont fait	ferai feras fera ferons ferez feront	ferais ferais ferait ferions feriez feraient	fasse fasses fasse fassions fassiez fassent
LIRE (to read) lu lisant	je lis tu lis il/elle lit nous lisons vous lisez ils/elles lisent	lisais lisais lisait lisions lisiez lisaient	ai lu as lu a lu avons lu avez lu ont lu	lirai liras lira lirons lirez liront	lirais lirais lirait lirions liriez liraient	lise lises lise lisions lisiez lisent
METTRE (to put) mis mettant	je mets tu mets il/elle met nous mettons vous mettez ils/elles mettent	mettais mettais mettait mettions mettiez mettaient	ai mis as mis a mis avons mis avez mis ont mis	mettrai mettras mettra mettrons mettrez mettront	mettrais mettrais mettrait mettrions mettriez mettraient	mette mettes mette mettions mettiez mettent
MOURIR (to die) mort mourant	je meurs tu meurs il/elle meurt nous mourons vous mourez ils/elles meurent	mourais mourais mourait mourions mouriez mouraient	suis mort(e) es mort(e) est mort(e) sommes mort(e)s êtes mort(e)(s) sont mort(e)s	mourrai mourras mourra mourrons mourrez mourront	mourrais mourrais mourrait mourrions mourriez mourraient	meure meures meure mourions mouriez meurent
OUVRIR (to open) ouvert ouvrant	j'ouvre tu ouvres il/elle ouvre nous ouvrons vous ouvrez ils/elles ouvrent	ouvrais ouvrais ouvrait ouvrions ouvriez ouvraient	ai ouvert as ouvert a ouvert avons ouvert avez ouvert ont ouvert	ouvrirai ouvriras ouvrira ouvrirons ouvrirez ouvriront	ouvrirais ouvrirais ouvrirait ouvririons ouvririez ouvriraient	ouvre ouvres ouvre ouvrions ouvriez ouvrent
PARTIR (to leave, to go away) parti partant	je pars tu pars il/elle part nous partons vous partez ils/elles partent	partais partais partait partions partiez partaient	suis parti(e) es parti(e) est parti(e) sommes parti(e)s êtes parti(e)(s) sont parti(e)s	partirai partiras partira partirons partirez partiront	partirais partirais partirait partirions partiriez partiraient	parte partes parte partions partiez partent

INFINITIF ET PARTICIPE PASSÉ/PRÉSENT	INDICATIF				CONDITIONNEL	SUBJONCTIF
	Présent	Imparfait	Passé composé	Futur	Présent	Présent
PEINDRE (to paint) peint peignant	je peins tu peins il/elle peint nous peignons vous peignez ils/elles peignent	peignais peignais peignait peignions peigniez peignaient	ai peint as peint a peint avons peint avez peint ont peint	peindrai peindras peindra peindrons peindrez peindront	peindrais peindrais peindrait peindrions peindriez peindraient	peigne peignes peigne peignions peigniez peignent
POUVOIR (to be able to) pu pouvant	je peux, puis tu peux il/elle peut nous pouvons vous pouvez ils/elles peuvent	pouvais pouvais pouvait pouvions pouviez pouvaient	ai pu as pu a pu avons pu avez pu ont pu	pourrai pourras pourra pourrons pourrez pourront	pourrais pourrais pourrait pourrions pourriez pourraient	puisse puisses puisse puissions puissiez puissent
PRENDRE (to take) pris prenant	je prends tu prends il/elle prend nous prenons vous prenez ils/elles prennent	prenais prenais prenait prenions preniez prenaient	ai pris as pris a pris avons pris avez pris ont pris	prendrai prendras prendra prendrons prendrez prendront	prendrais prendrais prendrait prendrions prendriez prendraient	prenne prennes prenne prenions preniez prennent
PROMETTRE (to promise) promis promettant	je promets tu promets il/elle promet nous promettons vous promettez ils/elles promettent	promettais promettais promettait promettions promettiez promettaient	ai promis as promis a promis avons promis avez promis ont promis	promettrai promettras promettra promettrons promettrez promettront	promettrais promettrais promettrait promettrions promettriez promettraient	promette promettes promette promettions promettiez promettent
RECEVOIR (to receive) reçu recevant	je reçois tu reçois il/elle reçoit nous recevons vous recevez ils/elles reçoivent	recevais recevais recevait recevions receviez recevaient	ai reçu as reçu a reçu avons reçu avez reçu ont reçu	recevrai recevras recevra recevrons recevrez recevront	recevrais recevrais recevrait recevrions recevriez recevraient	reçoive reçoives reçoive recevions receviez reçoivent
SAVOIR (to know) su sachant	je sais tu sais il/elle sait nous savons vous savez ils/elles savent	savais savais savait savions saviez savaient	ai su as su a su avons su avez su ont su	saurai sauras saura saurons saurez sauront	saurais saurais saurait saurions sauriez sauraient	sache saches sache sachions sachiez sachent
SERVIR (to serve) servi servant	je sers tu sers il/elle sert nous servons vous servez ils/elles servent	servais servais servait servions serviez servaient	ai servi(e) as servi(e) a servi(e) avons servi(e)s avez servi(e)(s) ont servi(e)s	servirai serviras servira servirons servirez serviront	servirais servirais servirait servirions serviriez serviraient	serve serves serve servions serviez servent

INFINITIF ET PARTICIPE PASSÉ/PRÉSENT	INDICATIF				CONDITIONNEL	SUBJONCTIF
	Présent	Imparfait	Passé composé	Futur	Présent	Présent
SORTIR (to go out) sorti sortant	je sors tu sors il/elle sort nous sortons vous sortez ils/elles sortent	sortais sortais sortait sortions sortiez sortaient	suis sorti(e) es sorti(e) est sorti(e) sommes sorti(e)s êtes sorti(e)(s) sont sorti(e)s	sortirai sortiras sortira sortirons sortirez sortiront	sortirais sortirais sortirait sortirions sortiriez sortiraient	sorte sortes sorte sortions sortiez sortent
TENIR (to hold) tenu tenant	je tiens tu tiens il/elle tient nous tenons vous tenez ils/elles tiennent	tenais tenais tenait tenions teniez tenaient	ai tenu as tenu a tenu avons tenu avez tenu ont tenu	tiendrai tiendras tiendra tiendrons tiendrez tiendront	tiendrais tiendrais tiendrait tiendrions tiendriez tiendraient	tienne tiennes tienne tenions teniez tiennent
VENIR (to come) venu venant	je viens tu viens il/elle vient nous venons vous venez ils/elles viennent	venais venais venait venions veniez venaient	suis venu(e) es venu(e) est venu(e) sommes venu(e)s êtes venu(e)(s) sont venu(e)s	viendrai viendras viendra viendrons viendrez viendront	viendrais viendrais viendrait viendrions viendriez viendraient	vienne viennes vienne venions veniez viennent
VOIR (to see) vu voyant	je vois tu vois il/elle voit nous voyons vous voyez ils/elles voient	voyais voyais voyait voyions voyiez voyaient	ai vu as vu a vu avons vu avez vu ont vu	verrai verras verra verrons verrez verront	verrais verrais verrait verrions verriez verraient	voie voies voie voyions voyiez voient
VOULOIR (to want) voulu voulant	je veux tu veux il/elle veut nous voulons vous voulez ils/elles veulent	voulais voulais voulait voulions vouliez voulaient	ai voulu as voulu a voulu avons voulu avez voulu ont voulu	voudrai voudras voudra voudrons voudrez voudront	voudrais voudrais voudrait voudrions voudriez voudraient	veuille veuilles veuille voulions vouliez veuillent

DICTIONNAIRE
FRANÇAIS-ANGLAIS

DICTIONNAIRE FRANÇAIS-ANGLAIS

(Bold print indicates new vocabulary presented in the vocabulary lists at the beginning of each lesson.)

A

à . . . . .at, to
à côté de . . . . .next to
à droite . . . . .to the right
à gauche . . . . .to the left
à l'aise . . . . . . .comfortable (for people)
à l'étranger . . . . .abroad
à travers . . . . .across
abandonner . . . .**to abandon**
abîmer . . . .**to damage, to ruin**
aboyer . . . .**to bark**
absent . . . . .absent
accident (l') (m.) . . . . .accident
accompagner . . . . .to accompany
accuser . . . .**to accuse**
acheter .to buy
acquérir . . . .**to acquire**
acteur/actrice (un/une) . . . .actor/actress
actif/active . . . . .active
actuel/actuelle . . . .**current**
addition (l') (f.) . .bill (e.g., in a restaurant)
admettre . . . . .to admit
admirateur/admiratrice (un/une) admirer
adolescent/adolescente (l')
(l'ado) (m./f.) . . . . .teenager
adorer . . . . .to adore
adresse (l') (f.) . . . . .address
adversaire (l') (m./f.) . . . . . . .opponent
adverse . . . . .opposite
aéroport (l') (m.) . . . . airport
affaires (les) (f.) . . . .**things,**
belongings, business
affection (l') (f.) . . . .**affection**
affectueux/affectueuse . . . . .affectionate
affiche (l') (f.) . . . . .poster
affreusement . . . . .terribly
affreux/affreuse . . . . .horrible
agaçant/agaçante . . . .**annoying**
agacé/agacée . . . . .annoyed
âgé/âgée .old
âge (l') (m.) . . . .**age**
agence de voyages (l') (f.)
. . . . .travel agency
agent de police (l') (m.),
(un/une) policier/policière . . .policeman
agneau (l') (m.) . . . . .lamb
aider .to help
aigu/aiguë . . . .**sharp**
ail (l') (m.) . . . . .garlic
aile (l') (f.) . . . .**wing**
aimable . . . . .pleasant
aimer . . . . .to like, to love
aimer mieux . . . . .to prefer
ajouter . . . .**to add**
alcool (l') (m.) . . . . .alcohol
algèbre (l') (f.) . . . . .algebra

aller . . . . .to go
aller à bicyclette . . . . . .to ride a bicycle
(faire du vélo)
aller à l'étranger . . . . .to go abroad
aller à la campagne . .to go to the country
aller à la montagne . . . . . . .to go to the
mountains
aller à pied . . . . .to walk
aller en avion . . . . .to fly
aller en train . . . . .to take a train
aller en voiture . . . . .to drive
aller au bord de la mer . . . . .to go to the
seaside
aller-retour (l') (m.) . . . .round trip ticket
aller simple (l') (m.) . . . . .one way ticket
aller voir . . . .**to visit someone**
allumer . . . .**to light,**
to turn on (electricity)
alors . . . . .then
amant/amante (l') (m./f.) . . . .**lover**
ambition (l') (f.) . . . . .ambition
amer/amère . . . .**bitter**
ami/amie (l') (m./f.) . . . . .friend
amitié (l') (f.) . . . .**friendship**
amour (l') (m.) . . . . .love
amoureux/amoureuse . . . .**in love**
amoureux/ . . . . .in love (with)
amoureuse (de)
ampoule (une) . . . . .a light bulb
amusant/amusante . . . .**amusing**
amuser . . . . to amuse
amuser (s') . . . .**to enjoy, to have**
a good time
analyste (un/une) . . . . .analyst
ananas (l') (m.) . . . . pineapple
ancien/ancienne . . . . . . .ancient, old
anglais/anglaise . . . .**English**
ange (l') (m.) . . . . .angel
animation . . . . . .animation, excitement
année (l') (f.) . . . . .year
anniversaire (l') (m.) . . . . .birthday,
anniversary
annoncer . . . . .to announce
antipathique . . .unattractive (as a person)
août .August
apparaître . . . .**to appear**
appareil (l') (m.) . . . . .machine
appareil photo (l') (m.) . . . . . . .camera
appartement (l') (m.) . . . . . . .apartment
appartenir à . . . .**to belong to**
appeler . . . . .to call
appeler (s') . . . . .to be called
applaudissement (l') (m.) . . . .applause
applaudir . . . . .to applaud
apporter . . . . .to bring
apprendre par cœur . .**to learn by heart**
appuyer (s') . . . .**to lean**

après . . . . .after
après-midi (l') (m./f.) . . . . . . .afternoon
arbitre (l') (m.) . . . . .referee
arbre (l') (m.) . . . . .tree
architecte (un/une) . . . . .architect
argent (l') (m.) . . . . .money
arracher . . . .**to tear out, to pull out**
arrêter . . . .**to stop**
arrière-grand-mère
(l') (f.) . . . . .great-grandmother
arrière-grand-père
(l') (m.) . . . . .great-grandfather
arrivée (l') (f.) . . . . .arrival
arriver . . . .**to arrive, to happen**
arrogant/arrogante . . . .**arrogant**
art (l') (m.) . . . . .art
artichaut (l') (m.) . . . . .artichoke
ascenseur (l') (m.) . . . . .elevator
asperge (l') (f.) . . . . .asparagus
aspirateur (l') (m.) . . . .vacuum cleaner
asseoir .to sit
asseoir (s') . . . . .to sit down
assez (de) . . . . .enough
assiette (l') (f.) . . . . .plate
assis .seated
assister à . . . .**to attend**
associer . . . . .to associate
attacher . . . . .to attach, to tie
attaquer . . . . .to attack
atteindre . . . .**to reach**
attendre . . . .**to wait for**
attendre à (s') . . . .**to expect**
attentif/attentive . . . .**attentive**
attirer . . . .**to attract**
attitude (l') (f.) . . . .**attitude**
attraper . . . . .to catch
au milieu de . . . . .in the middle of
au-dessous de . . . . .below
aube (l') (f.) . . . .**dawn**
aubergine (l') (f.) . . . . .eggplant
aucun/aucune (adj.) . . . . .no
augmenter . . . .**to increase**
aujourd'hui . . . . .today
aussi . . . . .also
aussitôt que . . . . .as soon as
autant . . . . .as much
autant que . . . . .as much as
auteur (l') (m.) . . . . .author
autobus (l') (m.) . . . . bus
automne (l') (m.) . . . . .autumn
autorisation (l') (f.) . . . .**permission**
autorité (l') (f.) . . . .**authority**
autoroute (l') (f.) . . . .**freeway, highway**
autre . . . .**other**
autruche (l') (f.) . . . . .ostrich
avant (de) . . . . .before
avantage (l') (m.) . . . .**advantage**

avare (l') (m.) . . . . .miser	*belle-sœur (la)* . . . . .sister-in-law	*but (le)* . . . .**aim, goal**
avertir . . . .**to warn**	*besoin (le)* . . . . .need	
avec . . . . .with	***bête*** . . . . **foolish, silly, stupid**	
avenue (l') (f.) . . . . .avenue	*bêtise (la)* . . . . .stupid action	
aveugle . . . .**blind**	*bibliothécaire (le/la)* . . . . .librarian	

avion (l') (m.) . . . . .airplane	*bibliothèque (la)* . . . . .library	*cachemire (le)* . . . . .cashmere
aviron (l') (m.) . . . . .rowing	*bicyclette (aller à)* . . . . .to ride a bicycle	*cadavre (le)* . . . . .corpse
avis (l') (m.) . . . . .opinion	(*faire du vélo*)	*cadeau (le)* . . . . .present
avocat/avocate (un/une) . . . . . . .lawyer	*bien* . . . . .well	***caché/cachée*** . . . .**hidden**
avoir . . . . .to have	*bien sûr* . . . . .of course	***cacher*** . . . .**to hide (something)**
avoir besoin de . . . . .to need	*bientôt* . . . . .soon	*café (le)* . . . . .coffee
avoir des ennuis . . . .**to have problems**	*bière (la)* .beer	*cafétéria (la)* . . . . .cafeteria
avoir envie (de) . . . .to want, to desire	***billet (le)*** . . . .**ticket**	*cage (la)* .cage
avoir faim . . . . .to be hungry	*biologie (la)* . . . . .biology	*calendrier (le)* . . . . .calendar
avoir honte (de) . . . . .to be ashamed of	*biscuit (le)* . . . . .cookie	*camarade (le)* . . . . . . .friend, comrade
avoir horreur de . . . . .**to hate, to loathe**	*blague (la)* . . . . .joke	*caméra (une)* . . . . .movie camera
avoir mal . . . .**to ache, to hurt**	*blanc/blanche* . . . . .white	*camion (le)* . . . . .truck
avoir peur (de) . . . . .to be afraid	***blessé/blessée*** . . . .**injured**	***campagne (la)*** . .**campaign, countryside**
avoir raison . . . . .to be right	***blesser*** . . . .**to wound**	*camper* . . . . .to go camping
avoir rendez-vous . . . .**to have an**	*bleu* . . . . .blue	*camping (le)* . . . . .camping
appointment	***blond/blonde*** . . . .**blond(e)**	***canadien/canadienne*** . . . .**Canadian**
avoir soif . . . . .to be thirsty	*boire* .to drink	*canapé (le)* . . . . .couch, sofa
avoir sommeil . . . . .to be sleepy	***bois (le)*** . . . . **forest, wood**	***capable*** . . . .**able**
avoir son diplôme . . . . .to graduate	*boisson (la)* . . . . .drink	*car (le)* . . . . .long distance bus
avoir tort . . . . .to be wrong	*boîte (la)* .box	***carotte (la)*** . . . .**carrot**
avril . . . . .April	***boîte aux lettres (la)*** . . . .**mailbox**	***carré/carrée*** . . . .**square**
	bon/bonne . . . .**good**	*carte (la)* . . . . .card, map
B	***bon marché*** . . . .**cheap**	(for countries or regions)
	bonbon (un) . . . . .candy	*carte de crédit (la)* . . . . .credit card
bagages (les) (m.) . . . .**luggage**	***bonheur (le)*** . . . .**happiness**	*cas (le)* .case
bague (la) . . . .**ring**	*bord (le)* . . . . .the edge	***casque (le)*** . . . .**helmet**
baignoire (la) . . . . .bathtub	*bottes (les) (f.)* . . . . .boots	*casquette (la)* . . . . .cap
bain (le) .bath	*bouc (le)* . . . . .billy goat	*casser (se)* . . . . .to break
baiser (le) . . . . .kiss	*bouche (la)* . . . . .mouth	*casserole (la)* . . . . .saucepan
bal (le) . . . . .ball	***bouclé/bouclée*** . . . . .**curly, buckled**	*catastrophique* . . . . .catastrophic
balai (le) . . . .**broom**	*boucle d'oreille (la)* . . . . .earring	***catholique*** . . . .**Catholic**
baleine (la) . . . . .whale	*bougie (la)* . . . . .candle	***causer*** . . . .**to cause**
balle (la) . . . . .ball (small)	*bouillir* . . . . .to boil	*ce/cet/cette/ces (adj.)* . . . . .this/these
ballet (un) . . . . .ballet	*boulanger/boulangère (le/la)* . . . .baker	*ceinture (la)* . . . . .belt
ballon (le) . . . . .ball (big)	***bourse (la)*** . . . . **scholarship**	*cela (pron.)* . . . . .this (one)
banane (la) . . . . .banana	*bouteille (la)* . . . . .bottle	*celui (pron.)* . . . . .this one
bande dessinée (une) . . . . . . .comic strip	*boutique (la)* . . . . .shop	***célèbre*** . . . .**famous**
banlieue (la) . . . . .suburbs	*bouton (le)* . . . . .button	*cent* .hundred
banque (la) . . . .**bank**	*bracelet (le)* . . . . .bracelet	*centre commercial (le)* . . .shopping mall
banquier/banquière (un/une) . . . .banker	***branché/branchée*** . . . .**plugged in, "in"**	*cependant* . . . . .however
barbe (la) . . . . .beard	**(in the know, connected)**	***certain/certaine*** . . . .**certain**
baseball (le) . . . . .baseball	*brancher* . . . . .to plug in	*céréales (les) (f.)* . . . . .cereal
basket (le) . . . . .basketball	*bras (le)* . . . . .arm	*cet/cette après-midi* . . . . . .this afternoon
baskets (les) (m.) . . . . .sneakers	*brebis (la)* . . . . .ewe	*chacun/chacune (pron.)* . . . . .each
bataille (la) . . . .**fight, battle**	***briller*** . . . .**to shine**	*chaîne (une)* . .stereo system, TV channel
bateau (le) . . . . .boat	*bronzage (le)* . . . . .tanning	*chaise (la)* . . . . .chair
bâtiment (le) . . . . .building	*bronzé/bronzée* . . . . .tanned	*chambre (la)* . . . . .bedroom
batterie (la) . . . . .drums	*bronzer* . . . . .to tan	*chameau (le)* . . . . .camel
battre (se) . . . .**to fight**	*brosser (se)* . . . . .to brush	*champ (le)* . . . . .field
bavarder . . . .**to chat**	*brouillard (le)* . . . . .fog	*champignon (le)* . . . . .mushroom
beau/belle . . . .**beautiful**	*bruit (le)* . . . . .noise	*champion/championne (le/la)* .champion
beau-frère (le) . . . . .brother-in-law	*brûler* . . . . .to burn	*championnat (le)* . . . . .championship
beau-père (le) . . . . .father-in-law	*brun* . . . . .brown (for hair)	*chance (la)* . . . . .luck
beaucoup . . . . .a lot	*bruyant/bruyante* . . . . .noisy	*chandelle (la)* . . . . .candle
bébé (le) . . . . .baby	*buisson (le)* . . . . .bush	*changer (se)* . . . . .to change
belle-mère (la) . . . . .mother-in-law	*bureau (le)* . . . . .desk, office	*chanson (une)* . . . . .a song
		chanter . . . . .to sing

chanteur/chanteuse (un/une) . . . . .singer
chapeau (le) . . . . .hat
chapitre (le) . . . . .chapter
chaque .each
charmant/charmante . . . . .charming
chat (le) .cat
château (le) . . . . .castle
chaud/chaude . . . .**hot, warm**
chauffer . . . .**to heat**
chaussettes (les) (f.) . . . . .socks
chaussures (les) (f.) . . . . .shoes
chauve . . . .**bald**
chef (le) . . . . .the boss
chemin (le) . . . .**path, direction**
chemise (la) . . . . .shirt
chemisier (le) . . . . .blouse
cher/chère . . . .**expensive**
chercher . . . . .to look for
chercheur/chercheuse (un/une) researcher
chèque (le) . . . . .check
cheval (le) . . . . .horse
chèvre (la) . . . . .goat
cheveux (les) (m.) . . . . .hair
chez (+ personne) . .at (someone's) house
chic . . . . .elegant
chien (le) . . . . .dog
chimie (la) . . . . .chemistry
chirurgien/chirurgienne (un/une) surgeon
chlore (le) . . . . .chlorine
choisir . . . .**to choose, to select**
chômage (au) . . . . .unemployed
choquant/choquante . . . . .shocking
choqué/choquée . . . . .shocked
chose (la) . . . . .thing
chrétien/chrétienne . . . .**Christian**
cinéma (le) . . . . .cinema, movie theater
cinq .five
cinquième . . . . .fifth
cintre (le) . . . .**hanger**
circonstance (la) . . . . .circumstance
cirque (le) . . . . .circus
ciseaux (les) (m.) . . . .**scissors**
civilisé . . . . .civilized
classe (la) . . . . .class
classique . . . . .classical
climat (le) . . . . .climate
climatisation (la) . . . . .air-conditioning
climatisé . . . . .air-conditioned
climatiseur (le) . . . . . . .air-conditioner
cloche (la) . . . .**bell**
code postal (le) . . . . .zip code
coiffer (se) . . . . .to do one's hair
coiffeur/coiffeuse (le/la) . . . .hairdresser
coin (le) . . . . .corner
colère (la) . . . .**anger**
collant (le) . . . . .pantyhose (tights)
collier (le) . . . . .necklace
combien? . . . . .how much?
combien de? . . .how much?, how many?
comédie musicale (une) . . . . .a musical

comédien/comédienne (un/une)
. . . . .actor, actress
commander . . . . .to order
comme .as
comme-ci comme-ça . . . . .more or less
commencer . . . . .to begin
comment? . . . . .how?
commerçant (un) . . . . .merchant
commerce (le) . . . .**business**
commissariat de
police (le) . . . . .police station
commode (la) . . . . .bureau
compact disque, CD (le)
. . . . .CD (compact disc)
compétition (la) . . . . .competition
complet/complète .full (only for a place)
comprendre . . . . .to understand
comptable (un/une) . . . . .accountant
compter . . . . .to count
comptoir (le) . . . . .counter
concert (un) . . . . .concert
concombre (le) . . . . .cucumber
conduire . . . . .to drive
conférence (la) . . . .**lecture**
confiance (la) . . . .**confidence**
confiture (la) . . . . .preserves, jam
confondre . . . .**to confuse**
confortable . . .**comfortable (for things)**
confus/confuse . . . .**embarrassed**
congélateur (le) . . . . .freezer
connaître . . . . .to know
connu . . . . .well-known
consciencieux/
conscientieuse . . . . . . .conscientious
conseil (le) . . . .**advice**
conseiller . . . .**to advise**
conseiller/conseillère (un/une) . .advisor
conte (le) . . . .**story, tale**
content/contente . . . . .happy
continent (le) . . . . .continent
continuer . . . . .to continue
contraire (le) . . . .**opposite**
contre . . . . .against
contribuer . . . . .to contribute
contrôle (le) . . . .**quiz**
copain/copine (le/la) . . . . .buddy
copier . . . . .to copy
coq (le) . . . . .rooster
coquillage (le) . . . . .seashell
corde (la) . . . . .rope
corps (le) . . . . .body
corriger . . . . .to correct
costume (le) . . . . .suit
côté (le) . . . . .side
coton (le) . . . .**cotton**
coucher (se) . . .to go to bed, to lie down
couette (la) . . . . .comforter
couleur (la) . . . . .color
couloir (le) . . . . .hallway
coupable . . . .**guilty**
couper . . . . .to cut

courant . . . . .fluent, common
courir . . . . .to run
couronne (la) . . . . .crown
courrier (le) . . . .**mail**
courrier électronique (le),
(le) e-mail, (le) mail . . . .**e-mail**
cours (le) . . . . .class, course
course (une) . . . . .race
court/courte . . . .**short**
cousin/cousine (le/la) . . . . .cousin
couteau (le) . . . . .knife
coûter . . . . .to cost
couvrir . . . .**to cover**
craie (la) . . . . .chalk
craindre . . . . .to fear
cravate (la) . . . . .tie
crayon (le) . . . . .pencil
crédule . . . . .gullible
crevé/crevée . . . .**burst, exhausted**
crier . . . . .to shout
croire . . . . .to believe
cru/crue . . . . .raw
cruel/cruelle . . . . .cruel
cuillère (la) . . . . .spoon
cuir (le) . . . . .leather
cuire . . . . .to cook
cuisine (la) . . . . .kitchen, cooking
cuisinier/cuisinière (un/une) . . . . . .cook
cuisinière (la) . . . . .stove
cuit/cuite . . . .**cooked**
curieux/curieuse . . . . .curious
curiosité (la) . . . . .curiosity

D

d'abord . . . . .at first
d'accord . . . . .OK
d'ailleurs . . . . .anyway
d'habitude . . . . .usually
d'où . . . . .from, where
dans .in
danse (la) . . . . .dance
danser . . . . .to dance
date (la) . . . . date (calendar)
de . . . . .of, from, about
de bonne heure . . . . .early
de nouveau . . . . .again
débarquer . . . . .to land, to get off
débarrasser (se) . . . . .to get rid of
debout . . . . .standing
débrancher . . . . .to unplug
débrouiller (se) . . . .**to manage**
décembre . . . . .December
décevoir . . . . .to disappoint
déchiré/déchirée . . . .**torn, ripped**
décider . . . . .to decide
déclaration (la) . . . . .declaration
découvrir . . . . .to discover
déçu/déçue . . . . .disappointed
dedans . . . . .inside
défaut (le) . . . .**defect**

défendre . . . . .to defend, to forbid
dégoûtant/dégoûtante . . . . .**disgusting**
déjà . . . . .already
déjeuner . . . . .to have lunch
déjouer . . . . .to outwit
délicieux/délicieuse . . . .**delicious**
demain . . . . .tomorrow
demander . . . . .to ask (for)
demander (se) . . . . **to wonder**
demander un renseignement . . . . .to ask
for information
déménager . . . . .to move (house)
demi (adj.) . . . . .half
démodé/démodée . . . . .out of fashion
dent (la) . . . . tooth
dentier (le) . . . . .denture, false teeth
départ (le) . . . . **departure**
dépêcher (se) . . . . to hurry
dépenser . . . . .to spend (money)
déposer . . . . .to drop off
déprimant . . . . .depressing
déprimer . . . . .to depress
déranger . . . .**to bother, to disturb**
dernier/dernière . . . .**last, past**
derrière . . . . .behind
dès que . . . . .as soon as
désagréable . . . . .unpleasant
descendre . . . . to go down
désert . . . . .deserted
déshabiller (se) . . . . .to undress
désirer . . . . .to desire
désobéir . . . . .to disobey
désolé/désolée . . . .**sorry**
désordre (le) . . . . .disorder, mess
dessert (le) . . . . .dessert
dessin (le) . . . .**drawing**
dessin animé (un) . . . . .cartoon
dessiner . . . . .to draw
destin (le) . . . .**destiny, fate**
détail (le) . . . .**detail**
détendre (se) . . . . .to relax
détendu/détendue . . . . .relaxed
détestable . . . . .horrible
détester . . . . .to hate
détruire . . . . .to destroy
dette (la) . . . .**debt**
deux fois, trois fois, etc. . . . .twice, three
times, etc.
deuxième . . . . .second
devant . . . . .in front of
devant (le) . . . . .front
développer . . . .**to develop**
devenir . . . . .to become
deviner . . . .**to guess**
devoir (+ infinitive) . . . . . . .to have to (do
something), must, to owe
devoirs (les) (m.) . . . .**homework**
dévorer . . . . .devour
différent/différente . . . .**different**
difficile . . . .**difficult**
difficulté (la) . . . . . .problem, difficulty

dimanche (le) . . . . .Sunday
diminuer . . . . .to diminish
dinde (la) . . . . .turkey
dîner . . . . .to have dinner
dire . . . . .to say, to tell
directeur/directrice . . . . . . .headmaster,
(un/une) head of company
discuter . . . .**to discuss**
disparaître . . . .**to disappear**
disputer . . . . .to quarrel
disputer (se) . . . .**to quarrel with**
distributeur de billets (le) . .ATM machine

divertir (se) . . . . .to entertain
divertissement (un) . . . . . .entertainment
dix . . . . .ten
dix-huit . . . . .eighteen
dix-neuf . . . . .nineteen
dix-sept . . . . .seventeen
dixième . . . . .tenth
documentaire (un) . . . . . . .documentary
doigt (le) . . . . finger
dominer . . . . .to rule, to be over
dommage (le) . . . . .damage
donc . . . . .therefore
donner . . . . .to give
dormir . . . . .to sleep
dortoir (le) . . . . .dormitory
dos (le) . . . . .back
douce/doux . . . . .soft, sweet
douceur (la) . . . . .gentleness
douche (la) . . . . .shower
doucher (se) . . . . .to shower
doué/douée . . . .**talented**
douleur (la) . . . .**pain, grief**
doute (le) . . . . .doubt
douter . . . . .to doubt
doux/douce . . . .**soft, sweet**
douze . . . . .twelve
drame (le) . . . . .drama
drap (le) . . . . .sheet
drapeau (le) . . . .**flag**
droit (le) . . . .**right, law, privilege**
drôle . . . .**funny**
dur/dure . . . .**hard**
durer . . . .**to last**
DVD (un) . . . . .DVD

E

eau (l') (f.) . . . . .water
éblouir . . . . .to blind
échapper (s') . . . . .to escape
écharpe (l') (f.) . . . . .scarf
échouer . . . . .to fail
éclaté/éclatée . . . .**burst**
éclater . . . .**to burst**
école (l') (f.) . . . . .school
économiser . . . .**to save money**
écouter . . . . .to listen to
écran (l') (m.) . . . .**screen**

écrire . . . . .to write
écrit/écrite . . . .**written**
écrivain (un) . . . . .writer
écureuil (l') (m.) . . . . .squirrel
éducatif/éducative . . . . .educational
effacer . . . .**to erase**
efficace . . . . .efficient
effrayant/effrayante . . . .**frightful,**
frightening
effrayer . . . .**to frighten, to scare**
égal .equal
église (l') (f.) . . . .**church**
égoïste . . . . .selfish
électrique . . . . .electric
élégant . . . . .elegant
élève (l') (m./f.) . . . . . . .pupil (student)
e-mail (le), (le) courriel, (le) courrier
électronique, (le) mail . . . .**e-mail**
embarrassé/embarrassée . . .embarrassed
embouteillage (l') (m.) . . . . .traffic jam
embrasser (s') . . . . .**to kiss, to embrace**
émission (l') (f.) . . . . . .television (radio)
program, show
empêcher . . . .**to prevent**
emploi (l') (m.) . . . . .job
emploi du temps (l') (m.) . . . . .**schedule**
employé/employée (l') (m./f.) . .**employee**
employer . . . . .to employ
emprunter . . . . .to borrow
en désordre . . . . .messy
en direct . . . . .live
en face de . . . . .across from
en même temps . . . . . .at the same time
en ordre . . . . .in order, tidy
en retard . . . . .late
enchanté/enchantée . . . .**pleased**
encore . . . . .still, more
endormir (s') . . . . .to go to sleep
endroit (l') (m.) . . . .**place**
énergie (l') (f.) . . . . .energy
énergie nucléaire
(l') (f.) . . . .**nuclear energy**
énergique . . . . .energetic
énervé/énervée . . . . . .**fidgety, nervous,**
exasperated
énerver (s') . . . . .to get exasperated
enfance (l') (f.) . . . .**childhood**
enfant (l') (m./f.) . . . . .child
enfin . . . . .finally
enfuir (s') . . . .**to run away**
enlever . . . .**to take off, to kidnap**
ennemi/ennemie (l') (m./f.) . . . . . .enemy
ennuyé/ennuyée . . . . .worried
ennuyer (s') . . . . .to be bored
ennuyeux/ennuyeuse . . . .**boring**
énorme . . . .**enormous**
enquête (une) . . . . .investigation
enregistrer . . . .to check in, to tape (e.g.,
video, song)
enseignant/enseignante . . . . . . .teacher
enseignement (l') (m.) . . . .**teaching**

enseigner . . . . to teach
ensemble . . . . .together
ensuite .then
entendre . . . . to hear, to understand
entendre avec (s') . . . .**to get along**
entendre dire . . . .**to hear (a rumor)**
entier/entière . . . .**entire**
entourer . . . .**to surround**
entraînement (l') (m.)
. . . .**training, practice**
entraîner (s') . . . . .to practice
entraîneur/entraîneuse (l') (m./f.)
. . . . .coach
entre .between
entrée (l') (f.) . . . .**entrance, first course**
entrer . . . . .to go in
entretenu/entretenue
. . . .**maintained, kept up**
entrevue (l') (f.) . . . .**interview**
envie (l') (f.) . . . . .envy
environ . . . . .more or less, about
environnement (l') (m.) . . . .environment
envoyer . . . . .to send
épeler . . . .**to spell**
épice (l') (f.) . . . . .spice
épinards (les) (m.) . . . . .spinach
épisode (l') (m.) . . . . .episode
équipe (l') (f.) . . . . .team
erreur (l') (f.) . . . . .error, mistake
escalader . . . . .to climb
escalier (l') (m.) . . . . .stairs
espérer . . . . .to hope
espion/espionne (un/une) . . . . .spy
essayer . . . .**to try, to try on**
essence (l') (f.) . . . . .gasoline
essuyer . . . . .to wipe, to dry
est (l') (m.) . . . . .east
et . . . . .and
étage (l') (m.) . . .floor (first, second . . .)
étagère (l') (f.) . . . . .shelf
état (l') (m.) . . . . .state, condition
été (l') (m.) . . . . .summer
éteindre . . . . .**to extinguish, to turn off**
étonnant . . . . .surprising
étonné . . . . .surprised
étonner . . . . .to surprise
étrange . . . .**strange**
étranger/étrangère . . . . .foreign
étranger/étrangère (l') (m./f.)
. . . . .foreigner, stranger
étranger (à l') . . . . .abroad
être . . . . .to be
être à l'heure . . . .**to be on time**
être à la mode . . . . .to be in fashion
être au courant . . . . .to be informed
être en colère . . . .**to be angry**
être en retard . . . .**to be late**
être ennuyé(e) . . . .**to be worried**
être ennuyeux . . . .**to be boring**
être pressé . . . .**to be in a hurry**
étroit/étroite . . . .**narrow, tight**

étudiant/étudiante (l') (m./f.) . . . .student
étudier . . . . .to study
eux . . . . . . .them (object of a preposition)
événement (l') (m.) . . . . .event
évident . . . . .obvious
évier (l') (m.) . . . . .kitchen sink
examen (l') (m.) . . . . .exam
exaspérer . . . . .exasperate, get on
one's nerves
excité/excitée . . . . .excited
exiger . . . .**to require, to demand**
expliquer . . . . .to explain
explorateur/exploriatrice (l') (m./f.)
. . . . .explorer
externe (l') (m./f.) . . . . .day student

F

fabriquer . . . . .to make, to do
fâché . . . . .angry, upset
fâcher (se) . . . .**to become angry**
facile . . . . .easy
façon (la) . . . . .the manner, way
facteur/factrice (le/la) . . . . . .mail carrier
facultatif/facultative . . . . .optional
faible . . . .**weak**
faim (la) . . . . .hunger
faire . . . . .to make, to do
faire attention . . . .**to pay attention**
faire attention à . . . . .to pay attention to
faire confiance . . . .**to trust**
faire des progrès . . . .**to improve**
faire du vélo . . . . .to ride a bicycle
(aller à bicyclette)
faire exprès . . . .**to do something**
on purpose
faire la cuisine . . . .**to cook**
faire la lessive . . . . . .to do the laundry
faire la queue . . . .**to wait in line**
faire la vaisselle . . . . . .to do the dishes
faire le tour de . . . .**to go around**
faire semblant de . . . . . .**to pretend to**
faire un tour . . . . .**to take a walk/drive**
faire un voyage . . . .**to take a trip**
faire une randonnée . . . . .to hike
falloir . . . . .to be necessary
familial/familiale . . . .**of the family**
fantôme (le) . . . . .ghost
fatigant . . . . .tiring
fatigue (la) . . . .**tiredness**
fatigué/fatiguée . . . .**tired**
faute (la) . . . . .mistake
fauteuil (le) . . . . .armchair
faux/fausse . . . . .wrong, false
félicitations (les) (f.) . . . .congratulations
féliciter . . . . .to congratulate
femme (la) . . . . .wife, woman
fenêtre (la) . . . . .window
fer (le) . . . . .iron
ferme (la) . . . .**farm**
fermé/fermée . . . .**closed**

fermer . . . . .to close, to shut
fermeture éclair (la) . . . . .zipper
fermier/fermière (un/une) . . . . . .farmer
festival (le) . . . . .festival
fête (la) . . . . .party
feu (le) . . . . .fire
feu rouge (le) . . . . .traffic light
feuille (la) . . . . .leaf
feuilleton (un) . . . . .soap opera
février . . . . .February
fidèle . . . .**faithful**
fier/fière . . . .**proud**
fille (la) . . . . .daughter, girl
film (le) . . . . .film
film d'amour (un) . . . . . .romantic movie
film d'horreur (un) . . . . . .horror movie
film policier (un) . . . . . .detective movie
fils (le) .son
fin (la) . . . .**end**
finir . . . . .to finish
flamme (la) . . . .**flame**
flatter . . . . .to flatter
flèche (la) . . . . .arrow
fleur (la) . . . . .flower
fleuve (le) . . . . .river
fonctionner . . . . .to function, to work
fond (le) . . . . .bottom
football (foot) (le) . . . . .soccer
football américain (le) . . . . . . .football
forêt (la) . . . . .forest
forêt tropicale (la) . . . . .rain forest
fort/forte . . . .**strong, loud**
fou/folle . . . .**crazy, mad**
foulard (le) . . . . .scarf
four (le) . . . . .oven
four à micro-ondes (le) . microwave oven
fourchette (la) . . . . .fork
fragile . . . . .fragile
frais/fraîche . . . . .fresh
fraise (la) . . . . .strawberry
frapper . . . . .to hit
frère (le) . . . . .brother
frire .to fry
froid/froide . . . .**cold**
fromage (le) . . . . .cheese
frontière (la) . . . .**border**
frustré/frustrée . . . . .frustrated
fumer . . . . .to smoke
furieux/furieuse . . . . . .**furious, angry**
futur (le) . . . .**future**

G

gagnant/gagnante (un/une) . . . . .winner
gagner . . . .**to earn, to win**
gagner de l'argent . . . . . .to earn money
gants (les) (m.) . . . . .gloves
garçon (le) . . . . .boy
garder . . . .**to keep**
gardien de but (un) . . . . .goalkeeper
gare (la) . . . . .train station

garer . . . . .to park
gâté/gâtée . . . .**spoiled**
gâteau (le) . . . . .cake
gauche . . . .**left**
gazelle (la) . . . . .gazelle
gazon (le) . . . . .grass
géant (le) . . . . .giant
geler . . . .**to freeze**
gêner . . . .**to embarrass, to bother**
généreux/généreuse . . . . .generous
genre (le) . . . .**kind, sort**
gens (les) (m.) . . . . .people
gentil/gentille . . . .**nice, kind**
géographie (la) . . . . .geography
géométrie (la) . . . . .geometry
gérant (le) . . . .**manager**
geste (le) . . . .**gesture**
gigantesque . . . . .huge
gilet (le) . . . . .vest
girafe (la) . . . . .giraffe
glace (la) . . . . .ice, ice cream
glace à la vanille (la)
. . . . .vanilla ice cream
glace au chocolat (la)
. . . . .chocolate ice cream
gorge (la) . . . . .throat
goût (le) . . . .**taste**
goûter . . . .to have an afternoon snack,
to taste
goutte (la) . . . .**drop**
gouvernement (le) . . . .**government**
gouverner . . . .**to govern**
grand/grande . . . .**big, tall**
grand magasin (le) . .**department store**
grand-mère (la) . . . . .grandmother
grand-père (le) . . . . .grandfather
grandir . . . .**to grow, to expand**
gratuit/gratuite . . . .**free of charge**
grave . . . .**serious**
grêle (la) . . . . .hail
grenouille (la) . . . . .frog
grille-pain (le) . . . . .toaster
griller . . . . .to broil, to grill
gris . . . . .grey
gronder . . . . .to scold
gros/grosse . . . .**big, fat**
grossir . . . . .to get bigger, to gain weight
groupe (le) . . . . .band
guichet (le) . . . . .ticket window
guide (le/la) . . . . .guide
guitare (la) . . . . .guitar
gymnase (le) . . . . .gymnasium

H

habile . . . . .skillful
habiller (s') . . . .to dress (to get dressed)
habitant/habitante (l') (m./f.) . .inhabitant
habiter . . . . .to live, to dwell
habitude (l') (f.) . . . . .habit
habituer (s') à . . . .**to get used to**

hamburger (le) . . . . .hamburger
haricots verts (les) (m.) . . . .green beans
haut/haute . . . . .high
hasard (le) . . . . .chance
herbe (l') (f.) . . . . .grass
hésiter . . . . .to hesitate
heure (l') (f.) . . . . .hour
heureux/heureuse . . . . .happy
hideux . . . . .hideous
hier . . . . .yesterday
hier soir . . . . .last night
histoire (l') (f.) . . . . . . .story, history
hiver (l') (m.) . . . . .winter
hockey (le) . . . . .hockey
hockey sur glace (le) . . . . .ice hockey
homme (l') (m.) . . . . .man
honnête . . . . .honest
honte (la) . . . .**embarrassment**
hôpital (l') (m.) . . . . .hospital
horaire (l') (m.)
. . . .**schedule (transportation)**
horreur (l') (f.) . . . . .horror
horrifié/horrifiée . . . . .horrified
hôte/hôtesse . . . . .host/hostess
hôtel (l') (m.) . . . . .hotel
hôtesse de l'air (l') (f.)
. . . . .flight attendant
huit . . . . .eight
huitième . . . . .eighth
humeur (l') (f.) . . . . .mood
humidité (l') (f.) . . . . .humidity

I

ici . . . . .here
idiot/idiote . . . . .stupid
idole (l') (f.) . . . . .idol
il est/c'est dommage . . . . .it is a pity
il paraît . . . . .it seems
il y a . . . . .there is, there are
île (l') (f.) . . . . .island
image (l') (f.) . . . .**picture**
immédiat/immédiate . . . . .immediate
immeuble (l') (m.)
. . . . .apartment building
impatience (l') (f.) . . . . .impatience
impatient/impatiente . . . .**eager**
imperméable (l') (m.) . . . . . . .raincoat
impoli/impolie, mal élevé/élevée
. . . .**impolite, rude**
impôt (l') (m.) . . . . .tax
impressionnant/impressionnante
. . . . .impressive
imprimante (l') (f.) . . . . .printer
imprimé/imprimée . . . .**printed**
imprimer . . . .**to print**
imprudent . . . . .not prudent,
carelessly daring
incendie (l') (m.) . . . . .fire (accident)
inconvénient (un) . . . . .a drawback
incroyable . . . .**unbelievable, incredible**

indignation (l') (f.) . . . . .indignation
indiquer . . . . .to indicate, to show
infini/infinie . . . .**infinite**
infirmerie (l') (f.) . . . . .infirmary
injuste . . . . .unfair
inquiéter (s') . . . . .to worry
inscription (l') (f.) . . . . . .**registration**
inscrire (s') . . . . .to register
instituteur/institutrice (l') . . . . . .teacher
insulter . . . . .to insult
intelligent/intelligente . . . . . .intelligent
interdire . . . . .to forbid
intéressant/intéressante . . . . .interesting
interne (l') (m./f.) . . . . .boarding student
interview (l') (f.) . . . . .interview
inutile . . . .**useless**
inventer . . . . .to invent
invité/invitée (un/une) . . . . .guest
inviter . . . . .to invite
irlandais/irlandaise . . . .**Irish**
italien/italienne . . . .**Italian**
ivre . . . .**drunk**

J

jaloux/jalouse . . . .**jealous**
jambe (la) . . . . .leg
jambon (le) . . . . .ham
janvier . . . . .January
japonais/japonaise . . . .**Japanese**
jardin (le) . . . . .garden, yard
jaune . . . . .yellow
jean (le) . . . . .jeans
jeter . . . .**to throw away**
jeu vidéo (un) . . . . .video game
jeudi . . . . .Thursday
jeune . . . .**young**
jeunesse (la) . . . .**youth**
joli/jolie . . . .**pretty**
jouer à . . . . .to play (a sport, cards, etc.)
jouer de . .to play (a musical instrument)
jouet (le) . . . . .toy
joueur/joueuse (un/une) . . . . .player
jour (le) . . . . .day
journal (le) . . . . .newspaper
journaliste (un/une) . . . . .journalist
journée (la) . . . . .day
juge (le) . . . . .judge
juger . . . .**to judge**
juif/juive . . . .**Jewish**
juillet . . . . .July
juin .June
jument (la) . . . . .mare
jupe (la) . . . . .skirt
jurer . . . .**to swear**
jus (le) . . . . .juice
jusqu'à (prep.) . . . . .until, up to
juste . . . . .fair, just

K

kilomètre (le) . . . . .kilometer

L

là . . . . there
là-bas . . . . .over there
lac (le) . . . . .lake
laid/laide . . . .**ugly**
laine (la) . . . . .wool
laisser . . . .**to leave**
laisser tomber . . . . .**to drop, to give up**
lait (le) . . . . .milk
lancer .to throw
langue (la) . . . .**language, tongue**
lapin (le) . . . . .rabbit
large . . . . .wide, large
lavabo (le) . . . . .bathroom sink
lave-linge (le) . . . . . . .washing machine
lave-vaisselle (le) . . . . .dishwasher
laver (se) . . . . .to wash
laverie (la) . . . . .laundromat
le/la/les . . . . .the
leçon (la) . . . . .lesson
légende (la) . . . .**legend**
léger/légère . . . .**light**
légume (le) . . . . .vegetable
lendemain (le) . . . . .the day after
lent/lente . . . .**slow**
lentement . . . . .slowly
lessive (la) . . . . .the wash (laundry)
lettre (la) . . . . .letter
leur/leurs . . . . .their
lever (se) . . . . .to get up
liberté (la) . . . . .freedom
libre . . . . .free (not busy, liberated)
lieu (le) . . . . .place
ligne (la) . . . . .line
limonade (la) . . . . .lemonade
lion (le) . . . . .lion
lire . . . . .to read
lit (le) . . . . .bed
livre (le) . . . . book
livrer . . . .**to deliver, to hand over**
locataire (le/la) . . . . .the tenant
loger . . . . .to dwell
loi (la) . . . . .the law
loin . . . . .far
loin de . . . . .far from
long/longue . . . . .long
longtemps . . . . .a long time
lorsque .when
loterie (la) . . . . .lottery
louer . . . .**to rent**
loup (le) . . . . .wolf
lourd/lourde . . . .**heavy**
loyer (le) . . . . .the rent
lundi .Monday
lune (la) . . . . .moon
lune de miel (la) . . . . .honeymoon

lunettes (les) (f.) . . . . .glasses (spectacles)
luxe (le) . . . . .luxury
lycée (le) . . . . .high school

M

ma/mon .my
machine (la) . . . . .machine
magasin (le) . . . . .store
magazine (le) . . . . .magazine
mai . . . . .May
maigre . . . .**thin**
maigrir . . . . .to lose weight
mail (le), (le) e-mail, (le) courriel
(le) courrier électronique . . . .**e-mail**
maillot de bain (le)
. . . . .bathing suit, swimsuit
main (la) . . . . .hand
maintenant . . . . .now
mais . . . . but
maïs (le) . . . . .corn
maison (la) . . . . .house
maître/maîtresse . . . . . . .master/mistress
mal . . . . .badly
mal élevé/élevée, impoli/impolie
. . . . .rude, impolite
malade . . . .**sick**
maladroit/maladroite . . . .**clumsy**
malheureux/malheureuse . . . . . .unhappy
malheureusement . . . . .unhappily
manche (la) . . . . .sleeve
manche (le) . . . . .handle
manière (la) . . . . .manner
manger . . . . .to eat
mangue (la) . . . . .mango
manque (le) . . . .**lack**
manquer . . . . .to miss (e.g., a train)
manteau (le) . . . . .coat
maquiller (se) . . . . . .to put on make-up
marchand/marchande (le/la) . .shopkeeper
marcher . . . . .to walk, to work
. . . .(to function)
mardi . . . . .Tuesday
mari (le) . . . . .husband
mariage (le) . . . .**wedding**
marié . . . . .married
marier (se) . . . . .to get married
marquer un but . . . . .to score a goal
marraine (la) . . . . .godmother
marrant/marrante . . . .**funny**
marron . . . .**brown**
mars . . . . .March
match (le) . . . . .game (sports)
matelas (le) . . . . .mattress
mathématiques (les) (f.) . . . .mathematics
matière (la) . . . . .subject
matin (le) . .in the morning, the morning
mauvais/mauvaise . . . . .bad
mécanicien/mécanicienne . . . .mechanic
(un/une)
méchant/méchante . . . . .mean

médecin (le) . . . . .doctor
meilleur/meilleure . . . .**better, best**
mélanger . . . .**to mix**
même .same
menacer . . . . .to threaten
mensonger/mensongère . . . . . .deceitful
menteur/menteuse (le/la) . . . . .liar
mentir . . . .**to lie**
mer (la) . . . . .sea
merci . . . . .thank you
mercredi . . . . .Wednesday
mère (la) . . . . .mother
mériter . . . .**to deserve**
merveilleux/merveilleuse . . . . .marvelous
mes (pl.) . . . . .my
mesurer . . . .**to measure**
météo (la) . . . . .weather report
métro (le) . . . . .subway
metteur en scène (le) . . . . . .the director
. . . . (play, movie)
mettre . . . . . .**to put, to place, to put on**
mettre à (se) . .**to start doing something**
mettre le couvert . . . . . .**to set the table**
midi . . . . .noon
mien (le) . . . . .mine
mieux (adv.) . . . . .better, best
mignon/mignonne . . . . . .**precious, cute**
milieu (le) . . . . .middle
mille . . . . .thousand
million (un) . . . . .million
mince (adj) . . . . .thin
minuit . . . . .midnight
miracle (le) . . . .**miracle**
miroir (le) . . . . .mirror
mobylette (la) . . . . .moped
moche . . . .**ugly, lousy, shoddy**
modeste . . . .**modest**
moi . . . . .me
moins . . . . .less
moins . . . que . . . . .less . . .than
mois (le) . . . . .month
moment (le) . . . . .moment
mon/ma . . . . .my
monde (le) . . . . .world
moniteur/monitrice (le/la) .coach, leader
monstre (le) . . . . .monster
montagne (la) . . . . .mountain
monter . . . . .to go up
montre (la) . . . . .watch
montrer . . . . .to show
moquer de (se) . . . . .to make fun of
morceau (le) . . . . . .**piece, bit, selection**
mordre . . . .**to bite**
mort/morte . . . .**dead**
mortel/mortelle . . . .**lethal**
mot (le) . . . . .word
moteur (le) . . . . .engine
moto (la) . . . . .motorcycle
mou/molle . . . .**soft, mushy**
mouchoir (le) . . . . .handkerchief
mouillé/mouillée . . . .**wet**

mouiller .to wet
mourir . . . . .to die
moustique (le) . . . . .mosquito
moutarde (la) . . . . .mustard
mouton (le) . . . . .sheep
moyen/moyenne . . . . .average
muet/muette . . . . .mute
municipal/municipale . . . . . .municipal
mûr . . . . .ripe
muscler . . . . .to develop muscle
musicien/musicienne (un/une) . .musician
musique (la) . . . . music
musulman/musulmane . . . . . .Muslim
mystère (le) . . . . .mystery
mystérieux/mystérieuse . . . . . mysterious

N

n'est-ce pas? . . . . .isn't that so?
n'importe qui . . . . .anyone
n'importe quoi . . . . .anything
nager . . . . .to swim
naïf (m.)/naïve (f.) . . . . .naïve
naître . . . . .to be born
natation (la) . . . . .swimming
nature (la) . . . . .nature
naturel/naturelle . . . . .natural
né/née . . . . .born
ne . . . aucun . . . . .none, no
ne . . . jamais . . . . .never
ne . . . ni . . . ni . . . . . .neither . . . nor
ne . . . personne . . . . . . .no one, nobody
ne . . plus . . . . .no longer, no more
ne . . . rien . . . . .nothing
nécessaire . . . . .necessary
neige (la) . . . . .snow
neiger . . . . .to snow
nerveux/nerveuse . . . . .nervous
nettoyer . . . . .to clean
neuf . . . . .nine
neuf/neuve . . . . .brand new
neveu (le) . . . . .nephew
neuvième . . . . .ninth
nez (le) . . . . .nose
nièce (la) . . . . .niece
nier .to deny
niveau (le) . . . . .level
noir/noire . . . . .black
nommer . . . . .to name
non . . . . .no
nord (le) . . . . .north
nos (pl.) . . . . .our
note (la) . . . . .grade
notre (sing.) . . . . .our
nourriture (la) . . . . .food
nouveau/nouvelle . . . . .new
nouvelles (les) (f.) . . . . .news
novembre . . . . .November
nuage (le) . . . . .cloud
nuit (la) . . . . .night
nul/nulle . . . . .no good, lousy

O

obéir . . . . .obey
obligatoire . . . . . .necessary, required
obliger . . . . .to oblige
observer . . . . .to observe
occupé/occupée . . . . .busy
octobre . . . . .October
œil (l') (m.) . . . . .eye
œuf (l') (m.) . . . . .egg
offrir . . . . .to offer
oignon (l') (m.) . . . . onion
oiseau (l') (m.) . . . . .bird
ombre (l') (f.) . . . . .shade, shadow
oncle (l') (m.) . . . . .uncle
ongle (l') (m.) . . . . . .fingernail, toenail
onze . . . . .eleven
orage (l') (m.) . . . . .storm
orange (l') (f.) . . . . .orange
ordinaire . . . . .common, ordinary
ordinateur (l') (m.) . . . . .computer
ordonner . . . . .to order
oreille (l') (f.) . . . . .ear
oreiller (l') (m.) . . . . .pillow
orgueil (l') (m.) . . . . .pride
original/originale . . . . .original
orthographe (l') (f.) . . . . .spelling
oser . . .to dare, to have the courage to
ou . . . . .or
où . . . . .where
oublier . . . . .to forget
ouest (l') (m.) . . . . .west
oui . . . . .yes
ours (l') (m.) . . . . .bear
ouvert/ouverte . . . . .open
ouvre-boîte (un) . . . . .can opener
ouvrir . . . . .to open
ouvrier/ouvrière (un/une)
. . . . .a factory worker

P

pain (le) . . . . .bread
paire (la) . . . . .pair
pantalon (le) . . . . .pants
panier (le) . . . . .basket
papier (le) . . . . .paper
paquet (le) . . . . .package
par . . . . .by
par-dessus . . . . .above
par exemple . . . . .for example
paraître . . . . .to seem, to appear
parapluie (le) . . . . .umbrella
parc (le) . . . . .park
parce que . . . . .because
parent (le) . . . . .parent
paresseux/paresseuse . . . . .lazy
parfois . . . . .sometimes
parking (le) . . . . .parking lot
parler . . . . .to speak
parmi . . . . .among

parole (la) . . . . .spoken word
partager . . . . .to share
partir . . . . .to go away, to leave
partir en vacances . . . .to go on vacation
partout . . . . .everywhere
passeport (le) . . . . .passport
passer . . . . .to spend (time)
passer (se) . . . . .to happen
passer l'aspirateur . . . . .to vacuum
passer un examen . . . . . .to take an exam
pasteur (le) . . . . .minister
patin (le) . . . . .skate
patinage (le) . . . . .skating
patiner . . . . .to skate
patron/patronne (le/la) . . . . .boss
pauvre . . . . .poor
payer . . . . .to pay
pays (le) . . . . .country
paysan/paysanne (le/la) . .peasant (farmer)
pêche (la) . . . . .peach, fishing
péché (le) . . . . .sin
peigner (se) . . . . .to comb
peignoir (le) . . . . .bathrobe
peindre . . . . .to paint
peint/peinte . . . . .painted
peinture (la) . . . . .painting
pelouse (la) . . . . .lawn
pellicule (la) . . . . .the film
pendant . . . . .during
pendant que . . . . .while
pendre . . . . .to hang
pénible . . . . .annoying, a pain
penser . . . . .to think
perdre . . . . .to lose
perdre (se) . . . . .to get lost
père (le) . . . . .father
permettre . . . . .to allow
permis/permise . . . . .allowed
permis de conduire (le) . .driver's license
personne (la) . . . . .person
persuader . . . . .to persuade
petit/petite . . . . .little, small, tiny
petit ami (le) . . . . .boyfriend
petite amie (la) . . . . .girlfriend
petit-fils (le) . . . . .grandson
petite-fille (la) . . . . .granddaughter
petits pois (les) (m.) . . . . .peas
peur (la) . . . . .fear
peut-être . . . . .maybe, perhaps
physique (la) . . . . .physics
physique (le) . . . . .physical appearance
piano (le) . . . . .piano
pièce (la) . . . . .room
pièce (de théâtre) (une) . . . . .play
pied (le) . . . . .foot
pierre (la) . . . . .stone
pilote (le) . . . . .pilot
pique-nique (le) . . . . .picnic
piquer . . . . .to sting
pire .worse
piscine (la) . . . . .swimming pool

placard (le) . . . . .closet	*précédent/précédente* . . . . .previous	*quantité (la)* . . . . .quantity
place (la) . . . . .seat	**préféré/préférée** . . . .**preferred, favorite**	*quart (le)* . . . . .quarter
plage (la) . . . . .beach	*préférer* . . . . .to prefer	**quartier (le)** . . . .**neighborhood,**
plaindre (se) . . . .**to complain**	**premier/première** . . . .**first**	**section, quarter**
plainte (la) . . . .**complaint**	*prendre* . . . . to take	*quatorze* . . . . .fourteen
plaisanterie (la) . . . . .joke	**prendre des notes** . . . . . .**to take notes**	*quatre* . . . . .four
plaisir (le) . . . . .pleasure	**prendre des photos** . . . . **to take photos**	*quatrième* . . . . .fourth
plan (le) . . . . .map of a city	**prendre soin de** . . . .**to take care of**	*que* . . . . that, which
plancher (le) . . . . .wooden floor	*prendre un bain* . . . . .to take a bath	*quel/quelle (adj.)* . . . . .which, what
plante (la) . . . . .plant	**prendre une décision**	*quelqu'un* . . . . .someone
planter . . . . .to plant	. . . .**to make a decision**	*quelque/quelques* . . . . .some
plat/plate . . . .**flat**	*prendre une douche* . . . .to take a shower	*quelque chose* . . . . .something
plat (le) . . . . .dish, course	*préoccupé, préoccupée* . . . . . . .worried	*quelquefois* . . . . .sometimes
plat principal (le) . . .main course, entree	*près* . . . . .near	*queue (la)* . . . . .line, tail
plateau (le) . . . .**tray**	*présentateur/présentatrice*	*quinze* . . . . .fifteen
plein/pleine . . . .**full**	*(un/une)* . . . . .TV host	**quitter** . . . .**to leave, to go away**
pleurer . . . .**to cry, to weep**	*présenter* . . . . .to introduce	**quotidien/quotidienne** . . . .**daily**
pleuvoir . . . . .to rain	*presque* . . . . .almost	
plier . . . .**to fold**	**presse (la)** . . . .**press**	
plombier (un) . . . . .plumber	**pressé/pressée** . . . .**in a hurry**	# R
plume (la) . . . .**feather**	**prêt/prête** . . . .**ready**	*raccrocher* . . . . .to hang up
plupart (la) . . . . .most	*prétentieux/prétentieuse* . . . .pretentious	**racine (la)** . . . .**root**
plus . . . . .more	*prêter* . . . . .to lend	**raconter** . . . .**to tell (a story)**
plus . . . que . . . . .more . . . than	**prévenir** . . . .**to warn**	*radio (la)* . . . . .radio
plusieurs . . . .**several, many**	*printemps (le)* . . . . .spring	**raide** . . . .**stiff**
poche (la) . . . . .pocket	*prise électrique (une)* . . . . .electric plug	*raison (la)* . . . . .reason
poêle (la) . . . . .frying pan	*prison (la)* . . . . .jail	*ramer* .to row
poème (le) . . . . .poem	**privé/privée** . . . .**private**	*randonnée (la)* . . . . .hike
poire (la) . . . . pear	*prix (le)* . . . . .prize, price	*rang (le)* . . . . .row
poison (le) . . . .**poison**	*problème (le)* . . . . .problem	**ranger** . . . .**to tidy, to put away**
poisson (le) . . . . .fish	**prochain/prochaine** . . . .**next**	*rapide* .fast
poivre (le) . . . . .pepper	*proche (adj.)* . . . . .near, close	**rapport (le)** . . . .**report**
poli/polie . . . .**courteous, polite**	*professeur (le)* . . . . .teacher	*raquette (la)* . . . . .racket
policier/policière (un/une) . . .policeman	*profond* . . . . .deep	**rare** . . . .**unusual, rare**
politicien/politicienne (le/la) . . .politician	*projet (le)* . . . . .a project	*raser (se)* . . . . .to shave
politique (la) . . . .**politics**	*promenade (la)* . . . . .a walk	*rasoir électrique (un)* . . . .electric shaver
pollué/polluée . . . . .polluted	*promener (se)* . . . . .to take a walk	*rassurer* . . . . .to reassure
pollution (la) . . . . .pollution	*promesse (la)* . . . . .promise	*rater* .to fail
pomme (la) . . . . .apple	**promettre** . . . .**to promise**	*ravi/ravie* . . . . .delighted
pompier (le) . . . . .fireman	**propre** . . . .**clean, own**	*rayon (le)* . . . . .department
pont (le) . . . . .bridge	*propriétaire (un/une)* . . . . .the owner	*récemment* . . . . .recently
porc (le) . . . . .pork	*protéger* . . . . .to protect	**récent/récente** . . . .**recent**
portable (le) . . . . .cell phone	**protestant/protestante** . . . . .**Protestant**	*recevoir* . . . .**to receive**
porte (la) . . . . .door, airport gate	*protester* . . . . .to protest	*réclame (la)* . . . . .advertisement, ad
porter . . . . .to wear, to carry	**prudent/prudente** . . . . .**prudent, careful**	*reconnaître* . . . . .to recognize
portrait (le) . . . .**picture, portrait**	**publicité (la), (la pub)** . . . .**advertising**	**réfléchir** . . . .**to reflect, to think**
poser une question . . .**to ask a question**	**advertisement (ad), announcement**	*réfrigérateur (le)* . . . . .refrigerator
poste (la) . . . . .post office	*puis* . . . . .then	*regarder* . . . . .to look
poste (le) . . . . . .employment position	*puisque* . . . . .since, because	*règlement (le)* . . . . .rule
poubelle (la) . . . . .garbage can	**puissant/puissante** . . . .**powerful**	**régner** . . . .**to reign**
poule (la) . . . . .hen	*pull (le)* . . . . .sweater	*regretter* . . . . .to regret
poulet (le) . . . . .chicken	**punir** . . . .**to punish**	*régulièrement* . . . . .regularly
poupée (la) . . . . .doll	**punition (la)** . . . .**punishment**	*relation (la)* . . . . .relationship
pour . . . . .for	*pupille (la)* . . . . .pupil (eye)	**remarquer** . . . .**to notice**
pourquoi? . . . . .why?	*purée de pommes de*	**remercier** . . . .**to thank**
pousser . . . . .to push, to grow	*terre (la)* . . . . .mashed potatoes	*remplacer* . . . . .to replace
pourtant . . . . .however	*pyjama (le)* . . . . .pajamas	**remplir** . . . .**to fill**
pourvu que . . . . .provided that		*remuer* . . . . .to stir
poussière (la) . . . .**dust**		*rencontrer* . . . . .to meet
pouvoir . . . . to be able (can)	# Q	*rendez-vous (un)* . . . . .appointment
pouvoir (le) . . . .**power**	*quai (le)* . . . . .train platform	**rendre** . . . .**to give back**
	quand .when	*rendre compte (se)* . . . . .to realize

renouveler ....renew
renseignement (le) ......**information**
rentrer ....to come back in
renverser ....**to spill**
réparer ....**to fix, to repair**
repas (le) ....meal
répéter ....to repeat
répondeur (le) ....**answering machine**
répondre .... to answer, to respond
réponse (la) ....answer, reply
reportage (un) ....newscast
reposer (se) ....**to rest**
réservation (la) ....reservation
réserver ....to make reservations
résolu ....determined
responsable ....responsible
ressembler à ....**to look like**
restaurant (le) ....restaurant
rester ....**to stay, to remain**
résoudre ....**to resolve, to solve
a problem**
résultat (le) ....result
résumé (le) ....**summary**
retourner ....to return
retard (le) ....**lateness**
retraite (la) ....retirement
retraite (à la) ....retired
retrouver ....to find again
réunion (la) ....meeting
réussir ...**to succeed, to pass (an exam)**
réveil (le) ....alarm clock
réveiller (se) ....to wake up
réveillon (le) ....New Year's Eve
revenir ....to come back
rêver....................to dream
révision (la) ....**review**
rez-de-chaussée (le)
...........ground floor (first floor)
riche ....rich
rideau (le) ....curtain
ridicule ....ridiculous
rire ....to laugh
rire (le) ....**laughter**
risque (le) ....**risk**
rivière (la) ....river
riz (le) ....rice
robe (la) ....dress
roi (le) ....king
roman (le) ....novel
ronfler ....to snore
rose (la) ....rose
rôti (le) ....roast
rôtir ....to roast
rouge ....red
rougir ....to blush, to turn red
rouillé/rouillée ....**rusty**
route (la) ....**road, route**
roux/rousse ....redhead
royaume (le) ....kingdom
rue (la) ....street
rusé/rusée ....sly

S

s'il vous plaît ....please

sa/son ....her, his
sable (le) ....**sand**
sac (le) ....**bag, handbag, purse**
sac à dos (le) ....backpack
sage ....**wise, intelligent**
saison (la) ....**season**
salade (la) ....salad
salaire (le) ....**salary**
sale ....dirty
salé/salée ....**salted**
salle (la) ....room
salle à manger (la) ....dining room
salle d'étude (la) ....study hall
salle de bains (la) ....bathroom
salon (le) ....sitting room
samedi ....Saturday
sanglant/sanglante ....bloody
sans ....without
sans goût .....**tasteless, without taste**
santé (la) ....health
satisfait/satisfaite ....**satisfied**
sauter ....to jump
sauvage ....wild
sauver ....**to save**
savoir ....to know
savoir (le) ....**knowledge**
savoir par cœur ......to know by heart
science-fiction (la) .....science fiction
sec/sèche ....**dry**
sèche-cheveux (un) ....hair dryer
sèche-linge (un) ....clothes dryer
sécher ....**to dry**
séchoir (le) ....clothes dryer
secret (le) ....secret
sécurité (la) ....**security, certainty**
seize ....sixteen
séjour (le) ....living room
sel (le) ....salt
semaine (la) ....week
sénateur/sénatrice (un/une) .....senator
sentiment (le) .....**sentiment, feeling**
sentir (se) ....to feel
sept ....seven
septembre ....September
septième ....seventh
série (la) ....**series**
sérieux/sérieuse ....**serious**
serpent (le) ....snake
serrer ....**to tighten, to squeeze**
serrure (la) ....keyhole
serveur/serveuse (un/une) ...waiter
serviette (la) ....towel, napkin
serviette de toilette (la) ....towel
servir ....to serve
servir à ....**to be used for/to**
servir de (se) ....**to use**
ses (pl.) ....his, her
seul/seule ....**alone**
seulement ....only
siècle (le) ....**century**
si ....if, so
siège (le) ....seat

sieste (la) ....siesta, nap
siffler ....to whistle
sifflet (le) ....whistle
signer ....**to sign**
silencieux/silencieuse ....quiet
singe (le) ....monkey
sinon ....otherwise
six ....six
sixième ....sixth
ski (le) ....skiing
slip (le) ....underpants
sœur (la) ....sister
soie (la) ....silk
soif (la) ....thirst
soigner ....**to care for**
soir (le) .....in the evening, the evening
soldat (un) ....soldier
soleil (le) ....sun
sombre ....dark
sommeil (le) ....sleep
sommet (le) ....summit
son ....her, his
son (le) ....**sound**
sonner ....**to ring**
sortie (la) ....**exit**
sortir .....to go out (for entertainment)
soudain ....suddenly
souhaiter ....to wish
soupçonner ....to suspect
soupe (la) ....soup
sourd/sourde ....**deaf**
sourire ....to smile
souris (la) ....a mouse
sous ....under
soutien-gorge (le) ....bra
souvenir (se) ....to remember
souvent ....often
spectateur/spectatrice (le/la) .. spectator
sportif/sportive ....**athletic, sporty**
station service (la) ....gas station
stationner ....to park
steak (le) .... steak
strophe (la) ....stanza
stylo (le) ....ink pen
succès (le) ....**success**
succession (la) ....succession
sucré/sucrée ....**sweet, sugary**
sucre (le) ....sugar
sud (le) ....south
suffisant/suffisante ....sufficient
suggérer ....suggest
suivre ....**to follow**
suivre un cours .....**to take a course**
supérieur/supérieure .**superior, better**
supermarché (le) ....supermarket
sur ....on
sûr/sûre ....**sure, certain**
surgelé/surgelée ....frozen
surpris/surprise ....**surprised**
surtout ....especially
surveiller ....to supervise
sympa ..**nice, attractive (as a person)**

sympathique . . . . .nice
synagogue (la) . . . . .synagogue
système (le) . . . .**system**

T

ta/ton . . . . .your
table (la) . . . . .table
tableau (le) . . . . . . .blackboard, painting
tâche (la) . . . .**task**
taille (la) . . . .**size, waist**
tailler . . . . .to sharpen (pencils)
taire (se) . . . . .to be quiet
talent (le) . . . .**talent**
tant . . . . .so much
tante (la) .aunt
tapis (le) . . . . .carpet, rug
tard . . . . .late
tarte (la) . . . . .pie
tarte aux pommes (la) . . . . . . .apple pie
tas (le) . . . .**heap, pile**
tasse (la) . . . . .cup
taureau (le) . . . . .bull
taxi (le) . . . . .taxi
tee-shirt (le) . . . . .T-shirt
téléphone (le) . . . . .telephone
télévision (la) . . . . .television
tellement . . . . . . .so, so much, so many
témoin (le) . . . .**witness**
tempête (la) . . . . .tempest, storm
temps (le) . . . . .time, weather
tenir . . . . .to hold
tennis (le) . . . . .tennis
tente (la) . . . .**tent**
terminer (se) . . . . .to end
terrain (le) . . . . .playing field
terrifiant . . . . .terrifying
terrifier . . . . .to terrify
tes (pl.) .your
tête (la) .head
têtu/têtue . . . .**stubborn**
texte (le) .text
thé (le) . . . . .tea
théâtre (le) . . . . .theater
ticket (le) . . . .**ticket (métro, bus)**
tigre (le) .tiger
timbre (le) . . . . .stamp
timide . . . . .shy, timid
tire-bouchon (le) . . . . .corkscrew
tirer sur . . . .**to shoot**
tiroir (le) . . . . .drawer
tissu (le) . . . . . .**fabric, cloth, material**
toi . . . . .you
toilettes (les) (f.) . . . . .toilet
toit (le) . . . .**roof**
tolérant . . . . .tolerant
tomate (la) . . . . .tomato
tomber . . . . .to fall
tomber amoureux de
. . . .**to fall in love with**
tomber en panne . . . . . . .to break down
tondeuse (une) . . . . .lawnmower
ton/ta . . . . .your
tondre . . . . .to mow

tortue (la) . . . .**turtle**
tôt . . . . .early
toujours . . . . .always
tour (le) .tour
tour (la) . . . . .tower
toujours . . . . .always
tourner . . .**to turn, to revolve, to rotate**
tousser . . . . .to cough
tout à coup . . . . .suddenly
tout de suite . . . . .right away
tout droit . . . . .straight ahead
tout le monde . . . . .everyone
tout le temps . . . . .all the time
tracteur (le) . . . . .tractor
traduire . . . . .to translate
train (le) . . . . .train
tranquille . . . .**calm, quiet**
transports en commun
(les) (m.) . . . . . .public transportation
travailler . . . . .to work
traverser . . . .**to go across, to cross**
treize . . . . .thirteen
trempé/trempée . . . .**soaked**
trente . . . . .thirty
très . . . . .very
trésor (le) . . . . .treasure
tricher . . . .**to cheat**
trimestre (le) . . . . .term
triste . . . . .sad
trois .three
troisième . . . . .third
tromper . . . .**to deceive**
tromper (se) . . . .**to be mistaken,**
to make a mistake
trompette (la) . . . . .trumpet
trompeur/trompeuse . . . . .deceiving
trop (de) . . . . .too much, too many
trottoir (le) . . . . .sidewalk
troupeau (le) . . . .**herd**
trouver . . . . .to find
tu . . . . .you
tuer . . . .**to kill**
tulipe (la) . . . . .tulip
typique . . . . .typical

U

un/une . . . . .a, one
un peu . . . . .a little
une fois . . . . .once
université (l') (f.) . . . . .university
urbaniste (l') (m./f.) . . . . . . .city planner
usine (une) . . . . .factory
utile . . . . .useful
utiliser . . . . .to use

V

vacances (les) (f.) . . . .**vacation**
vache (la) . . . . .cow
vague (la) . . . .**wave**
vaisselle (la) . . . . .dishes
valise (la) . . . .**suitcase**
valoir la peine . .**to be worth the trouble**

vélo (le) . . . . .bicycle
vendeur/vendeuse (un/une) .**store clerk**
vendre . . . . .to sell
vendredi . . . . .Friday
vengeance (la) . . . .**revenge, vengeance**
venir . . . . .to come
vent (le) . . . . .wind
ventilateur (un) . . . . .fan
vérifier . . . . .to check
vérité (la) . . . . .truth
verre (le) . . . . .glass
vers . . . . .toward
verser . . . .**to pour**
vert .green
veste (la) . . . . .jacket
vêtement (le) . . . . .piece of clothing
vêtements (les) (m.) . . . . .clothes
viande (la) . . . . .meat
victime (la) . . . .**victim**
vidéo (la) . . . . .videocassette
vie (la) . . . . .life
vieillesse (la) . . . .**old age**
vieux/vieille . . . .**old**
village (le) . . . . .village
villageois/villageoise (le/la)
. . . . .person living in a village
ville (la) . . . . .city
vin (le) . . . . .wine
vingt . . . . .twenty
violence (la) . . . .**violence**
violet/violette . . . . .purple
violon (le) . . . . .violin
visiter . . . . .to visit (a place)
vite . . . . .fast, quickly
vitesse (la) . . . . .speed
voir . . . . .to see
voisin/voisine (un/une) . . . . . .neighbor
voiture (la) . . . . .car
voix (la) . . . . .voice
vol (le) . . . .**flight, theft**
volé/volée . . . .**stolen**
voler . . . . .to steal, to fly
voleur/voleuse (un/une) . . . . .thief
vos .your
vote (le) . . . .**vote**
votre . . . . .your
vouloir . . . . .to want
vous . . . . .you
voyage (le) . . . . .trip
voyager . . . . .to travel
vrai .true

W

wagon (le) . . . . .wagon

Y

yeux (les) (m.) . . . . .eyes

Z

zèbre (le) . . . . .zebra

DICTIONNAIRE
ANGLAIS-FRANÇAIS

DICTIONNAIRE ANGLAIS-FRANÇAIS

(Bold print indicates new vocabulary presented in the vocabulary lists at the beginning of each lesson.)

A

a, one . . . .*un/une*
a little . . . .*un peu*
a lot . . . .*beaucoup*
abandon (to) . . . .***abandonner***
able . . . .***capable***
about, from, of . . . .*de*
about, more or less . . . .*environ*
above . . . .*par-dessus*
abroad . . . .*à l'étranger*
abroad (to go) . . . .*aller à l'étranger*
absent . . . .*absent*
accident . . . .*(l') accident (m.)*
accompany (to) . . . .*accompagner*
accountant . . . .*(un/une) comptable*
accuse (to) . . . .***accuser***
ache (to), to hurt . . . .***avoir mal***
acquire (to) . . . .***acquérir***
across . . . .*à travers*
across (to go), to cross . . . . . .***traverser***
across from . . . .*en face de*
active . . . .*actif*
actor/actress . . . .*(un/une) acteur/actrice*
  (un/une) comédien/comédienne
add (to) . . . .***ajouter***
address . . . .*(l') adresse (f.)*
admirer . . . .*(l') admirateur (m.)*
admit (to) . . . .*admettre*
adore (to) . . . .*adorer*
advantage . . . .***(l') avantage (m.)***
advertisement, ad . . . .*(la) réclame*
advertisement (ad), advertising,
  announcement .***(la) publicité (la pub)***
advice . . . .***(le) conseil***
advise (to) . . . .***conseiller***
advisor . .*(un/une) conseiller/conseillère*
affection . . . .***(l') affection (f.)***
affectionate . . . . .*affectueux/affectueuse*
afraid (to be) . . . .*avoir peur (de)*
after . . . .*après*
afternoon . . . .*(l') après-midi (m./f.)*
afternoon snack (to have an) . . . . .*goûter*
again . . . .*de nouveau*
against . . . .*contre*
age . . . .***(l') âge (m.)***
aim, goal . . . .***(le) but***
air-conditioned . . . .*climatisé*
air-conditioner . . . .*(le) climatiseur*
air-conditioning . . . . . .*(la) climatisation*
airplane . . . .*(l') avion (m.)*
airport . . . .*(l') aéroport (m.)*
airport gate, door . . . .*(la) porte*
alarm clock . . . .*(le) réveil*
alcohol . . . .*(l') alcool (m.)*
algebra . . . .*(l') algèbre (f.)*
all the time . . . .*tout le temps*

allow (to) . . . .*permettre*
allowed . . . .*permis/permise*
almost . . . .*presque*
alone . . . .***seul/seule***
already . . . .*déjà*
also . . . .*aussi*
always . . . .*toujours*
ambition . . . .*(l') ambition (f.)*
among . . . .*parmi*
amuse (to) . . . .*amuser*
amusing . . . .***amusant/amusante***
analyst . . . .*(un/une) analyst/analyste*
ancient, old . . . .*ancien/ancienne*
and . . . .*et*
angel . . . .*(l') ange (m.)*
anger . . . .***(la) colère***
angry (to be) . . . .*être en colère*
angry (to become) . . . .*(se) fâcher*
angry, furious . . . . .***furieux/furieuse***
angry, upset . . . .*fâché*
animation, excitement . . . . . .*animation*
anniversary, birthday
  . . . .*anniversaire (l') (m.)*
announce (to) . . . .*annoncer*
announcement, advertisement (ad)
  . . . .***(la) publicité (la pub)***
annoyed . . . .*agacé/agacée*
annoying . . . .***agaçant/agaçante***
annoying, a pain . . . .***pénible***
answer (to), to respond . . . . . .*répondre*
answering machine . . . .***(le) répondeur***
anyone . . . .*n'importe qui*
anything . . . .*n'importe quoi*
anyway . . . .*d'ailleurs*
apartment . . . .*(l') appartement (m.)*
apartment building . . .*(l') immeuble (m.)*
appear (to) . . . .***apparaître***
appear (to), to seem . . . . . .***paraître***
applaud (to) . . . .*applaudir*
applause . . . . .*(l') applaudissement (m.)*
apple . . . .*(la) pomme*
apple pie . . . .*(la) tarte aux pommes*
appointment . . . .*(un) rendez-vous*
appointment (to have an)
  . . . .***avoir rendez-vous***
April . . . .*avril*
architect . . . .*(un/une) architecte*
arm . . . .*(le) bras*
armchair . . . .*(le) fauteuil*
arrival . . . .*(l') arrivée (f.)*
arrive (to) . . . .*arriver*
arrogant . . . .***arrogant/arrogante***
arrow . . . .*(la) flèche*
art . . . .*(l') art (m.)*
artichoke . . . .*(l') artichaut (m.)*
as . . . .*comme*
as much . . . .*autant*

as much as . . . .*autant que*
as soon as . . . .*dès que, aussitôt que*
ashamed of (to be) . . . . .*avoir honte (de)*
ask (for) (to) . . . .*demander*
ask a question (to) . .***poser une question***
ask (for) (to) . . . .*demander*
asparagus . . . .*(l') asperge (f.)*
associate (to) . . . .*associer*
at, to . . . .*à*
at first . . . .*d'abord*
at (someone's) house . .*chez (+ personne)*
at the same time . . . .*en même temps*
athletic, sporty . . . .*sportif/sportive*
ATM machine
  . . . .*(le) distributeur de billets*
attach (to), to tie . . . .*attacher*
attack (to) . . . .*attaquer*
attend (to) . . . .***assister à***
attention (to pay) . . . . .***faire attention***
attentive . . . .***attentif/attentive***
attitude . . . .***(l') attitude (f.)***
attract (to) . . . .***attirer***
attractive (as a person), nice . . . . .*sympa*
August . . . .*août*
aunt . . . .*(la) tante*
author . . . .*(l') auteur (m.)*
authority . . . .***(l') autorité (f.)***
autumn . . . .*(l') automne (m.)*
avenue . . . .*(l') avenue (f.)*
average . . . .***moyen/moyenne***

B

baby . . . .*(le) bébé*
back . . . .*(le) dos*
backpack . . . .*(le) sac à dos*
bad . . . .*mauvais/mauvaise*
badly . . . .*mal*
bag, handbag, purse . . . .***(le) sac***
baker . . . . .*(le/la) boulanger/boulangère*
bald . . . .***chauve***
ball . . . .*(le) bal*
ball (big) . . . .*(le) ballon*
ball (small) . . . .*(la) balle*
ballet . . . .*(un) ballet*
banana . . . .*(la) banane*
band . . . .*(le) groupe*
bank . . . .***(la) banque***
banker . . . .*(un/une) banquier/banquière*
bark (to) . . . .***aboyer***
baseball . . . .*(le) baseball*
basket . . . .*le panier*
basketball . . . .*(le) basket*
bath . . . .*(le) bain*
bath (to take a) . . . .*prendre un bain*
bathing suit, swimsuit
  . . . .*(le) maillot de bain*

bathrobe . . . .*(le) peignoir*
bathroom . . . .*(la) salle de bains*
bathroom sink . . . .*(le) lavabo*
bathtub . . . .*(la) baignoire*
battle . . . .*(la) bataille*
be (to) . . . . *être*
be able (to) (can) . . . .*pouvoir*
be over (to), to rule . . . .*dominer*
beach . . . .*(la) plage*
bear . . . .*(l') ours (m.)*
beard . . . .*(la) barbe*
beautiful . . . .**beau/belle**
because . . . .*parce que*
because, since . . . .*puisque*
become (to) . . . .*devenir*
bed . . . .*(le) lit*
bed (to go to), to lie down . .*(se) coucher*
bedroom . . . .*(la) chambre*
beer . . . .*(la) bière*
before . . . .*avant (de)*
begin (to) . . . .*commencer*
behind . . . .*derrière*
believe (to) . . . .*croire*
bell . . . .**(la) cloche**
belong to (to) . . . .**appartenir à**
belongings, things, business
. . . .**(les) affaires (f.)**
below . . . .*au-dessous de*
belt . . . .*(la) ceinture*
better, best . . . .**meilleur/meilleure**
better, best (adv.) . . . .*mieux*
better, superior . . .**supérieur/supérieure**
between . . . .*entre*
bicycle . . . .*(le) vélo*
bicycle (to ride a) . . . . .*aller à bicyclette*
(*faire du vélo*)
big, fat, tall . .*gros/grosse, grand/grande*
bill (e.g., in a restaurant) . .*(l') addition (f.)*
billy goat . . . .*(le) bouc*
biology . . . .*(la) biologie*
bird . . . .*(l') oiseau (m.)*
birthday, anniversary
. . . .*(l') anniversaire (m.)*
bit, piece, selection . . . . . .**(le) morceau**
bite (to) . . . .**mordre**
bitter . . . .**amer/amère**
black . . . .*noir/noire*
blackboard, painting . . . . . .*(le) tableau*
blind . . . .**aveugle**
blind (to) . . . .*éblouir*
blond(e) . . . .**blond/blonde**
bloody . . . .*sanglant/sanglante*
blouse . . . .*(le) chemisier*
blue . . . .*bleu*
blush (to), to turn red . . . .*rougir*
boarding student . . . . .*(l') interne (m./f.)*
boat . . . .*(le) bateau*
body . . . .*(le) corps*
boil (to) . . . .*bouillir*
book . . . .*(le) livre*
boots . . . .*(les) bottes (f.)*

border . . . .**(la) frontière**
bored (to be) . . . .*(s') ennuyer*
boring . . . .**ennuyeux/ennuyeuse**
boring (to be) . . . .**être ennuyeux**
born . . . .**né/née**
born (to be) . . . .*naître*
borrow (to) . . . .*emprunter*
boss . . .*(le/la) patron/patronne, (le) chef*
bother (to), to disturb . . . . . .**déranger**
bother (to), to embarrass . . . . . .**gêner**
bottle . . . .*(la) bouteille*
bottom . . . .*(le) fond*
box . . . .*(la) boîte*
boy . . . .*(le) garçon*
boyfriend . . . .*(le) petit ami*
bra . . . .*(le) soutien-gorge*
bracelet . . . .*(le) bracelet*
brand new . . . .*neuf/neuve*
bread . . . .*(le) pain*
break (to) . . . .*(se) casser*
break down (to) . . . . . .*tomber en panne*
bridge . . . .*(le) pont*
bring (to) . . . .*apporter*
broil (to), to grill . . . .*griller*
broom . . . .**(le) balai**
brother . . . .*(le) frère*
brother-in-law . . . .*(le) beau-frère*
brown . . . .**marron**
brown (for hair) . . . .*brun*
brush (to) . . . .*(se) brosser*
buckled, curly . . . . . .**bouclé/bouclée**
buddy . . . .*(le/la) copain/copine*
building . . . .*(le) bâtiment*
bull . . . .*(le) taureau*
bureau . . . .*(la) commode*
burn (to) . . . .*brûler*
burst, exhausted . . . .**crevé/crevée**
burst . . . .**éclaté/éclatée**
burst (to) . . . .**éclater**
bus . . . .*(l') autobus (m.)*
bush . . . .*(le) buisson*
business . . . .**(le) commerce**
business, belongings, things
. . . .**(les) affaires (f.)**
busy . . . .**occupé/occupée**
but . . . .*mais*
button . . . .*(le) bouton*
buy (to) . . . .*acheter*
by . . . .*par*

C

cafeteria . . . .*(la) cafétéria*
cage . . . .*(la) cage*
cake . . . .*(le) gâteau*
calendar . . . .*(le) calendrier*
call (to) . . . .*appeler*
called (to be) . . . .*(s') appeler*
calm . . . .**tranquille**
camel . . . .*(le) chameau*
camera . . . .*(l') appareil photo (m.)*

campaign . . . .**(la) campagne**
camping . . . .*(le) camping*
camping (to go) . . . .*camper*
can opener . . . .*(un) ouvre-boîte*
Canadian . . . .**canadien/canadienne**
candle . . . .*(la) bougie, (la) chandelle*
candy . . . .*(un) bonbon*
cap . . . .*(la) casquette*
car . . . .*(la) voiture*
card, map (for countries
or regions) . . . .*(la) carte*
care for (to) . . . .**soigner**
careful, prudent . . . .*prudent*
carelessly daring, not prudent
. . . .*imprudent*
carpet, rug . . . .*(le) tapis*
carrot . . . .**(la) carotte**
carry (to), to wear . . . .*porter*
cartoon . . . .*(un) dessin animé*
case . . . .*(le) cas*
cashmere . . . .*(le) cachemire*
castle . . . .*(le) château*
cat . . . .*(le) chat*
catastrophic . . . .*catastrophique*
catch (to) . . . .*attraper*
Catholic . . . .**catholique**
cause (to) . . . .**causer**
cautious . . . .**prudent/prudente**
CD (compact disc)
. . . .*(le) disque compact, (le) CD*
cell phone . . . .*(le) portable*
century . . . .**(le) siècle**
cereal . . . .*(les) céréales (f.)*
certain . . . .**certain/certaine**
certain, sure . . . .**sûr/sûre**
certainty, security . . . .**(la) sécurité**
chair . . . .*(la) chaise*
chalk . . . .*(la) craie*
champion . .*(le/la) champion/championne*
championship . . . .*(le) championnat*
chance . . . .*(le) hasard*
change (to) . . . .*(se) changer*
charming . . . .*charmant/charmante*
chat (to) . . . .**bavarder**
cheap . . . .**bon marché**
cheat (to) . . . .**tricher**
check . . . .*(le) chèque*
check (to) . . . .*vérifier*
check in (to), to tape
(e.g., film, song) . . . .*enregistrer*
cheese . . . .*(le) fromage*
chemistry . . . .*(la) chimie*
chicken . . . .*(le) poulet*
child . . . .*(l') enfant (m./f.)*
childhood . . . .**(l') enfance (f.)**
chlorine . . . .*(le) chlore*
chocolate ice cream
. . . .*(la) glace au chocolat*
choose (to) . . . .*choisir*
Christian . . . .**chrétien/chrétienne**
church . . . .**(l') église (f.)**

cinema, movie theater . . . . . .*(le) cinéma*
circumstance . . . .*(la) circonstance*
circus . . . .*(le) cirque*
city . . . .*(la) ville*
city planner . . . .*(l') urbaniste (m./f.)*
civilized . . . .*civilisé*
class . . . .*(la) classe*
class, course . . . .*(le) cours*
classical . . . .*classique*
clean . . . .*propre*
clean (to) . . . .*nettoyer*
climate . . . .*(le) climat*
climb (to) . . . .*escalader*
close, near (adj.) . . . .*proche*
close (to), to shut . . . .*fermer*
closed . . . .*fermé/fermée*
closet . . . .*(le) placard*
cloth, material, fabric . . . .*(le) tissu*
clothes . . . .*(les) vêtements (m.)*
clothes dryer . . . .*(un) sèche-linge,*
                              (le) séchoir
cloud . . . .*(le) nuage*
clumsy . . . .*maladroit/maladroite*
coach . . . .*(l') entraîneur/*
                  entraîneuse (m./f.)
coach, leader . .*(le/la) moniteur/monitrice*
coat . . . .*(le) manteau*
coffee . . . .*(le) café*
cold . . . .*froid/froide*
color . . . .*(la) couleur*
comb (to) . . . .*(se) peigner*
come (to) . . . .*venir*
come back (to), to return . . . . . .*revenir*
come back in (to) . . . .*rentrer*
comfortable (for people) . . . .*à l'aise*
comfortable (for things) . . . .*confortable*
comforter . . . .*(la) couette*
comic strip . . . .*(une) bande dessinée*
common, fluent . . . .*courant*
common, ordinary . . . .*ordinaire*
compact disc (CD)
       . . . .*(le) disque compact, (le) CD*
competition . . . .*(la) compétition*
complain (to) . . . .*(se) plaindre*
complaint . . . .*(la) plainte*
computer . . . .*(l') ordinateur (m.)*
concert . . . .*(un) concert*
condition, state . . . .*(l') état (m.)*
confidence . . . .*(la) confiance*
confuse (to) . . . .*confondre*
congratulate (to) . . . .*féliciter*
congratulations . . . .*(les) félicitations (f.)*
connected, plugged in
       . . . .*branché/branchée*
conscientious . . . .*consciencieux/*
                  consciencieuse
continent . . . .*(le) continent*
continue (to) . . . .*continuer*
contribute (to) . . . .*contribuer*
cook . . . . .*(un/une) cuisinier/cuisinière*
cook (to) . . . .*cuire, faire la cuisine*

cooked . . . .*cuit*
cookie . . . .*(le) biscuit*
cooking, kitchen . . . .*(la) cuisine*
copy (to) . . . .*copier*
corkscrew . . . .*(le) tire-bouchon*
corn . . . .*(le) maïs*
corner . . . .*(le) coin*
corpse . . . .*(le) cadavre*
correct (to) . . . .*corriger*
cost (to) . . . .*coûter*
cotton . . . .*(le) coton*
couch, sofa . . . .*(le) canapé*
cough (to) . . . .*tousser*
count (to) . . . .*compter*
counter . . . .*(le) comptoir*
country . . . .*(le) pays*
country (to go to the)
       . . . .*aller à la campagne*
countryside . . . .*(la) campagne*
courage to (to have the), to dare . .*oser*
course, class . . . .*(le) cours*
course, dish . . . .*(le) plat*
courteous, polite . . . .*poli/polie*
cousin . . . .*(le/la) cousin/cousine*
cover (to) . . . .*couvrir*
cow . . . .*(la) vache*
crazy, mad . . . .*fou/folle*
credit card . . . . . .*(la) carte de crédit*
cross (to), to go across . . . . . .*traverser*
crown . . . .*(la) couronne*
cruel . . . .*cruel/cruelle*
cry (to) . . . .*pleurer*
cucumber . . . .*(le) concombre*
cup . . . .*(la) tasse*
curious . . . .*curieux/curieuse*
curiosity . . . .*(la) curiosité*
curly, buckled . . . .*bouclé/bouclée*
current . . . .*actuel/actuelle*
curtain . . . .*(le) rideau*
cut (to) . . . .*couper*
cute, precious . . . . . .*mignon/mignonne*

D

daily . . . .*quotidien/quotidienne*
damage . . . .*(le) dommage*
damage (to), to ruin . . . .*abîmer*
dance . . . .*(la) danse*
dance (to) . . . .*danser*
to dare, to have the courage to . . .*oser*
dark . . . .*sombre*
date (calendar) . . . .*(la) date*
daughter, girl . . . .*(la) fille*
dawn . . . .*(l') aube (f.)*
day . . . . .*(le) jour, (la) journée*
day (the) . . . .*(la) journée*
day after (the) . . . .*(le) lendemain*
day student . . . .*(l') externe (m./f.)*
dead . . . .*mort/morte*
deaf . . . .*sourd/sourde*
debt . . . .*(la) dette*

deceitful . . . .*mensonger/mensongère*
deceive (to) . . . .*tromper*
deceiving . . . .*trompeur/trompeuse*
December . . . .*décembre*
decide (to) . . . .*décider*
declaration . . . .*(la) déclaration*
deep . . . .*profond*
defect . . . .*(le) défaut*
defend (to), to forbid . . . .*défendre*
delicious . . . .*délicieux/délicieuse*
delighted . . . .*ravi/ravie*
deliver (to), to hand over . . . . . .*livrer*
demand (to), to require . . . .*exiger*
denture, false teeth . . . .*(le) dentier*
deny (to) . . . .*nier*
department . . . .*(le) rayon*
department store . . .*(le) grand magasin*
departure . . . .*(le) départ*
depress (to) . . . .*déprimer*
depressing . . . .*déprimant*
deserted . . . .*désert*
deserve (to) . . . .*mériter*
desire (to) . . . .*désirer*
desire (to), to want . . . . .*avoir envie (de)*
desk, office . . . .*(le) bureau*
dessert . . . .*(le) dessert*
destiny, fate . . . .*(le) destin*
destroy (to) . . . .*détruire*
detail . . . .*(le) détail*
detective movie . . . . .*(un) film policier*
determined . . . .*résolu*
develop (to) . . . .*développer*
devour . . . .*dévorer*
die (to) . . . .*mourir*
different . . . .*différent/différente*
difficult . . . .*difficile*
difficulty, problem . . . .*(la) difficulté*
diminish (to) . . . .*diminuer*
dining room . . . .*(la) salle à manger*
dinner (to have) . . . .*dîner*
direction, path . . . .*(le) chemin*
director (play, movie)
       . . . .*le metteur en scène*
dirty . . . .*sale*
disappear (to) . . . .*disparaître*
disappoint (to) . . . .*décevoir*
disappointed . . . .*déçu/déçue*
discover (to) . . . .*découvrir*
discuss (to) . . . .*discuter*
disgusting . . . . .*dégoûtant/dégoûtante*
dish, course . . . .*(le) plat*
dishes . . . .*(la) vaisselle*
dishes (to do the) . . . . .*faire la vaisselle*
dishwasher . . . .*(le) lave-vaisselle*
disobey (to) . . . .*désobéir*
disorder, mess . . . .*(le) désordre*
disturb (to), to bother . . . .*déranger*
do (to) . . . .*faire*
do one's hair (to) . . . .*(se) coiffer*
doctor . . . .*(le) médecin*
documentary . . . .*(un) documentaire*

dog . . . .*(le) chien*	*embarrassé/embarrassée*	fair, just . . . .*juste*
doll . . . .*(la) poupée*	**embarrassment** . . . .**(la) honte**	**faithful** . . . .**fidèle**
door, airport gate . . . .*(la) porte*	employ (to) . . . .*employer*	fall (to) . . . .*tomber*
dormitory . . . .*(le) dortoir*	**employee** . . . .**(l') employé/**	**fall in love with (to)**
doubt . . . .*(le) doute*	*employée (m./f.)*	. . . .**tomber amoureux de**
doubt (to) . . . .*douter*	employment position . . . .*(le) poste*	false, wrong . . . .*faux/fausse*
drama . . . .*(le) drame*	**end** . . . .**(la) fin**	false teeth, denture . . . .*(le) dentier*
draw (to) . . . .*dessiner*	end (to) . . . .*(se) terminer*	**family (of the)** . . . . .**familial/familiale**
drawback (a) . . . .*(un) inconvénient*	enemy . . . . . .*(l') ennemi/ennemie (m./f.)*	**famous** . . . .**célèbre**
drawer . . . .*(le) tiroir*	energetic . . . .*énergique*	fan . . . .*(un) ventilateur*
drawing . . . .**(le) dessin**	energy . . . .*(l') énergie (f.)*	far . . . .*loin*
dream (to) . . . .*rêver*	engine . . . .*(le) moteur*	far from . . . .*loin de*
dress . . . .*(la) robe*	**English** . . . .*anglais/anglaise*	**farm** . . . .**(la) ferme**
dress (to) (to get dressed) . . .*(s') habiller*	**enjoy (to), to have a good time**	farmer . . . . . .*(un/une) fermier/fermière*
drink . . . .*(la) boisson*	. . . .*(s') amuser*	fashion (to be in) . . . . . .*être à la mode*
drink (to) . . . .*boire*	**enormous** . . . .**énorme**	fast . . . .*rapide*
drive (to) . . . .*conduire*	enough . . . .*assez*	fast, quickly . . . .*vite*
drive to (to) . . . .*aller en voiture*	entertain (to) . . . .*(se) divertir*	**fat, big, tall** . .*gros/grosse, grand/grande*
driver's license . .*(le) permis de conduire*	entertainment . . . . . .*(un) divertissement*	**fate, destiny** . . . .**(le) destin**
drop . . . .**(la) goutte**	**entire** . . . .**entier/entière**	father . . . .*(le) père*
drop (to), to give up . . . .**laisser tomber**	**entrance, first course** . . . .**(l') entrée (f.)**	father-in-law . . . .*(le) beau-père*
drop off (to) . . . .*déposer*	entree, main course . . .*(le) plat principal*	**favorite, preferred** . . . .**préféré/préférée**
drums . . . .*(la) batterie*	environment . . . . .*(l') environnement (m.)*	fear . . . .*(la) peur*
drunk . . . .**ivre**	envy . . . .*(l') envie (f.)*	fear (to) . . . .*craindre*
dry . . . .**sec/sèche**	episode . . . .*(l') épisode (m.)*	**feather** . . . .**(la) plume**
dry (to) . . . .**sécher**	equal . . . .*égal*	February . . . .*février*
during . . . .*pendant*	**erase (to)** . . . .**effacer**	feel (to) . . . .*(se) sentir*
dust . . . .**(la) poussière**	error, mistake . . . .*(l') erreur (f.)*	**feeling, sentiment** . . . . . .**(le) sentiment**
DVD . . . .*(un) DVD*	escape (to) . . . .*(s') échapper*	festival . . . .*(le) festival*
dwell (to), to live . . . .*habiter, loger*	especially . . . .*surtout*	**fidgety, nervous**
	event . . . .*(l') événement (m.)*	**exasperated** . . . .**énervé/énervée**
# E	everyone . . . .*tout le monde*	field . . . .*(le) champ*
	everywhere . . . .*partout*	fifteen . . . .*quinze*
each (adj.) . . . .*chaque*	ewe . . . .*(la) brebis*	fifth . . . .*cinquième*
each (pron.) . . . .*chacun/chacune*	exam . . . .*(l') examen (m.)*	**fight** . . . .**(la) bataille**
eager . . . .*impatient/impatiente*	exam (to take an) . . . .*passer un examen*	**fight (to)** . . . .**(se) battre**
ear . . . .*(l') oreille (f.)*	exasperate, get on one's nerves	**fill (to)** . . . .**remplir**
early . . . .*de bonne heure, tôt*	. . . .*exaspérer*	film . . . .*(la) pellicule, (le) film*
earn (to), to win . . . .**gagner**	exasperated, fidgety,	finally . . . .*enfin*
earring . . . .*(la) boucle d'oreille*	nervous . . . .*énervé/énervée*	find (to) . . . .*trouver*
east . . . .*(l') est (m.)*	exasperated (to get) . . . .*(s') énerver*	find again (to) . . . .*retrouver*
easy . . . .*facile*	**exhausted, burst** . . . .**crevé/crevée**	finger . . . .*(le) doigt*
eat (to) . . . .*manger*	excited . . . .*excité/excitée*	**fingernail, toenail** . . . . .**(l') ongle (m.)**
edge (the) . . . .*(le) bord*	excitement, animation . . . .*animation*	finish (to) . . . .*finir*
educative . . . .*éducatif/éducative*	**exit** . . . .**(la) sortie**	fire . . . .*(le) feu*
efficient . . . .*efficace*	**expand (to), to grow** . . . .**grandir**	fire (accident) . . . .*(l') incendie (m.)*
egg . . . .*(l') œuf (m.)*	**expect (to)** . . . .**(s') attendre à**	fireman . . . .*(le) pompier*
eggplant . . . .*(l') aubergine (f.)*	**expensive** . . . .**cher/chère**	**first** . . . .**premier/première**
eight . . . .*huit*	explain (to) . . . .*expliquer*	**first course, entrance** . . . .**(l') entrée (f.)**
eighteen . . . .*dix-huit*	explorer . . . .*(l') explorateur (m.)*	fish . . . .*(le) poisson*
eighth . . . .*huitième*	**extinguish (to), to turn off** . . . .**éteindre**	fishing, peach . . . .*(la) pêche*
electric . . . .*électrique*	eye . . . .*(l') œil (m.)*	five . . . .*cinq*
electric plug . . . . . .*(une) prise électrique*	eyes . . . .*(les) yeux (m.)*	**fix (to), to repair** . . . .**réparer**
electric shaver . . . .*(un) rasoir électrique*		**flag** . . . .**(le) drapeau**
elegant . . . .*chic, élégant*	# F	**flame** . . . .**(la) flamme**
elevator . . . .*(l') ascenseur (m.)*		**flat** . . . .**plat/plate**
eleven . . . .*onze*	fabric, cloth, material . . . .*(le) tissu*	flatter (to) . . . .*flatter*
e-mail . . . . . .**(le) courrier électronique,**	factory . . . .*(une) usine*	**flight, theft** . . . .**(le) vol**
(le) courriel, (le) e-mail, (le) mail	factory worker (a)	flight attendant . .*(l') hôtesse de l'air (f.)*
embarrass (to), to bother . . . . . .**gêner**	. . . .*(un/une) ouvrier/ouvrière*	floor (first, second . . .) . . .*(l') étage (m.)*
embarrassed . . . .**confus/confuse,**	fail (to) . . . .*échouer, rater*	flower . . . .*(la) fleur*

fluent, common . . . .*courant*
fly (to) . . . .*voler*
fly to (to) . . . .*aller en avion*
fog . . . .*(le) brouillard*
fold (to) . . . .*plier*
follow (to) . . . .*suivre*
food . . . .*(la) nourriture*
foolish, silly, stupid . . . .*bête*
food . . . .*(la) nourriture*
foot . . . .*(le) pied*
football . . . .*(le) football américain*
for . . . .*pour*
for example . . . .*par exemple*
forbid (to), to defend . .*défendre, interdire*
foreign . . . .*étranger/étrangère*
foreigner . .*(l') étranger/étrangère (m./f.)*
forest . . . .*(la) forêt*
forest, wood . . . .*(le) bois*
for example . . . .*par exemple*
forget (to) . . . .*oublier*
fork . . . .*(la) fourchette*
four . . . .*quatre*
fourteen . . . .*quatorze*
fourth . . . .*quatrième*
fragile . . . .*fragile*
free (not busy, liberated) . . . .*libre*
free of charge . . . .*gratuit/gratuite*
freedom . . . .*(la) liberté*
freeway, highway . . . .*(l') autoroute (f.)*
freeze (to) . . . .*geler*
freezer . . . .*(le) congélateur*
fresh . . . .*frais/fraîche*
Friday . . . .*vendredi*
friend . . . .*(l') ami/amie (m./f.)*
friendship . . . .*(l') amitié (f.)*
frighten (to), to scare . . . .*effrayer*
frightful, frightening
. . . .*effrayant/effrayante*
frog . . . .*(la) grenouille*
from, about, of . . . .*de*
from, where . . . .*d'où*
front . . . .*(le) devant*
frozen . . . .*surgelé/surgelée*
frustrated . . . .*frustré/frustrée*
fry (to) . . . .*frire*
frying pan . . . .*(la) poêle*
full . . . .*plein/pleine*
full (only for a place) . .*complet/complète*
function (to), to work . . . . .*fonctionner*
funny . . . .*drôle, marrant/marrante*
furious, angry . . . . . .*furieux/furieuse*
future . . . .*(le) futur*

G

gain weight (to), to get bigger . . .*grossir*
game (sports) . . . .*(le) match*
garbage can . . . .*(la) poubelle*
garden, yard . . . .*(le) jardin*
garlic . . . .*(l') aïl (m.)*
gas station . . . .*(la) station service*
gasoline . . . .*(l') essence (f.)*

gazelle . . . .*(la) gazelle*
generous . . . .*généreux/généreuse*
gentleness . . . .*(la) douceur*
geography . . . .*(la) géographie*
geometry . . . .*(la) géométrie*
gesture . . . .*(le) geste*
get along (to) . . . .*(s') entendre avec*
get bigger (to), to gain weight . . .*grossir*
get married (to) . . . .*(se) marier*
get off (to), to land . . . .*débarquer*
get rid of (to) . . . .*(se) débarrasser*
get up (to) . . . .*(se) lever*
get used to (to) . . . . . .*(s') habituer à*
ghost . . . .*(le) fantôme*
giant . . . .*(le) géant*
giraffe . . . .*(la) girafe*
girl, daughter . . . .*(la) fille*
girlfriend . . . .*(la) petite amie*
give (to) . . . .*donner*
give back (to) . . . .*rendre*
give up (to), to drop . . .*laisser tomber*
glass . . . .*(le) verre*
glasses (spectacles) . . . .*(les) lunettes (f.)*
gloves . . . .*(les) gants (m.)*
go (to) . . . .*aller*
go across (to), to cross . . . . . .*traverser*
go around (to) . . . .*faire le tour de*
go away (to), to leave . . .*partir, quitter*
go down (to) . . . .*descendre*
go in (to) . . . .*entrer*
go out (to) (for entertainment) . . . .*sortir*
go to bed (to), to lie down . .*(se) coucher*
go to sleep (to) . . . .*(s') endormir*
go up (to) . . . .*monter*
goal, aim . . . .*(le) but*
goal (to score a) . . . . . .*marquer un but*
goalkeeper . . . .*(un) gardien de but*
godmother . . . .*la marraine*
good . . . .*bon/bonne*
good time (to have a),
to enjoy . . . .*(s') amuser*
govern (to) . . . .*gouverner*
government . . . .*(le) gouvernement*
grade . . . .*(la) note*
graduate (to) . . . .*avoir son diplôme*
granddaughter . . . .*(la) petite-fille*
grandfather . . . .*(le) grand-père*
grandmother . . . .*(la) grand-mère*
grandson . . . .*(le) petit-fils*
grass . . . .*(le) gazon, (l') herbe (f.)*
great grandfather
. . . .*(l') arrière grand-père (m.)*
great grandmother
. . . .*(l') arrière grand-mère (f.)*
green . . . .*vert*
green beans . . . .*(les) haricots verts (m.)*
grey . . . .*gris*
grief, pain . . . .*(la) douleur*
grill (to), to broil . . . .*griller*
ground floor (first floor)
. . . .*(le) rez-de-chaussée*
grow (to), to expand . . . .*grandir*

grow (to), to push . . . .*pousser*
guess (to) . . . .*deviner*
guest . . . .*(l') invité/ invitée*
guide . . . .*(le/la) guide*
guilty . . . .*coupable*
guitar . . . .*(la) guitare*
gullible . . . .*crédule*
gymnasium . . . .*(le) gymnase*

H

habit . . . .*(l') habitude (f.)*
hail . . . .*(la) grêle*
hair . . . .*(les) cheveux (m.)*
hair dryer . . . .*(un) sèche-cheveux*
hairdresser . . . .*(le/la) coiffeur/coiffeuse*
half (adj.) . . . .*demi*
hallway . . . .*(le) couloir*
ham . . . .*(le) jambon*
hamburger . . . .*(le) hamburger*
hand . . . .*(la) main*
handbag, bag, purse . . . .*(le) sac*
handkerchief . . . .*(le) mouchoir*
handle . . . .*(le) manche*
hand over (to), to deliver . . . . . .*livrer*
hang (to) . . . .*pendre*
hang up (to) . . . .*raccrocher*
hanger . . . .*(le) cintre*
happen (to) . . . .*arriver*
happen (to) . . . .*(se) passer*
happiness . . . .*(le) bonheur*
happy . . . .*heureux/heureuse,*
content/contente
hard . . . .*dur/dure*
hat . . . .*(le) chapeau*
hate (to) . . . .*détester*
hate (to), to loathe . . . .*avoir horreur de*
have (to) . . . .*avoir*
have to (to) (do something),
must, to owe . . . . .*devoir (+ infinitive)*
have a good time (to),
to enjoy . . . .*(s') amuser*
have lunch (to) . . . .*(le) déjeuner*
have problems (to) . . .*avoir des ennuis*
have the courage to (to) . . . .*oser*
head . . . .*(la) tête*
headmaster, head of company
. . . .*(un/une) directeur/directrice*
health . . . .*(la) santé*
heap, pile . . . .*(le) tas*
hear (to), to understand . . . .*entendre*
hear (a rumor) (to) . . . . .*entendre dire*
heat (to) . . . .*chauffer*
heavy . . . .*lourd/lourde*
helmet . . . .*(le) casque*
help (to) . . . .*aider*
hen . . . .*(la) poule*
her . . . .*sa/son/ses*
herd . . . .*(le) troupeau*
here . . . .*ici*
hesitate (to) . . . .*hésiter*
hidden . . . .*caché/cachée*

hide (something) (to) . . . . *cacher*
hideous . . . . *hideux*
high . . . . *haut/haute*
high school . . . . *(le) lycée*
highway, freeway . . . *(l') autoroute (f.)*
hike . . . . *(la) randonnée*
hike (to) . . . . *faire une randonnée*
his . . . . *sa/son/ses*
history, story . . . . *(l') histoire (f.)*
hit (to) . . . . *frapper*
hockey . . . . *(le) hockey*
hold (to) . . . . *tenir*
homework . . . . *(les) devoirs (m.)*
honest . . . . *honnête*
honeymoon . . . . *(la) lune de miel*
hope (to) . . . . *espérer*
horrified . . . . *horrifié/horrifiée*
horrible . . . . . *détestable, affreux/affreuse*
horror . . . . *(l') horreur (f.)*
horror movie . . . . *(un) film d'horreur*
horse . . . . *(le) cheval*
hospital . . . . *(l') hôpital (m.)*
host/hostess . . . . *hôte/hôtesse*
hot, warm . . . . *chaud/chaude*
hotel . . . . *(l') hôtel (m.)*
hour . . . . *(l') heure (f.)*
house . . . . *(la) maison*
how? . . . . *comment?*
how much?, how many? . . . *combien de?*
however . . . . *cependant, pourtant*
huge . . . . *gigantesque*
humidity . . . . *(l') humidité (f.)*
hunger . . . . *(la) faim*
hungry (to be) . . . . *avoir faim*
hurry (in a) . . . . *pressé/pressée*
hurry (to) . . . . *(se) dépêcher*
hurry (to be in a) . . . . *être pressé*
hurt (to), to ache . . . . *avoir mal*
husband . . . . *(le) mari*

I

ice, ice cream . . . . *(la) glace*
ice hockey . . . . . *(le) hockey sur glace*
idol . . . . *(l') idole (f.)*
if, so . . . . *si*
immediate . . . . *immédiat/immédiate*
impatience . . . . *(l') impatience (f.)*
impolite, rude . . . . *impoli/impolie,*
mal élevé/élevée
impressive . . . . *impressionnant/*
impressionnante
in . . . . *dans*
"in" (in the know, connected)
. . . . *branché/branchée*
in front of . . . . *devant*
in order, tidy . . . . *(en) ordre*
in the evening, the evening . . . . *(le) soir*
in the middle of . . . . *au milieu de*
in the morning, the morning . . *(le) matin*
increase (to) . . . . *augmenter*

incredible . . . . *incroyable*
indicate (to), to show . . . . *indiquer*
indignation . . . . . *(l') indignation (f.)*
infinite . . . . *infini/infinie*
infirmary . . . . *(l') infirmerie (f.)*
information . . . . *(le) renseignement*
information (to ask for)
. . . . *demander un renseignement*
informed (to be) . . . . . . *être au courant*
inhabitant . . *(l') habitant/habitante (m./f.)*
injured . . . . *blessé/blessée*
ink pen . . . . *(le) stylo*
inside . . . . *dedans*
insult (to) . . . . *insulter*
intelligent, wise . . . . . *sage, intelligent/*
intelligente
interesting . . . . . *intéressant/intéressante*
interview . . . . *(l') entrevue (f.)*
introduce (to) . . . . *présenter*
invent (to) . . . . *inventer*
investigation . . . . *(une) enquête*
invite (to) . . . . *inviter*
Irish . . . . *irlandais/irlandaise*
iron . . . . *(le) fer*
island . . . . *(l') île (f.)*
isn't that so? . . . . *n'est-ce pas?*
it is a pity . . . . . *il est/c'est dommage*
it seems . . . . *il paraît*
Italian . . . . *italien/italienne*

J

jacket . . . . *(la) veste*
jail . . . . *(la) prison*
jam, preserves . . . . *(la) confiture*
January . . . . *janvier*
Japanese . . . . *japonais/japonaise*
jealous . . . . *jaloux/jalouse*
jeans . . . . *(le) jean*
Jewish . . . . *juif/juive*
job . . . . *(l') emploi (m.)*
joke . . . . . . *(la) plaisanterie, (la) blague*
journalist . . . . *(un/une) journaliste*
judge . . . . *(le) juge*
judge (to) . . . . *juger*
juice . . . . *(le) jus*
July . . . . *juillet*
jump (to) . . . . *sauter*
June . . . . *juin*
just, fair . . . . *juste*

K

keep (to) . . . . *garder*
kept up, maintained
. . . . *entretenu/entretenue*
keyhole . . . . *(la) serrure*
kidnap (to), to take off . . . . . . *enlever*
kill (to) . . . . *tuer*
kilometer . . . . *(le) kilomètre*
kind, nice . . . . *gentil/gentille*

kind, sort . . . . *(le) genre*
king . . . . *(le) roi*
kingdom . . . . *(le) royaume*
kiss . . . . *(le) baiser*
kiss (to), to embrace . . . . *(s') embrasser*
kitchen, cooking . . . . *(la) cuisine*
kitchen sink . . . . *(l') évier (m.)*
knife . . . . *(le) couteau*
know (to) . . . . *connaître, savoir*
know by heart (to) . . . . *savoir par cœur*
knowledge . . . . *(le) savoir*

L

lack . . . . *(le) manque*
lake . . . . *(le) lac*
lamb . . . . *(l') agneau (m.)*
land (to), to get off . . . . *débarquer*
language, tongue . . . . *(la) langue*
large, wide . . . . *large*
last, past . . . . *dernier/dernière*
last (to) . . . . *durer*
last night . . . . *hier soir*
late . . . . *tard, en retard*
late (to be) . . . . *être en retard*
lateness . . . . *(le) retard*
laugh (to) . . . . *rire*
laughter . . . . *(le) rire*
laundromat . . . . *(la) laverie*
laundry (to do the) . . . . . *faire la lessive*
law (the) . . . . *(la) loi*
lawn . . . . *(la) pelouse*
lawnmower . . . . *(une) tondeuse*
law, privilege, right . . . . *(le) droit*
lawyer . . . . *(un/une) avocat/avocate*
lay down (to), to put to bed . . . *coucher*
lazy . . . . *paresseux/paresseuse*
leader, coach . . *(le/la) moniteur/monitrice*
leaf . . . . *(la) feuille*
lean (to) . . . . *(s') appuyer*
learn by heart (to)
. . . . *apprendre par cœur*
leather . . . . *(le) cuir*
leave (to), to go away
. . . . *laisser, quitter, partir*
lecture . . . . *(la) conférence*
left . . . . *gauche*
left (to the) . . . . *à gauche*
leg . . . . *(la) jambe*
legend . . . . *(la) légende*
lemonade . . . . *(la) limonade*
lend (to) . . . . *prêter*
less . . . . *moins*
less . . than . . . . *moins . . . que*
lesson . . . . *(la) leçon*
letter . . . . *(la) lettre*
level . . . . *(le) niveau*
lethal . . . . *mortel/mortelle*
liar . . . . *(le/la) menteur/menteuse*
liberty . . . . *(la) liberté*
librarian . . . . *(le/la) bibliothécaire*

library . . . . (la) bibliothèque
lie (to) . . . .***mentir***
lie down (to), to go to bed . . .(se) coucher
life . . . .(la) vie
light . . . .***léger/légère***
light (to), to turn on . . . .***allumer***
light bulb (a) . . . .(une) ampoule
like (to), to love . . . . .aimer
line . . . .(la) ligne
line, tail . . . .(la) queue
lion . . . .(le) lion
listen to (to) . . . . .écouter
little, tiny, small . . . .***petit/petite***
live . . . .(en) direct
live (to), to dwell . . . . .habiter
living room . . . .(le) séjour
loathe (to), to hate . . . .***avoir horreur de***
long . . . . .long/longue
long distance bus . . . .(le) car
long time (a) . . . . .longtemps
look (to) . . . . .regarder
look for (to) . . . . .chercher
look like (to) . . . .***ressembler à***
lose (to) . . . . .perdre
lose weight (to) . . . . .maigrir
lost (to get) . . . .(se) perdre
lottery . . . .(la) loterie
loud, strong . . . .***fort/forte***
lousy, no good . . . . .nul
lousy, shoddy, ugly . . . .***moche***
love . . . .(l') amour (m.)
love (to), to like . . . . .aimer
love (in) . . . .***amoureux/amoureuse***
love (with) (in) . . . . .amoureux/
amoureuse (de)
lover . . . .***(l') amant/amante (m./f.)***
luck . . . .(la) chance
luggage . . . .***(les) bagages (m.)***
lunch (to have) . . . . .déjeuner
luxury . . . .(le) luxe

M

machine . . . .(la) machine,
(l') appareil (m.)
mad, crazy . . . . .fou/folle
magazine . . . .(le) magazine
mail carrier . . . . . .(le/la) facteur/factrice
mailbox . . . .***(la) boîte aux lettres***
main course, entree . . .(le) plat principal
maintained, kept up
. . . .***entretenu/entretenue***
make a decision (to)
. . . .***prendre une décision***
make (to) . . . . .fabriquer
make fun of (to) . . . .(se) moquer de
make-up (to put on) . . . . . . .se maquiller
man . . . .(l') homme (m.)
manage (to) . . . .(se) débrouiller
manager . . . .***(le) gérant***
mango . . . .(la) mangue

manner . . . .(la) manière
manner (the), way . . . .(la) façon
many, several . . . .***plusieurs***
map (for countries
or regions), card . . . .(la) carte
map of a city . . . .(le) plan
March .mars
mare . . . .(la) jument
married . . . . .marié
marvelous . . . . .merveilleux/merveilleuse
mashed potatoes
. . . .(la) purée de pommes de terre
master/mistress . . . . . .maître/maîtresse
material, cloth, fabric . . . . . .***(le) tissu***
mathematics . . . .(les) mathématiques (f.)
mattress . . . .(le) matelas
May .mai
maybe, perhaps . . . . .peut-être
me .moi
meal . . . .(le) repas
mean . . . . .méchant/méchante
measure (to) . . . .***mesurer***
meat . . . .(la) viande
meet (to) . . . . .rencontrer
meeting . . . .(la) réunion
mechanic . . . .(un/une) mécanicien/
mécanicienne
merchant . . . .(un) commerçant
mess, disorder . . . .(le) désordre
messy . . . .(en) désordre
microwave oven (a)
. . . .(un) four à micro-ondes
middle . . . .(le) milieu
midnight . . . . .minuit
milk . . . .(le) lait
million . . . . .un million
mine . . . .(le) mien
minister . . . .(le) pasteur
miracle . . . .***(le) miracle***
mirror . . . .(le) miroir
miser . . . .(l') avare (m.)
miss (to) (e.g., a train) . . . . . . .manquer
mistake, error . . .(l') erreur (f.), (la) faute
mistake (to make a),
to be mistaken . . . .***se tromper***
mix (to) . . . .***mélanger***
modest . . . .***modeste***
moment . . . .(le) moment
Monday . . . . .lundi
money . . . .(l') argent (m.)
money (to earn) . . . .gagner de l'argent
monkey . . . .(le) singe
monster . . . .(le) monstre
month . . . .(le) mois
mood . . . .(l') humeur (f.)
moon . . . .(la) lune
moped . . . .(la) mobylette
more . . . than . . . . .plus . . . que
more .plus
more, still . . . . .encore
more or less . . . . . .comme ci comme ça

more or less, about . . . . .environ
mosquito . . . .(le) moustique
most . . . .(la) plupart
mother . . . .(la) mère
mother-in-law . . . .(la) belle-mère
motorcycle . . . .(la) moto
mountain . . . .(la) montagne
mountains (to go to the)
. . . . .aller à la montagne
mouse . . . .(la) souris
mouth . . . .(la) bouche
move (to) (house) . . . . .déménager
movie theater, cinema . . . . .(le) cinéma
movie camera . . . .(une) caméra
mow (to) . . . . .tondre
municipal . . . . . .municipal/municipale
muscle (to develop) . . . . .muscler
mushroom . . . .(le) champignon
mushy, soft . . . .***mou/molle***
music . . . .(la) musique
musical (a) . . . . .(une) comédie musicale
musician . .(un/une) musicien/musicienne
Muslim . . . .***musulman/musulmane***
must, to have to, to owe . . . . . . .devoir
mustard . . . .(la) moutarde
mute . . . .***muet/muette***
my . . . . .mon, ma, mes
mysterious . . . . .mystérieux/mystérieuse
mystery . . . .***(le) mystère***

N

naïve . . . .***naïf (m.)/naïve (f.)***
name (to) . . . .***nommer***
nap, siesta . . . .(la) sieste
napkin, towel . . . .(la) serviette
narrow, tight . . . .***étroit/étroite***
natural . . . . .naturel/naturelle
nature . . . .***(la) nature***
near . . . . .près (de)
near, close (adj.) . . . . .proche
necessary . . . . . .***nécessaire, obligatoire***
necessary (to be) . . . . .falloir
necklace . . . .(le) collier
need (the) . . . .(le) besoin
need (to) . . . . .avoir besoin de
neighbor . . . .(un/une) voisin/voisine
neighborhood, section,
quarter . . . .***(le) quartier***
neither . . . nor . . . . .ne . . . ni . . . ni
nephew . . . .(le) neveu
nervous . . . . .nerveux/nerveuse
nervous, fidgety,
exasperated . . . .***énervé/énervée***
never . . . . .ne . . . jamais
new . . . .***nouveau/nouvelle***
New Year's Eve
. . . .(le) réveillon du Nouvel An
news . . . .***(les) nouvelles (f.)***
newscast . . . .(un) reportage
newspaper . . . .(le) journal

next . . . .*prochain/prochaine*
next to . . . .*à côté de*
nice . . . .*sympathique*
nice, attractive (as a person) . . . .*sympa*
nice, kind . . . .*gentil/gentille*
niece . . . .*(la) nièce*
night . . . .*(la) nuit*
nine . . . .*neuf*
nineteen . . . .*dix-neuf*
ninth . . . .*neuvième*
no . . . .*non*
no (adj.) . . . .*aucun/aucune*
no good, lousy . . . .*nul*
no longer, no more . . . .*ne . . . plus*
no one, nobody . . . . . .*ne . . . personne*
noise . . . .*(le) bruit*
noisy . . . .*bruyant/bruyante*
none, no . . . .*ne . . . aucun*
noon . . . .*midi*
north . . . .*(le) nord*
nose . . . .*(le) nez*
not prudent, carelessly daring
. . . .*imprudent*
nothing . . . .*ne . . . rien*
notice (to) . . . .*remarquer*
novel . . . .*(le) roman*
November . . . .*novembre*
now . . . .*maintenant*
nuclear energy
. . . .*(l') énergie nucléaire (f.)*

O

obey . . . .*obéir*
oblige (to) . . . .*obliger*
observe (to) . . . .*observer*
obvious . . . .*évident*
October . . . .*octobre*
of, from, about . . . .*de*
of course . . . .*bien sûr*
offer (to) . . . .*offrir*
office, desk . . . .*(le) bureau*
often . . . .*souvent*
OK . . . .*d'accord*
old . . . .*âgé/âgée, vieux/vieille*
old, ancient . . . .*ancien/ancienne*
old age . . . .*(la) vieillesse*
on . . . .*sur*
on purpose (to do something)
. . . .*faire exprès*
on time (to be) . . . .*être à l' heure*
once . . . .*une fois*
one, a . . . .*un/une*
one way ticket . . . . .*(l') aller simple (m.)*
onion . . . .*(l') oignon (m.)*
only . . . .*seulement*
only, alone . . . .*seul/seule*
open . . . .*ouvert/ouverte*
open (to) . . . .*ouvrir*
opinion . . . .*(l') avis (m.)*
opponent . . . .*(l') adversaire (m.)*
opposite . . . .*(le) contraire,*

(l') adversaire (m.)
optional . . . .*facultatif/facultative*
or . . . .*ou*
orange . . . .*(l') orange (f.)*
order (to) . . . .*commander, ordonner*
ordinary, common . . . .*ordinaire*
original . . . .*original/originale*
ostrich . . . .*(l') autruche (f.)*
other . . . .*autre*
otherwise . . . .*sinon*
our (pl.) . . . .*nos*
our (sing.) . . . .*notre*
out of fashion . . . .*démodé/démodée*
outwit (to) . . . .*déjouer*
oven . . . .*(le) four*
over there . . . .*là-bas*
owe (to), to have to, must . . . . . .*devoir*
own . . . .*propre*
owner (the) . . . .*(un/une) propriétaire*

P

package . . . .*(le) paquet*
pain (a), annoying . . . .*pénible*
pain, grief . . . .*(la) douleur*
paint (to) . . . .*peindre*
painted . . . .*peint/peinte*
painting . . . .*(la) peinture*
painting, blackboard . . . .*(le) tableau*
pair . . . .*(la) paire*
pajamas . . . .*(le) pyjama*
paper . . . .*(le) papier*
parent . . . .*(le) parent*
pants . . . .*(le) pantalon*
pantyhose (tights) . . . .*(le) collant*
park . . . .*(le) parc*
park (to) . . . .*garer, stationner*
parking lot . . . .*(le) parking*
party . . . .*(la) fête*
pass (to) (an exam),
to succeed . . . .*réussir*
passport . . . .*(le) passeport*
past, last . . . .*dernier/dernière*
path, direction . . . .*(le) chemin*
pay (to) . . . .*payer*
pay attention (to) . . . . .*faire attention*
pay attention to (to) . . . .*faire attention à*
peach, fishing . . . .*(la) pêche*
pear . . . .*(la) poire*
peas . . . .*(les) petits pois (m.)*
peasant (farmer) . . . . . .*(le/la) paysan/*
paysanne
pencil . . . .*(le) crayon*
people . . . .*(les) gens (m.)*
pepper . . . .*(le) poivre*
perhaps, maybe . . . .*peut-être*
permission . . . .*(l') autorisation (f.)*
person . . . .*(la) personne*
person living in a village
. . . .*(le/la) villageois/villageoise*
persuade (to) . . . .*persuader*
photos (to take) . . . .*prendre des photos*

physical appearance . . . . . .*(le) physique*
physics . . . .*(la) physique*
piano . . . .*(le) piano*
picnic . . . .*(le) pique-nique*
picture . . . .*(l') image (f.)*
picture, portrait . . . .*(le) portrait*
pie . . . .*(la) tarte*
piece, bit, selection . . . . . .*(le) morceau*
piece of clothing . . . .*(le) vêtement*
pile, heap . . . .*(le) tas*
pillow . . . .*(l') oreiller (m.)*
pilot . . . .*(le) pilote*
pineapple . . . .*(l') ananas (m.)*
place . . . .*(l') endroit (m.), (le) lieu*
place (to), to put . . . .*mettre*
plant . . . .*(la) plante*
plant (to) . . . .*planter*
plate . . . .*(l') assiette (f.)*
platform . . . .*(le) quai*
play . . . .*(une) pièce (de théâtre)*
play (to) (a sport) . . . .*jouer à*
play (to) (a musical instrument)
. . . .*jouer de*
player . . . .*(un/une) joueur/joueuse*
playing field . . . .*(le) terrain*
pleasant . . . .*aimable*
please . . . .*s'il vous plaît*
pleased . . . .*enchanté/enchantée*
pleasure . . . .*(le) plaisir*
plug in (to) . . . .*brancher*
plugged in, connected
. . . .*branché, branchée*
plumber . . . .*(un) plombier*
pocket . . . .*(la) poche*
poem . . . .*(le) poème*
poison . . . .*(le) poison*
police station
. . . .*(le) commissariat de police*
policeman . . . . .*(l') agent de police (m.),*
(un/une) policier/policière
polite, courteous . . . .*poli/polie*
politician . .*(le/la) politicien/politicienne*
politics . . . .*(la) politique*
polluted . . . .*pollué/polluée*
pollution . . . .*(la) pollution*
poor . . . .*pauvre*
pork . . . .*(le) porc*
portrait, picture . . . .*(le) portrait*
poster . . . .*(l') affiche (f.)*
post office . . . .*(la) poste*
pour (to) . . . .*verser*
power . . . .*(le) pouvoir*
powerful . . . .*puissant/puissante*
practice . . . .*(l') entraînement (m.)*
practice (to) . . . .*(s') entraîner*
precious, cute . . . . .*mignon/mignonne*
prefer (to) . . . .*préférer, aimer mieux*
preferred, favorite . . . .*préféré/préférée*
present . . . .*(le) cadeau*
preserves, jam . . . .*(la) confiture*
press . . . .*(la) presse*
pretend to (to) . . . . .*faire semblant de*

pretentious . . . . .*prétentieux/prétentieuse*
pretty . . . .*joli/jolie*
prevent (to) . . . .*empêcher*
previous . . . .*précédent/précédente*
price, prize . . . .*(le) prix*
pride . . . .*(l') orgueil (m.)*
print (to) . . . .*imprimer*
printed . . . .*imprimé/imprimée*
printer . . . .*(l') imprimante (f.)*
private . . . .*privé/privée*
privilege, law, right . . . .*(le) droit*
prize, price . . . .*(le) prix*
problem . . . .*(le) problème*
problems (to have) . . .*avoir des ennuis*
problem, difficulty . . . .*(la) difficulté*
project . . . .*(le) projet*
promise . . . .*(la) promesse*
promise (to) . . . .*promettre*
protect (to) . . . .*protéger*
protest (to) . . . .*protester*
Protestant . . . . .*protestant/protestante*
proud . . . .*fier/fière*
provided that . . . .*pourvu que*
prudent, careful . . . .*prudent*
public transportation
. . . . .*(les) transports en commun (m.)*
pull out (to), to tear out . . . . .*arracher*
punish (to) . . . .*punir*
punishment . . . .*(la) punition*
pupil, student . . . .*(l') élève,*
(l') étudiant/étudiante (m./f.)
pupil (eye) . . . .*(la) pupille*
purple . . . .*violet/violette*
purse, bag, handbag . . . .*(le) sac*
push (to), to grow . . . .*pousser*
put (to) . . . .*mettre*
put away (to), to tidy . . . .*ranger*
put on (to) . . . .*mettre*

Q

quantity . . . .*(la) quantité*
quarrel (to) . . . .*disputer*
quarrel with (to) . . . .*(se) disputer*
quarter . . . .*(le) quart*
quarter, neighborhood,
section . . . .*(le) quartier*
quickly, fast . . . .*vite*
quiet . . . .*silencieux/silencieuse,*
tranquille
quiet (to be) . . . .*(se) taire*
quiz . . . .*(le) contrôle*

R

rabbit . . . .*(le) lapin*
race . . . .*(une) course*
racket . . . .*(la) raquette*
radio . . . .*(la) radio*
rain (to) . . . .*pleuvoir*
rain forest . . . . .*(la) forêt tropicale*

raincoat . . . .*(l') imperméable (m.)*
rare, unusual . . . .*rare*
raw . . . .*cru/crue*
reach (to) . . . .*atteindre*
read (to) . . . .*lire*
ready . . . .*prêt/prête*
realize (to) . . . .*(se) rendre compte*
reason . . . .*(la) raison*
reassure (to) . . . .*rassurer*
receive (to) . . . .*recevoir*
recent . . . .*récent/récente*
recently . . . .*récemment*
recognize (to) . . . .*reconnaître*
red . . . .*rouge*
red (to turn), to blush . . . .*rougir*
redhead . . . .*roux/rousse*
referee . . . .*(l') arbitre (m.)*
reflect (to) . . . .*réfléchir*
refrigerator . . . .*(le) réfrigérateur*
register (to) . . . .*(s') inscrire*
registration . . . .*(l') inscription (f.)*
regret (to) . . . .*regretter*
regularly . . . .*régulièrement*
reign (to) . . . .*régner*
relationship . . . .*(la) relation*
relax (to) . . . .*(se) détendre*
relaxed . . . .*détendu/détendue*
remain (to), to stay . . . .*rester*
remember (to) . . . .*(se) souvenir*
renew . . . .*renouveler*
rent (the) . . . .*(le) loyer*
rent (to) . . . .*louer*
repair (to), to fix . . . .*réparer*
repeat (to) . . . .*répéter*
replace (to) . . . .*remplacer*
reply . . . .*(la) réponse*
report . . . .*(le) rapport*
require (to), to demand . . . .*exiger*
required . . . .*obligatoire*
researcher . . . .*(un/une) chercheur/*
chercheuse
reservation . . . .*(la) réservation*
reservations (to make) . . . .*réserver*
resolve (to), to solve a
problem . . . .*résoudre*
respond (to), to answer . . . . . .*répondre*
responsible . . . .*responsable*
rest (to) . . . .*(se) reposer*
restaurant . . . .*(le) restaurant*
result . . . .*(le) résultat*
retired . . . .*à la retraite*
retirement . . . .*(la) retraite*
return (to) . . . .*retourner*
revenge, vengeance . . . .*(la) vengeance*
review . . . .*(la) révision*
revolve (to), to turn,
to rotate . . . .*tourner*
rice . . . .*(le) riz*
rich . . . .*riche*
ridiculous . . . .*ridicule*
right (to be) . . . .*avoir raison*

right (to the) . . . .*à droite*
right away . . . .*tout de suite*
right, law, privilege . . . .*(le) droit*
ring . . . .*(la) bague*
ring (to) . . . .*sonner*
ripe . . . .*mûr*
ripped, torn . . . .*déchiré/déchirée*
risk . . . .*(le) risque*
river . . . .*(le) fleuve, (la) rivière*
road, route . . . .*(la) route*
roast . . . .*(le) rôti*
roast (to) . . . .*rôtir*
romantic movie . . . . .*(un) film d'amour*
roof . . . .*(le) toit*
room . . . .*(la) salle, (la) pièce*
rooster . . . .*(le) coq*
root . . . .*(la) racine*
rope . . . .*(la) corde*
rose . . . .*(la) rose*
rotate (to), to turn,
to revolve . . . .*tourner*
round trip ticket . . . . .*(l') aller-retour (m.)*
route, road . . . .*(la) route*
row . . . .*(le) rang*
row (to) . . . .*ramer*
rowing . . . .*(l') aviron (m.)*
rude, impolite . . . .*mal élevé/élevée,*
impoli/impolie
rug, carpet . . . .*(le) tapis*
ruin (to), to damage . . . .*abîmer*
rule . . . .*(le) règlement*
rule (to), to be over . . . .*dominer*
run (to) . . . .*courir*
run away (to) . . . .*(s') enfuir*
rusty . . . .*rouillé/rouillée*

S

sad . . . .*triste*
salad . . . .*(la) salade*
salary . . . .*(le) salaire*
salt . . . .*(le) sel*
salted . . . .*salé/salée*
same . . . .*même*
sand . . . .*(le) sable*
satisfied . . . .*satisfait/satisfaite*
Saturday . . . .*samedi*
saucepan . . . .*(la) casserole*
save (to) . . . .*sauver*
save money (to) . . . .*économiser*
say (to), to tell . . . .*dire*
scare (to), to frighten . . . .*effrayer*
scarf . . . . . .*(le) foulard, (l') écharpe (f.)*
schedule . . . . .*(l') emploi du temps (m.)*
schedule (transportation)
. . . .*(l') horaire (m.)*
scholarship . . . .*(la) bourse*
school . . . .*(l') école (f.)*
science fiction . . . . . .*(la) science-fiction*
scissors . . . .*(les) ciseaux (m.)*
scold (to) . . . .*gronder*

screen . . . .*(l') écran (m.)*
sea . . . .*(la) mer*
seashell . . . .*(le) coquillage*
seaside (to go to the)
. . . .*aller au bord de la mer*
season . . . .*(la) saison*
seat . . . .*(la) place, (le) siège*
seated . . . .*assis*
second . . . .*deuxième*
secret . . . .*(le) secret*
section, quarter,
neighborhood . . . .*(le) quartier*
security, certainty . . . .*(la) sécurité*
see (to) . . . .*voir*
seem (to), to appear . . . .*paraître*
select (to), to choose . . . .*choisir*
selection, bit, piece . . . . . .*(le) morceau*
selfish . . . .*égoïste*
sell (to) . . . .*vendre*
senator . . . . *(un/une) sénateur/sénatrice*
send (to) . . . .*envoyer*
sentiment, feeling . . . . . .*(le) sentiment*
September . . . .*septembre*
series . . . .*(la) série*
serious . . . .*sérieux/sérieuse, grave*
serve (to) . . . .*servir*
set the table (to) . . . . .*mettre le couvert*
seven . . . .*sept*
seventeen . . . .*dix-sept*
seventh . . . .*septième*
several, many . . . .*plusieurs*
shadow, shade . . . .*(l') ombre (f.)*
share (to) . . . .*partager*
sharp . . . .*aigu/aiguë*
sharpen (to) (pencils) . . . .*tailler*
shave (to) . . . .*(se) raser*
sheep . . . .*(le) mouton*
sheet . . . .*(le) drap*
shelf . . . .*(l') étagère (f.)*
shine (to) . . . .*briller*
shirt . . . .*(la) chemise*
shocked . . . .*choqué/choquée*
shocking . . . .*choquant/choquante*
shoddy, lousy, ugly . . . .*moche*
shoes . . . .*(les) chaussures (f.)*
shoot (to) . . . .*tirer sur*
shop . . . .*(la) boutique*
shopkeeper . .*(le/la) marchand/marchande*
shopping mall
. . . .*(le) centre commercial*
short . . . .*court/courte*
shout (to) . . . .*crier*
show, television (radio)
program . . . .*(une) émission*
show (to), to indicate . .*montrer, indiquer*
shower . . . .*(la) douche*
shower (to) . . . .*(se) doucher*
shower (to take a)
. . . .*prendre une douche*
shut (to), to close . . . .*fermer*
shy, timid . . . .*timide*

sick . . . .*malade*
side . . . .*(le) côté*
sidewalk . . . .*(le) trottoir*
siesta, nap . . . .*(la) sieste*
sign (to) . . . .*signer*
silly, stupid, foolish . . . .*bête*
sin . . . .*(le) péché*
since, because . . . .*puisque*
sing (to) . . . .*chanter*
singer . . . .*(le/la) chanteur/chanteuse*
silk . . . .*(la) soie*
sister . . . .*(la) sœur*
sister-in-law . . . .*(la) belle-sœur*
sit (to) . . . .*asseoir*
sit down (to) . . . .*(s') asseoir*
sitting room . . . .*(le) salon*
six . . . .*six*
sixteen . . . .*seize*
sixth . . . .*sixième*
size, waist . . . .*(la) taille*
skate . . . .*(le) patin*
skate (to) . . . .*patiner*
skating . . . .*(le) patinage*
skiing . . . .*(le) ski*
skillful . . . .*habile*
skirt . . . .*(la) jupe*
sleep . . . .*(le) sommeil*
sleep (to) . . . .*dormir*
sleepy (to be) . . . .*avoir sommeil*
sleeve . . . .*(la) manche*
slow . . . .*lent/lente*
slowly . . . .*lentement*
sly . . . .*rusé/rusée*
small, tiny, little . . . .*petit/petite*
smart, wise . . . .*prudent/prudente*
smile (to) . . . .*sourire*
smoke (to) . . . .*fumer*
snack (to), to taste . . . .*goûter*
snake . . . .*(le) serpent*
sneakers . . . .*(les) baskets (m.)*
snore (to) . . . .*ronfler*
snow . . . .*(la) neige*
snow (to) . . . .*neiger*
so, if . . . .*si*
so, so much, so many . . . .*tellement*
so much . . . .*tant*
soaked . . . .*trempé/trempée*
soap opera . . . .*(un) feuilleton*
soccer . . . .*(le) football (foot)*
socks . . . .*(les) chaussettes (f.)*
sofa, couch . . . .*(le) canapé*
soft, mushy . . . .*mou/molle*
soft, sweet . . . .*doux/douce*
soldier . . . .*(un) soldat*
solve a problem (to),
to resolve . . . .*résoudre*
some . . . .*quelque/quelques*
someone . . . .*quelqu'un*
something . . . .*quelque chose*
sometimes . . . .*quelquefois, parfois*
son . . . .*(le) fils*

song (a) . . . .*(une) chanson*
soon . . . .*bientôt*
sort, kind . . . .*(le) genre*
sound . . . .*(le) son*
soup . . . .*(la) soupe*
south . . . .*(le) sud*
speak (to) . . . .*parler*
spectator . . .*(le/la) spectateur/spectatrice*
speed . . . .*(la) vitesse*
spell (to) . . . .*épeler*
spelling . . . .*(l') orthographe (f.)*
spend (money) (to) . . . .*dépenser*
spend (time) (to) . . . .*passer*
spice . . . .*(l') épice (f.)*
spill (to) . . . .*renverser*
spinach . . . .*(les) épinards (m.)*
spoiled . . . .*gâté/gâtée*
spoken word . . . .*(la) parole*
spoon . . . .*(la) cuillère*
sporty, athletic . . . .*sportif/sportive*
spring . . . .*(le) printemps*
spy . . . .*(un/une) espion/espionne*
square . . . .*carré/carrée*
squeeze (to), to tighten . . . .*serrer*
squirrel . . . .*(l') écureuil (m.)*
stairs . . . .*(l') escalier (m.)*
stamp . . . .*(le) timbre*
standing . . . .*debout*
stanza . . . .*(la) strophe*
start doing something (to)
. . . .*(se) mettre à*
state, condition . . . .*(l') état (m.)*
stay (to), to remain . . . .*rester*
steak . . . .*(le) steak*
steal (to) . . . .*voler*
stereo system, TV channel . *(une) chaîne*
stiff . . . .*raide*
still, more . . . .*encore*
sting (to) . . . .*piquer*
stir (to) . . . .*remuer*
stolen . . . .*volé/volée*
stone . . . .*(la) pierre*
stop (to) . . . .*arrêter, (s') arrêter*
store . . . .*(le) magasin*
store clerk (the)
. . . .*(le/la) vendeur/vendeuse*
storm . . . .*(l') orage (m.)*
storm, tempest . . . .*(la) tempête*
story (to tell a) . . . .*raconter*
story, history . . . .*(l') histoire (f.)*
story, tale . . . .*(le) conte*
stove . . . .*(la) cuisinière*
straight ahead . . . .*tout droit*
strange . . . .*étrange*
strawberry . . . .*(la) fraise*
street . . . .*(la) rue*
strong, loud . . . .*fort/forte*
stubborn . . . .*têtu/têtue*
student, pupil . . . .*(l') élève,*
(un/une) étudiant/étudiante
study (to) . . . .*étudier*

study hall . . . .*(la) salle d'étude*
stupid . . . .*idiot/idiote*
stupid, silly, foolish . . . .***bête***
stupid action . . . .*(la) bêtise*
subject . . . .*(la) matière*
suburbs . . . .*(la) banlieue*
subway . . . .*(le) métro*
succeed (to), to pass
 (an exam) . . . .***réussir***
success . . . .*(le) succès*
succession . . . .*(la) succession*
suddenly . . . .*soudain, tout à coup*
sufficient . . . .*suffisant/suffisante*
sugar . . . .*(le) sucre*
sugary, sweet . . . .***sucré/sucrée***
suggest . . . .*suggérer*
suit . . . .*(le) costume*
suitcase . . . .***(la) valise***
summary . . . .***(le) résumé***
summer . . . .*(l') été (m.)*
summit . . . .*(le) sommet*
sun . . . .*(le) soleil*
Sunday . . . .*(le) dimanche*
superior, better . . .***supérieur/supérieure***
supermarket . . . .*(le) supermarché*
supervise (to) . . . .*surveiller*
sure, certain . . . .***sûr/sûre***
surgeon . . . .*(un/une) chirurgien/*
 chirurgienne
surprise (to) . . . .*étonner*
surprised . . . . .*surpris/surprise, étonné*
surprising . . . .*étonnant*
suspect (to) . . . .*soupçonner*
surround (to) . . . .***entourer***
swear (to) . . . .***jurer***
sweater . . . .*(le) pull*
sweet, soft . . . .***doux/douce***
sweet, sugary . . . .***sucré/sucrée***
swim (to) . . . .*nager*
swimming . . . .*(la) natation*
swimming pool . . . .*(la) piscine*
swimsuit, bathing suit
 . . . .*(le) maillot de bain*
synagogue . . . .*(la) synagogue*
system . . . .***(le) système***

T

table . . . .*(la) table*
tail, line . . . .*(la) queue*
take (to) . . . .*prendre*
take a course (to) . . . .*suivre un cours*
take a drive (to)/walk . . . *faire un tour*
take a trip (to) . . . . . . *faire un voyage*
take a walk (to)/drive . . . *faire un tour*
take care of (to) . . . . .*prendre soin de*
take off (to), to kidnap . . . . . .*enlever*
take notes (to) . . . . .*prendre des notes*
tale, story . . . .*(le) conte*
talent . . . .*(le) talent*
talented . . . .*doué/douée*

tall, big, fat . . *grand/grande, gros/grosse*
tan (to) . . . .*bronzer*
tanned . . . .*bronzé/bronzée*
tanning . . . .*(le) bronzage*
tape (to), to check in, to record
 . . . .*enregistrer*
task . . . .***(la) tâche***
taste . . . .***(le) goût***
taste (to), to snack . . . .*goûter*
tasteless, without taste . . . . .***sans goût***
tax . . . .*(l') impôt (m.)*
taxi . . . .*(le) taxi*
tea . . . .*(le) thé*
teach (to) . . . .*enseigner*
teacher . . . . .*(l') enseignant/enseignante*
 (m./f.), (le) professeur
teaching . . . . . .***(l') enseignement (m.)***
team . . . .*(l') équipe (f.)*
tear out (to), to pull out . . . . .***arracher***
teenager . . . .*(l') adolescent/adolescente*
 (l'ado) (m../f.)
telephone . . . .*(le) téléphone*
television . . . .*(la) télévision*
television (radio)
 program, show . . . . . .*(l') émission (f.)*
tell (to), to say . . . .*dire*
tell (a story) (to) . . . .***raconter***
tempest, storm . . . .*(la) tempête*
ten . . . .*dix*
tenant (the) . . . .*(le/la) locataire*
tennis . . . .*(le) tennis*
tent . . . .***(la) tente***
tenth . . . .*dixième*
term . . . .*(le) trimestre*
terribly . . . .*affreusement*
terrify (to) . . . .*terrifier*
terrifying . . . .*terrifiant*
text . . . .*(le) texte*
thank (to) . . . .***remercier***
thank you . . . .*merci*
that, which . . . .*que*
the . . . .*le/la/les*
theater . . . .*(le) théâtre*
their . . . .*leur/leurs*
theft, flight . . . .***(le) vol***
them (object of a preposition) . . . .*eux*
then . . . .*ensuite, alors, puis*
there . . . .*là*
there is, there are . . . .*il y a*
therefore . . . .*donc*
these/this . . . . . .*ces/ce/cet/cette (adj.)*
thief . . . .*(un/une) voleur/voleuse*
thin . . . .***maigre***
thin (adj.) . . . .*mince*
thing . . . .*(la) chose*
things, belongings, business
 . . . .***(les) affaires (f.)***
think (to) . . . .*penser*
third . . . .*troisième*
thirst . . . .*(la) soif*
thirsty (to be) . . . .*avoir soif*

thirteen . . . .*treize*
thirty . . . .*trente*
this/these . . . .*ce/cet/cette/ces (adj.)*
this (pron.) . . . .*cela*
this afternoon . . . . . .*cet/cette après-midi*
this (one) . . . .*celui (pron.)*
three . . . .*trois*
thousand . . . .*mille*
threaten (to) . . . .*menacer*
throat . . . .*(la) gorge*
throw (to) . . . .*lancer*
throw away (to) . . . .***jeter***
Thursday . . . .*jeudi*
ticket . . . .***(le) billet***
ticket (subway, bus) . . . .*(le) ticket*
ticket window . . . .*(le) guichet*
tidy, in order . . . .*(en) ordre*
tidy (to), to put away . . . .***ranger***
tie . . . .*(la) cravate*
tie (to), to attach . . . .*attacher*
tiger . . . .*(le) tigre*
tight, narrow . . . .***étroit/étroite***
tighten (to), to squeeze . . . .***serrer***
time, weather . . . .*(le) temps*
timid, shy . . . .*timide*
tiny, small, little . . . .***petit/petite***
tired . . . .***fatigué/fatiguée***
tiredness . . . .***(la) fatigue***
tiring . . . .*fatigant*
to, at . . . .*à*
toaster (a) . . . .*(un) grille-pain*
today . . . .*aujourd'hui*
toenail, fingernail . . . . . .***(l') ongle (m.)***
together . . . .*ensemble*
toilet . . . .*(les) toilettes (f.)*
tolerant . . . .*tolérant/tolérante*
tomato . . . .*(la) tomate*
tomorrow . . . .*demain*
tongue, language . . . .*(la) langue*
too much, too many . . . .*trop (de)*
tooth . . . .*(la) dent*
torn, ripped . . . .***déchiré/déchirée***
tour . . . .*(le) tour*
toward . . . .*vers*
towel, napkin . . . .*(la) serviette*
towel . . . .*(la) serviette de toilette*
tower . . . .*(la) tour*
toy . . . .*(le) jouet*
tractor . . . .*(le) tracteur*
traffic jam . . . . . .*(l') embouteillage (m.)*
traffic light red/green
 . . . .*(le) feu rouge/vert*
train . . . .*(le) train*
train to (to take a) . . . .*aller en train*
training . . . .***(l') entraînement (m.)***
train platform . . . .*(le) quai*
train station . . . .*(la) gare*
translate . . . .*traduire*
travel (to) . . . .*voyager*
travel agency
 . . . .*(l') agence de voyages (f.)*

tray . . . .*(le) plateau*
treasure . . . .*(le) trésor*
tree . . . .*(l') arbre (m.)*
trip . . . .*(le) voyage*
truck . . . .*(le) camion*
true . . . .*vrai*
trumpet . . . .*(la) trompette*
trust (to) . . . .*faire confiance*
truth . . . .*(la) vérité*
try (to), to try on . . . .**essayer**
T-shirt . . . .*(le) tee-shirt*
Tuesday . . . .*mardi*
tulip . . . .*(la) tulipe*
turkey . . . .*(la) dinde*
turtle . . . .*(la) tortue*
turn (to), to revolve,
  to rotate . . . .**tourner**
turn off (to), to extinguish . . . .*éteindre*
turn on (to), to light . . . .*allumer*
TV channel, stereo system .*(une) chaîne*
TV host . . . .*(un/une) présentateur/*
                          présentatrice
twelve . . . .*douze*
twenty . . . .*vingt*
twice, three times, etc. . . . . . .*deux fois,*
                          trois fois, etc.

typical . . . .*typique*

U

ugly . . . .*laid/laide*
ugly, lousy, shoddy . . . .*moche*
umbrella . . . .*(le) parapluie*
unattractive (as a person) . . .*antipathique*
unbelievable . . . .*incroyable*
uncle . . . .*(l') oncle (m.)*
under . . . .*sous*
underpants . . . .*(le) slip*
understand (to) . . .*comprendre, entendre*
undress (to) . . . .*(se) déshabiller*
unemployed . . . .*au chômage*
unfair . . . .*injuste*
unhappily . . . .*malheureusement*
unhappy . . . . .*malheureux/malheureuse*
university . . . .*(l') université (f.)*
unpleasant . . . .*désagréable*
unplug (to) . . . .*débrancher*
until, up to (prep.) . . . .*jusqu'à*
unusual, rare . . . .*rare*
upset . . . .*ennuyé/ennuyée*
upset, angry . . . .*fâché/fâchée*
use (to) . . . .*(se) servir de, utiliser*
used for/to (to be) . . . .*servir à*
useful . . . .*utile*
useless . . . .*inutile*
usually . . . .*d'habitude*

V

vacation . . . .*(les) vacances (f.)*

vacation (to go on) .*partir en vacances*
vacuum (to) . . . .*passer l'aspirateur*
vacuum cleaner . . . . .*(l') aspirateur (m.)*
vanilla ice cream ..*(la) glace à la vanille*
vegetable . . . .*(le) légume*
vengeance, revenge . . . .*(la) vengeance*
very . . . .*très*
vest . . . .*(le) gilet*
victim . . . .*(la) victime*
video game . . . .*(un) jeu vidéo*
village . . . .*(le) village*
violin . . . .*(le) violon*
violence . . . .*(la) violence*
visit (to) (a place) . . . .*visiter*
visit someone (to) . . . .*aller voir*
voice . . . .*(la) voix*
vote . . . .*(le) vote*

W

wagon . . . .*(le) wagon*
waist, size . . . .*(la) taille*
wait for (to) . . . .*attendre*
wait in line (to) . . . .*faire la queue*
waiter . . . .*(le/la) serveur/serveuse*
wake up (to) . . . .*(se) réveiller*
walk (a) . . . .*(la) promenade*
walk (to) . . . .*marcher*
walk to (to) . . . .*aller à pied*
walk (to take a) . . . .*(se) promener*
want (to) . . . .*vouloir*
want (to), to desire . . . . .*avoir envie (de)*
warm, hot . . . .*chaud/chaude*
warn (to) . . . .*avertir, prévenir*
wash (the) (laundry) . . . .*(la) lessive*
wash (to) . . . .*(se) laver*
washing machine . . . .*(le) lave-linge*
watch . . . .*(la) montre*
water . . . .*(l') eau (f.)*
wave . . . .*(la) vague*
weak . . . .*faible*
wear (to), to carry . . . .*porter*
weather, time . . . .*(le) temps*
weather report . . . .*(la) météo*
wedding . . . .*(le) mariage*
Wednesday . . . .*mercredi*
week . . . .*(la) semaine*
weep (to), to cry . . . .*pleurer*
well . . . .*bien*
well-known . . . .*connu*
west . . . .*(l') ouest (m.)*
wet . . . .*mouillé/mouillée*
wet (to) . . . .*mouiller*
whale . . . .*(la) baleine*
when . . . .*lorsque, quand*
where . . . .*où*
where from . . . .*d'où*
which, that . . . .*que*
which, what (adj.) . . . .*quel/quelle*
while . . . .*pendant que*
whistle . . . .*(le) sifflet*

whistle (to) . . . .*siffler*
white . . . .*blanc/blanche*
why? . . . .*pourquoi?*
wide, large . . . .*large*
wife, woman . . . .*(la) femme*
wild . . . .*sauvage*
win (to), to earn . . . .**gagner**
wind . . . .*(le) vent*
window . . . .*(la) fenêtre*
wine . . . .*(le) vin*
wing . . . .*(l') aile (f.)*
winner . . . . .*(un/une) gagnant/gagnante*
winter . . . .*(l') hiver (m.)*
wipe (to), to dry . . . .*essuyer*
wise, intelligent . . . .*sage*
wise, smart . . . .*prudent/prudente*
wish (to) . . . .*souhaiter*
with . . . .*avec*
without . . . .*sans*
without taste, tasteless . . . . .*sans goût*
witness . . . .*(le) témoin*
wolf . . . .*(le) loup*
woman, wife . . . .*(la) femme*
wonder (to) . . . .*(se) demander*
wood, forest . . . .*(le) bois*
wooden floor . . . .*(le) plancher*
wool . . . .*(la) laine*
word . . . .*(le) mot*
work (to) . . . .*travailler*
work (to), to function,
  to walk . . . .*fonctionner, marcher*
world . . . .*(le) monde*
worse . . . .*pire*
worth the trouble (to be)
  . . . .*valoir la peine*
worried (to be) . . . .*être ennuyé(e)*
worry (to) . . . .*(s') inquiéter, préoccuper*
wound (to) . . . .*blesser*
write (to) . . . .*écrire*
writer . . . .*(un) écrivain*
written . . . .*écrit/écrite*
wrong, false . . . .*faux/fausse*
wrong (to be) . . . .*avoir tort*

Y

yard, garden . . . .*(le) jardin*
year . . . .*(l') année (f.)*
yellow . . . .*jaune*
yes . . . .*oui*
yesterday . . . .*hier*
you . . . .*toi, tu, vous*
young . . . .*jeune*
your . . . .*votre, vos, ton, ta, tes*
youth . . . .*(la) jeunesse*

Z

zebra . . . .*(le) zèbre*
zip code . . . .*(le) code postal*
zipper . . . .*(la) fermeture éclair*

❧❧ INDEX ❧❧